Alfred Vincent Kidder
and the
Development of
Americanist Archaeology

frontis: Alfred Vincent Kidder, 1885–1963. (Photo 1960, courtesy of Faith Kidder Fuller)

ALFRED VINCENT KIDDER
AND THE
DEVELOPMENT OF
AMERICANIST ARCHAEOLOGY

Douglas R. Givens

UNIVERSITY OF NEW MEXICO PRESS
ALBUQUERQUE

Library of Congress Cataloging-in-Publication Data

Givens, Douglas R.
    Alfred Vincent Kidder and the development of Americanist
archaeology / Douglas R. Givens.
        p.   cm.
    Includes bibliographical references and index.
    ISBN 0-8263-1351-5
    1. Kidder, Alfred Vincent, 1885–1963.   2. Anthropologists—United
States—Biography.   3. Archaeology—United States—History.
4. Pecos National Monument (N.M.)   5. Indians of Mexico—
Antiquities.   6. Indians of Central America—Antiquities.
7. America—Antiquities.   I. Title.
GN21.K5G58   1992
973.9'092—dc20
[B]   91-43853
                                                                   CIP

iv

DEDICATED
IN APPRECIATION TO
RICHARD B. WOODBURY,
LINDA WEST GIVENS,
AND
HELEN GIVENS WILKENING

CONTENTS

PREFACE

In 1956, with the assistance of Fay-Cooper Cole, J. O. Brew, and Gordon R. Willey, A. V. Kidder began the task of collecting bits and pieces of material from his personal papers to construct an autobiography. This material includes a humorous description of his chosen career:

That I became an archaeologist was due partly, I think, to heredity; partly, I believe to what might be called conditioning; and in very large part, I know, to pure accident. If heredity was involved, the responsible gene was strung on my father's chromosome, not my mother's, for her whole interest was in living men and women (AVK I:1, AVK III:1).

Alfred Vincent Kidder held a central position in the development of Americanist archaeology from 1915 until his death in 1963. His long and illustrious career is evidenced in the awards, honors, titles, and achievements he collected during his lifetime. Kidder retired on November 1, 1950, and shortly thereafter colleagues from all over the country joined in creating the Alfred Vincent Kidder Award for achievement in American archaeology. The award is made for work in the southwestern United States and in Middle America, the two fields to which he contributed so much. In his honor one hundred medals were cast (the medals were designed by Tatiana Proskouriakoff) and were deposited in the Peabody Museum (Harvard University). Every three years since its inception, a recipient designated by the American Anthropological Association has received the award (Woodbury 1973:81). Other recognition during his professional career included honorary degrees from the University of New Mexico (1934), the University of Michigan (1949), the National University of Mexico (1951), and the University of San Carlos,

Guatemala (1955). Kidder was also named Commander, Order of the Quetzal, by the Republic of Guatemala, in 1955. He was the first Viking Fund Medalist in Archaeology (1946); he also received the Lucy Wharton Drexel Medal from the University Museum, University of Pennsylvania, and the Medal of Merit conferred by the University of Arizona on the occasion of its seventy-fifth anniversary. Kidder also had served as an officer and active member of the American Philosophical Society and was a member of the National Academy of Sciences (Wauchope 1965:164).

The papers of Alfred Vincent Kidder were made available to me by his daughter, Faith Kidder Fuller. I had unrestricted use of the papers prior to their deposit in various archives on the campus of Harvard University. At the time, both the Harvard University Archives and the Tozzer Library contained portions of Kidder's papers; all papers are now in the Harvard University Archives. It was shortly after their deposit that I had the pleasure of meeting Tristram R. Kidder, son of A. V. Kidder's son James. Tristram Kidder and A. V. Kidder's son Alfred II are the only members of A. V. Kidder's family to make archaeology their vocation.

I used several methods to obtain information for this book. First I read and sorted all the unpublished materials sent to me by Faith Kidder Fuller. This enabled me to work out a fairly detailed biography of Kidder from the diaries and papers. The research process also involved interviews with a number of scholars who knew Kidder well. I spent a total of ten hours, on two different occasions, interviewing Richard B. Woodbury, a long-time friend and colleague of A. V. Kidder. Our meetings were held at Lambert Saint Louis International Airport, while he was awaiting connections at various times. During our airport meetings, Dick was able to add a great deal to my knowledge about Kidder as an archaeologist. The interview process with Dick Woodbury also involved many telephone calls and considerable written correspondence over a three-year period. Periodic contact with him also enabled me to answer certain questions that came to mind during the reading of Kidder's unpublished papers and diaries. Watson Smith, whom I also interviewed in person and by letter, recounted some of his memories of Kidder and his place in Americanist archaeology. I received twenty-seven letters from him, and he was able to provide information not discussed in Kidder's unpublished papers. Finally, I spent a total of twelve hours with Randolph A. Kidder, on two separate occasions, to solicit his recollections of his father's Pecos work. On these occasions he was able to give me a detailed account of his father's work there and of Charles and Anne Lindbergh's visit to the pueblo.

Gordon Willey (Personal Communication, 12 October 1982) has indicated to me that he borrowed a tape recorder and received a small grant from the Wenner-Gren Foundation for Anthropological Research for the purpose of taking down Dr. Kidder's reminiscences in interview form. The contents of the tape and Dr. Willey's notes were typed up. Only one copy of the transcript was made, and it was given to Mrs. Madeleine Kidder. Dr. Willey asked her if she wished it prepared for publication; she declined. Dr. Willey indicated that the conversations with Kidder were taped with Kidder and Willey alone. He does not remember any sessions with Fay-Cooper Cole and J. O. Brew as part of the interview team. The transcript was a part of the A. V. Kidder papers on loan to me by Kidder's daughter, Faith Kidder Fuller; it does contain questions directed to Kidder by both Cole and Brew.

AVK I, II, and III refer to Kidder's unpublished autobiographical notes, which synthesize certain of his diaries. See Appendix I (and bibliography) for complete notation forms here.

There are other sources of material pertaining to Kidder that I have not yet pursued. These include the Peabody Museum archives, where the Kluckhohn and other materials from the Kidder era are housed, and the American Philosophical Society, where materials pertaining to Kidder are housed. I have not interviewed Faith Kidder Fuller in a formal way about her recollections of her father's work.

This book is not a study in the history of ideas, nor is it a study in the philosophy of science. My aim was to find out as much as possible about Kidder as a man and as an archaeologist, with special attention to his contributions to the development of Americanist archaeology.

Acknowledgments

Without Faith Kidder Fuller's generous offer to allow me access to her father's papers, this book would not have been possible. I am deeply grateful to her. I have also received aid and encouragement from A. V. Kidder's son, Randolph A. Kidder, and his wife, Dotty. Richard B. Woodbury has spent many hours discussing Kidder's life and work with me, and has been an unfailing source of inspiration and support. Watson Smith has kindly corresponded with me about Kidder and the American Southwest; his assistance is much appreciated.

Douglas R. Givens
Saint Louis, Missouri
Summer 1991

CHAPTER ONE

FROM ORNITHOLOGIST TO ARCHAEOLOGIST

Alfred Vincent Kidder was born 29 October 1885, in Marquette, Michigan, the scion of two venerable New England families. His father, Alfred Kidder, was a descendant of James Kidder, an Englishman who emigrated to Boston about 1649 and was killed in King Phillip's War, in 1679. His mother, Kate Dalliba, also came from a long line of New Englanders, including one ancestor who fought in the revolutionary war and another who was related by marriage to the inventor Eli Whitney.

Alfred Vincent was the youngest of five children, two of whom died in infancy before he was born. The only siblings he ever knew were his two older brothers, Howard and Homer. In 1870 their father had moved the family from Boston to Marquette, on Michigan's Upper Peninsula, when he took a job with an iron-mining company there. The elder Kidder joined the firm as a clerk and bookkeeper, but gradually worked his way into a better-paying position as a mining engineer. Although he had no formal training in this area, he apparently possessed a sharp intellect and easily taught himself what he needed to know. He remained with the company for more than twenty years.

About 1892, when A. V. Kidder was six or seven, the family returned to Massachusetts, settling in the college town of Cambridge. At first they lived with Kate Kidder's mother, at 96 Brattle Street; by the mid-1890s they had built their own house, at the corner of Brattle and Fayerweather streets. Kidder's father befriended some of the best scientific minds of the day, including the geologists Raphael Pumpelly and Alexander Agassiz and the anthropologists Lewis Henry Morgan and Frederic Ward Putnam. Despite having had only a high-school education himself, Alfred Kidder did not feel out of place in their company. Besides being a self-taught engineer and structural geologist, the elder Kidder was also an

1

avid amateur antiquarian and naturalist, and had accumulated a large library, including numerous books on American Indians, both modern and prehistoric. Among them were George Catlin's *North American Indians* and John L. Stephens's *Incidents of Travel in Central America, Chiapas and Yucatan* (two of young Ted Kidder's favorites), as well as complete sets of the annual reports of the American Bureau of Ethnology, the Harvard Peabody Museum, and the Smithsonian National Museum (AVK II:5–6). There can be little doubt that growing up in this fertile environment laid the foundations of A. V. Kidder's career in anthropology and archaeology.

Ted Kidder was apparently quite close to his father, and the bond between them became even stronger as the boy grew up. In his unpublished memoirs, Kidder included a sonnet his brother Homer had written to their father in 1896, explaining that it expressed how he himself felt about him:

> *To My Father*
> *Ev'n as a child, 'ere my thought had begun*
> *To know itself, I know thou could'st endure*
> *No harm to me, and in thy care secure*
> *I dwelt, as bees that trust the kindly sun.*
> *A boy, I walked with thee and knew thee one*
> *Of whose unfailing love I could be sure.*
> *Whether by fortune though were rich or poor,*
> *Until thy life its latest sands had run,*
> *And now that to young manhood I am grown,*
> *Looking about me on the world to see*
> *In whom perfection is the nearest shown,*
> *My heart, my reason, tell me thou are he*
> *Of all the souls of men that I have known*
> *Whose like it were my dearest wish to be. (AVK I:21)*

His mother and father were a devoted couple and never exchanged a cross word, although they had different interests. Kidder (AVK I:27) remembers that his mother really ran the family, and all the planning was done by her. His father was certainly not henpecked but, given his books

(Lyell, Parkman, Prescott, Emerson, Marryatt, and the memoirs of the Civil War generals), he rarely became involved in muhdane family matters. His wife's planning was so "well conceived and so obviously inspired by intense love [for] her family that there was never any possible cause for controversy" (AVK I:27).

SCHOOL DAYS

Like all proper Cambridge children of the day, Ted Kidder began his school career at the Buckingham School (ca. 1893), then located at the corner of Garden and Buckingham streets. His teachers, a Miss Markham and a Miss Mansen, were a strong influence on him, especially in inculcating the "proper behavior" expected of children. The elementary school experience that Kidder detested most was dancing class. Whenever he had a choice of partners, he always seemed to dance with "a largish, very solid little girl who had a kind of pom-pon on the back of her dress that [he] could use to steer . . . her through the . . . hopelessly tricky maneuver of the 'reverse' " (AVK I:33).

Concerning the little girls at Buckingham School, Kidder recalls no sentimental attachment of that period, but he does recollect "cordial dislike" for one girl with pigtails, who sat two or three desks behind him. They never did get along. One day this little girl passed by Kidder's desk and yelled "ouch," which brought on him "an understandable, but false, suspicion of pencil-poking" (AVK I:33–34). However, he got even. There was a low-branching apple tree in the yard of the school, and one day, toward the end of recess, he saw her climbing down from it. He "had no pencil to prod her with, but . . . reached up and gave her behind a most satisfying pinch" (AVK I:33–34). She scrambled back up, out of reach. "Just then the bell rang and I ran for the door. She couldn't get down before it was shut. Whether or not she was 'kept after school', the usual penalty for coming in late from recess, I can't remember. I guess not, as she was what would now be called an 'apple polisher'."

Kidder confessed this action years later to a new headmistress of the Buckingham School, and she replied: "Your apple tree has been replaced by an inferior and less climbable one. The children everyone says are so wild are *much* tamer nowadays. No one has trapped a little girl in a tree by your Caruso-like [Crusoe-like] method" (AVK I:34). Kidder added:

"This I resent. The action, I admit, was identical, but not its motivation."

After completing the primary grades at the Buckingham School, Kidder was enrolled, in 1896, in the Preparatory Division of the Browne and Nichols School, in Cambridge. The curriculum included English, French, German, and mathematics, as well as seemingly endless instruction in dancing, which he continued to despise.

During Kidder's elementary school years, the family spent their summers away from Cambridge, first in Florida (from about 1892 to 1896) and later back at Marquette, Michigan, where the eldest son, Howard, was working as a mine engineer. They spent much of their time there at the Huron Mountain Club, a private resort on the shore of Lake Superior. Kidder's father was one of the club's early trustees (AVK I:36).

Summers spent at the Huron Club nurtured Kidder's interest in the study of nature, which continued in Cambridge. There Kidder and some of his boyhood friends established a bird club with the aid of Lieutenant Wirt Robinson, a military sciences instructor at Harvard, who was also an amateur naturalist. In addition to birding, Robinson also introduced the boys to the study of small mammals and insects and taught them to be observant of the natural world around them, not only in the countryside, but in the city as well (AVK I:50). This activity led—at the age of fifteen—to Kidder's first published paper, "A Bittern at Close Range," which appeared in the journal *Bird Lore*.

In Cambridge Kidder's two best friends were Richard Eustis and Eustis Russell. Euie Russell and Kidder were together at Browne and Nichols, at La Villa Aukenthaler School (at Ouchy, Switzerland), and at Harvard College. Euie was best man at Kidder's wedding and married Kidder's cousin Josephine Dorr. After a career as an attorney in Boston and Saint Paul, Minnesota, and service in the marines during World War I, Russell died in 1932 (AVK I:51).

Near the turn of the century, the Kidder family was rocked by Howard's death, from typhoid, on 6 December 1898. After his death the parents decided to spend a winter in Europe and in California. This was partly the result of the recent family tragedy, but also because A. V. Kidder was not making satisfactory progress at Browne and Nichols, and his parents thought it wise to take him out of school for a time. Apparently they felt that travel would be a stimulating alternative to books and classrooms.

Kidder's first sight of Europe (probably in 1900), was of Naples. There for the first time he saw beggars, many of them deformed. These experiences must have been shocking to a youngster who took for granted the comforts provided by his family in Marquette and Cambridge. Perhaps Kidder's travels in Italy and throughout Europe stimulated an early concern for the lifeways of other cultures and fueled his interest in anthropology. He visited Capri and its Blue Grotto, Sorrento, Pompeii, Herculaneum, and Rome. This experience may have contributed to Kidder's later interest in Old World archaeology.

From Rome Kidder and his family traveled to Florence, Venice, and then Switzerland. Kidder's recollections of this period contain descriptions of his interest in other cultures. Implicit in these recollections is his feeling of the absence of a more mature individual to guide and cultivate his interests. Evidently he felt he had missed a great deal.

The family next visited Paris, a good place to be in 1900. It was the year of l'Exposition Universelle, a magnificent display of the peoples and crafts of every land (AVK I:63). He saw it in the best of company, for his brother Homer had come over from Cambridge as soon as college was out and he was free from duty as an instructor in English at Harvard and Radcliffe. "No boy of fifteen could have had a more perfect companion than Homer, for I was then becoming old enough to profit from the maturity of his knowledge of almost every humanistic field" (AVK I:63). Kidder's appreciation for architecture in France and throughout Europe was developed under Homer's careful tutelage. A. V. Kidder's son, Randolph (personal communication, July 1983), suggests that Homer might have been the catalytic agent for introducing Ted to the world of anthropology. Homer had long been interested in the American Indian and had recorded some of the oral traditions of the Ojibwa (H. Kidder, 1899). In any case Homer apparently provided just the kind of guidance required by a young and curious mind. The two brothers spent most of their time studying the cathedral structure of Notre Dame, Saint Denis, Sainte Chapelle, and that of the city of Cologne. Homer became his best friend (AMK I:52); he was a patient teacher and the younger brother benefited from his friendly manner as well as his knowledge. Homer explained what they saw during their travels in France and provided a logical structure for it. Homer also gave his brother an interest in English literature—especially that of the poets and the Elizabethan dramatists— and in the early history of the Lake Superior country and its Indians (AVK

I:64). Homer's varied reading must have encouraged Ted to expand his own horizons. Beginning with his unpublished diaries of 1940, Kidder revealed his broad interests by listing the books he read each year. Titles ranged from Greek classics to Agatha Christie mystery novels.

The trip to Europe and the relationship with his academically oriented older brother perhaps provided the impetus for Kidder to become more serious about his studies. His boyhood interests had been less than scholarly, and some might even be called frivolous. It seems that Homer instilled in his brother a seriousness about life and intellectual activity that previously was lacking.

The family returned from Europe in August of 1901, and Kidder returned to the Browne and Nichols School with newfound enthusiasm. He began his long love affair with the German language, and it was the elementary grounding in German he received at Browne and Nichols and later, instruction in German at La Villa, that Kidder credited when he easily passed the language entrance examination on his application to Harvard University (AVK I:72).

The new start at Browne and Nichols was slightly more successful regarding mathematics—always his worst subject—than previous years had been. This situation was mainly due to Kidder's algebra teacher, Edgar Nichols. In spite of Kidder's poor performance even in his class, Nichols was not a poor teacher in Kidder's estimation. He had a custom of calling his class to the blackboard to "work out some wretched problem about a man who could row so many yards when bucking a current which ran, etc., etc.,—the kind that becomes all full of x's and y's" (AVK I:73). This no doubt contributed to the math anxiety that dogged Kidder throughout his life. The only pleasure young Kidder had in Mr. Nichols's algebra class was to see how white his teacher could get in an hour; he used his hand instead of an eraser to wipe his blackboard clear, wiping the chalk dust on the seat of his pants (AVK I:73–74).

Kidder did better in English. Under the direction of Mr. Browne, Kidder acquired his ability in writing and his taste for fine literature.

In the autumn of 1902, Kidder's parents enrolled him at the La Villa School, in Ouchy, Switzerland. They had planned to spend a considerable time living in Europe (made possible by Alfred's retirement, in 1901), and they thought it better, because of logistics, that their son accompany them. La Villa proved to be an extraordinary school. It provided a chance for him to interact with boys from a variety of countries. Attending the school were students from Scotland, Great Britain, Turkey, Argentina, Bolivia, Cuba, and Brazil. The teachers of the school were also of many nationalities.

La Villa prided itself on preparing its students in advanced language study and liberal arts. This school was instrumental, just as the Browne and Nichols School had been, in helping young Kidder acquire the skills he would need to enter Harvard in 1904. The year saw him mature scholastically and broaden his worldly experience as well.

One highlight of Kidder's year at La Villa was his attendance at a play that starred Sarah Bernhardt. Sitting in the wings, offstage, Kidder saw Bernhardt being brought from her dressing room by her maid and her manager. Ceremoniously giving her his arm, her manager led her to a special armchair that was always ready in the wings. There she sat, relaxed, "an old lady with a knitted gray shawl over her shoulders" (AVK I:95–96). At the sound of her cue she rose and sailed out on the stage. Then the unthinkable happened:

> *The dialogue called for her to smoke. But the property man had failed to have the wherewithal ready to have {a cigarette} on the table. Ad-libbing, the man filling in with some sort of business, she strolled laughing over to us, half-turned her back to the audience and hissed directly at me, 'Une cigarette! Vite! Vite! Vite!' I had a box of Rameses in my pocket, I yanked it open, held one out. She plucked it from my hand, turned, drifted back center, where her partner, who had it ready, struck a match and gave her a light. After a couple of puffs she sank into her chair and took, or rather started to take, a deep inhalation. Calamity! Rameses were not really strong cigarettes, but they were evidently not the very mild sort that should have been provided. A choking sound, a desperate gulp, then a terrible spell of coughing. The man—he was a hero then, no matter what the author may have made him—played up nobly, created what I believe is known as a scene-stealing diversion, and almost at once the curtain came down. (AVK I:97)*

In 1903 Kidder left La Villa to attend the Noble and Greenough School, in the Boston area. It was hard for him to leave La Villa, but his parents decided it would be best (AVK I:31). In his personal papers and diaries, he mentions his parents' decision concerning the transfer, but does not elaborate on their reasons. Perhaps they had in mind a more "Americanized" education for him, to better prepare him to enter Harvard College. La Villa had served its purpose; his experiences there gave him the confidence to strike out on his own, knowing that he could handle himself in any social situation.

HARVARD

Ted Kidder entered Harvard College in the fall of 1904, just a few weeks before his nineteenth birthday. Harvard was then nearing the end of an era of educational reform initiated by Charles W. Eliot when he took over the presidency of the school, in 1869. Among other things Eliot had discarded the old system of a strictly prescribed curriculum, in favor of an elective system in which each student enjoyed considerable latitude in organizing his own course of study.

The elective system was well suited to Kidder's varied interests and allowed him the freedom to explore many subject areas. He mentions in his diaries the subjects he found especially to his liking: French, German, Latin, ancient history, modern European history, and American history. With a few exceptions, notably zoology and ornithology, he focused on the humanities during his first two years at Harvard. Apparently he had trouble deciding on a major. At first he had considered a career in medicine, but his dislike of math and a distaste for chemistry quickly ruled that out.

His aversion for chemistry developed from his experiences in the basic chemistry course required for entrance into medical school; he did very poorly in that course. It met in Boylston Hall, "an antiquated, badly ventilated, evil smelling building. The laboratories in the basement smelled even worse and one had to spend hours down there" (AVK II:6–7). His instructor, Professor Jackson, no doubt contributed to Kidder's disillusionment. Not being interested in the subject of chemistry, Kidder would often read books during Professor Jackson's lectures, although he knew that the professor got very annoyed with students who did this. One fateful day Kidder was discovered reading *The Virginian* in class. During the lecture Professor Jackson interjected:

'Will the gentleman who is reading the book please speak to me after the lecture,' so I went down after the lecture and there were four other fellows who went down too. He fixed his eye on me {and} these other fellows just sort of evaporated. (AVK I:8).

Professor Jackson simply noted the book Kidder had been reading; to his surprise, he was not thrown out of class.

Kidder's memoirs note how he despised his time in Boylston Hall. For that reason he applauded a decision many years later to let the building serve the study of modern languages instead of chemistry.

But medicine's loss was anthropology's gain. Like most undergraduates—of his day and ours—Kidder was inclined to enroll in those courses that required the least amount of work. Thus he elected, in his sophomore year, to take a course on the ethnology of the American Indian in lieu of a dreaded mathematics class. The course, designated Anthropology 5, sounded interesting to him and, "better yet, it came on Monday, Wednesday, and Friday at nine—as I was much averse to courses that met on Saturdays. Furthermore, the course was favorably spoken of by some of my less studious friends who had taken it in former years" (Woodbury 1973:5). The course was taught by Professor Roland B. Dixon, later a valued friend of Kidder's, under whom he did some of his graduate work. Dixon's assistant was Vilhjalmur Stefansson, future ethnographer of the Arctic (Woodbury 1973:5). It was this course—the first of several he took as an undergraduate—that Kidder remembered as being the starting point of his interest in an archaeological career.

His decision to study anthropology made Kidder something of a pioneer. The discipline was in its infancy in those days. The anthropology community at Harvard was not even officially a department, but rather the sideline of a few professors in other fields. It had close ties to the Peabody Museum, and its funding came mostly from public and private endowments. Because of its small size, relations among members of the community were close. Students enjoyed much individual attention from faculty members, who served more as advisors or tutors than as classroom teachers. Kidder's own mentor was his father's old friend, Professor Frederic Ward Putnam, with whom he shared a mutual interest in ornithology.

In the spring of 1907, almost by accident, Kidder made a decision that launched his career as a field archaeologist. He had planned to spend the summer with his long-time childhood friend, Eustis Russell, a classmate at Harvard, but for some reason that plan fell through (AVK I:51), leaving Kidder at loose ends (AVK II:6). Then, at breakfast one morning, he accidentally noticed an announcement in the Harvard *Crimson* (the student newspaper) that three men who had specialized in anthropology might be accepted as volunteers on an expedition to the cliff-dweller country of the Southwest, under the auspices of the Archaeological Institute of America. Those interested, the notice read, should apply to Dr. A. M. Tozzer, at Thayer Hall (AVK II:6). Kidder presented himself at Dr. Tozzer's room, and there he found and for the first time really talked with, two men who were to become his life-long friends and close associates: Alfred Tozzer and Sylvanus Morley.

> *The third man was John Gould Fletcher, of Little Rock, a poet given to free verse, already a protégé of Amy Lowell and later the author of a very good book on his native Arkansas. Morley, Fletcher, and I, being the only applicants, were all accepted. I can't remember that we were given any definite instructions, except that early in July we were to meet Edgar L. Hewett, the leader of a University of Utah party, at a place called Bluff City, Utah. (AVK II:7)*

CHAPTER TWO

FIELDWORK:
PUSHED OFF THE PIER

Throughout the remaining weeks of that spring semester of his junior year, Kidder looked forward to his upcoming summer of fieldwork in the Southwest. Finally, his classes and examinations behind him, the twenty-one-year-old Kidder boarded a train bound for Colorado.

Kidder (AVK II:7) implies that this trip to Utah was the first time that he did anything really on his own. He (or his parents) must have paid his transportation and funded most of his first field season. His unpublished papers and diaries do not mention that Tozzer or Hewett provided such funding. He made the journey alone, for some reason, leaving a day ahead of Fletcher and Morley. He had never before been west of Chicago, so every day offered new sights and new experiences. Nothing Kidder had been familiar with back East could be taken for granted in the West. Even his Bostonian dialect could get him in trouble, as he discovered one morning when he tried to order breakfast on the train:

I ordered dropped eggs. The waitress looked at me as if she thought I was making game of her; nevertheless, she went and talked to someone through the scuttle in the back wall. Then she turned and called across to me 'The chef says to quit your kidding!' Never having heard the word poached and as those were the days when there was a cook in every proper kitchen, I was entirely unable to explain how an egg should be dropped. I compromised on hot cakes. (AVK I:71).

At Alamosa, Colorado, Kidder transferred to a narrow-gauge line to take him to Durango. The ride on the little, clanky train lasted all day. The track skirted the edge of the gorge uncomfortably, and an elderly bridgebuilder who was smoking his cigar on the back platform took

11

pleasure in showing Kidder where, in the spring, a locomotive had rolled off, and "where, 'back in '81, a stage went down killin' nine'" (AVK III. 1:30).

The train climbed over 10,200 feet stopped at a watering station; but we had not yet crossed the Continental Divide. The train began to descend, crossed the Divide, which is on the West of the Pass itself, and came into the long, broken valleys along the sides of which we traveled the rest of the day. (AVK III:30–31)

Kidder finally reached Durango at 5:30 P.M. and took a room for the night.

The next morning, Sunday, 30 June, Kidder continued on by train to Mancos, Colorado, where he hired a buggy to take him to Cortez, twenty miles away. But his final destination, Bluff City, Utah, still lay more than fifty miles farther west, and there was no railroad. Kidder would have to find his own transportation.

While in Mancos he had been told about a man named Jesse Majors, who had a government contract to carry the mail between there and Bluff. At Cortez he talked with Majors and arranged to be taken to Bluff with a mail rider. They traveled by horse-drawn buggy rather than on horseback, much to Kidder's delight. On the way Kidder had his first look at the San Juan River, which he described as a "swirling, chocolate-colored [river] so laden with earth from the torn banks of up-stream arroyos" (AVK II:18). [1]

In his travels throughout the San Juan country, Kidder noted that "eastern people" were made to feel quite welcome. Traders would take in the weary traveler and feed both man and beast. Even perfect strangers were treated in this manner. Later the custom changed out of economic necessity. Kidder recalled that it nearly broke John Wetherill's hospitable heart, toward the end of his life, when improved roads brought so many sightseers through Kayenta on their way to Rainbow Bridge that he had to charge them or go broke (AVK II:18–19).

The last day of Kidder's journey to Bluff was spent, in part, in a trading post and general store in Aneth, Utah. The little store at Aneth was like every other of the time in the Navajo country. The store's counter was highly polished by the Indians, who always lounged on it while doing business or just being there. "No Navajo, male or female, was ever in a hurry whether buying a can of peaches and a pound of wool or blanket . . . (AVK II:20). After resting, Kidder and the mail carrier left for Bluff and arrived there the night of 1 July 1907. Kidder was dropped off at the house of a couple named Raplee, who took him in for the night.

The next morning Ted Kidder and Edgar Hewett met for the first time, at the breakfast table of Mr. and Mrs. Raplee. Thus began a professional association that would continue—though not always cordially—for years to come. Kidder's introduction to field archaeology soon followed. After breakfast Hewett and Kidder walked up to the base of the cliffs, where there was a long, flat-topped mount that he told Kidder was the site of an ancient pueblo. The site was strewn with hammerstones and potsherds, thousands of them, of every sort—black, white, red, coarse, and fine. Across the canyon was an encampment of the renegade Utes who used to live about the valley: a cluster of shelters, poles hung with cottonwood boughs to keep off the sun. They found a dozen or so of the men lying around a blanket, deep in some game of cards (AVK II:25).

After a short day of site surveying (cut short by the fierce heat), Kidder returned to Bluff, where he met several students from Utah who were also working for Hewett in the San Juan watershed. They were mostly seniors or first-year graduates at the state university, and Kidder thought them seemingly older men than the upperclassmen at Harvard (AVK II:26). Kidder then returned to the Raplees' ranch to await the arrival of Hewett, about 5 o'clock that afternoon.

HOVENWEEP

After supper Hewett and Kidder set off on horseback for McElmo Canyon, a remote area straddling the Utah-Colorado border, some thirty-five miles away. They rode several miles up the San Juan in the long summer evening before making camp for the night. Next morning at daybreak they continued their journey, arriving later that day at an isolated ranch house near the junction of McElmo and Yellow Jacket canyons. The ranch, operated by a Mr. James Holley and his family, would be their headquarters during the coming weeks of fieldwork. Fletcher and Morley joined them there later the same day, and together they set up camp.

The next day was the Fourth of July, Independence Day. The date was ironic, because the three Harvard men were about to have bestowed upon them more independence than they probably wanted. Hewett took them to the top of a nearby mesa and gave them their assignment: "He waved an arm, taking in it seemed, about half the world, 'I want you boys to make an archaeological survey of this country. I'll be back in three weeks'" (AVK III:39). Hewett then left them, offering only one bit of advice to guide them: They would find ruins, he said, on mesas that overlook the junctions of important drainages. And that was all he told them. The rest they would have to figure out on their own. Such was Hewett's "education" of would-be field archaeologists. As he later recalled:

I have applied something that I learned on the waterfront of Lake Michigan when all the kids in the southern part of Chicago swam in the lake as a matter of inalienable right. I noticed one young leader who was obviously the boss of the waterfront. I observed that all the new recruits of the gang swam like a fish in a day or two. I said to this young ruffian, 'Who teaches these kids to swim so quickly and so well?' He said, 'I do.'

'Well, how do you do it?'

'Push 'em off de pier.' (Hewett 1943:149)

Today Hewett's sink-or-swim approach has been replaced with training involving the scrutiny of every movement of field students, each activity being carefully analyzed and criticized by the instructor. Hewett (1943: 151–52) continues:

Kidder's first workout was a fifty mile ride across the mesa with me on the roughest bronco I could find for him. He came through it a chastened man, but game. Fletcher was horse wrangler in charge of the team, a venerable horse and a wicked looking mule. A run-in with the latter resulted in his getting tangled in the mule's picket rope and dragged a quarter of a mile or so over the rocky terrain. He was not favorably disposed to this first phase of his 'training'. Morley undertook the commissary; put plaster of Paris in his biscuit dough in lieu of baking powder; spread the camp beds in the dry irrigation ditch (water turned on at four in the morning); moved their

Harvard crimson blankets to Mr. Holley's haystacks where in the early morning downpour the colors 'ran' copiously over Mr. Holley's new mown alfalfa. The next transfer was to a neighboring group of anthills. A high wind scattered their note paper and garments over the valley . . .

I planned their work so they wouldn't lie about the camp; told them to make a complete archaeological survey of McElmo mesa and have their report ready in six weeks {sic}. I had to join a group of western students two hundred miles down the San Juan. Helplessly they watched me ride off into the sunset.[2]

Kidder and Fletcher had no idea what an "archaeological survey" was, nor what it entailed. Their anthropology courses at Harvard had provided no training in field archaeology. Morley was somewhat better prepared, having done fieldwork in the Yucatan the year before (Brunhouse 1971: 32), so Hewett had put him in charge. Lacking any sort of plan, and with only Morley's limited experience and Hewett's terse instructions to guide them, the three men set to work.

The area to be surveyed lay mostly to the north of the Holley ranch headquarters, in the area of what is now Hovenweep National Monument. Much of this territory had already been surveyed (Bandelier 1890b), although Hewett was apparently unaware of that. One of the major problems encountered by Kidder and his two colleagues was that they had to make their own map as they went along, since Hewett had given them none. As a matter of fact, no really good map of the area existed at the time. Morley gave the mapping job to Kidder.

Knowing no formal methodology, the men improvised their own. Each ruin found was mapped, measured, and described in notebooks. Morley wrote the field notes, and Kidder kept a journal of their activities. Both Morley and Kidder drew up plans of the structures they found, and all three of them did the measuring (AVK III:34).

Fletcher, whose fingers were all thumbs, turned out, though willing, to be of little use except to hold one end of the tape. Said tape, supplied by Hewett, was a 50-foot cloth one; {Kidder} brought along a cheap pocket compass, Morley and Kidder each had a kodak.

Notwithstanding our primitive equipment, we did a pretty good job. But it was all due to Vay {Morley}. He was an indefatigable worker, full of energy, invariably cheerful, whistling and singing as he stumbled about among the ruins. Very nearsighted, it was a miracle that he didn't break a leg or pitch himself over any of the cliffs to the very edges of which many of the little canyon-head pueblos clung. His example kept us going, in spite of the great heat, and various minor discomforts, the worst of which was the clinging of the swarms of flies . . . (AVK III:43)[3]

Their workdays, which began at daybreak, were long and exhausting. Kidder (AVK III:44) recalled that one of the greatest pleasures after a day's work was to go to the irrigation ditch at the Holleys' ranch, lie in the wet sand at the bottom of the ditch, and read. Appreciation of the cool, wet sand was shared by the dogs and chickens of the ranch, but this did not prevent him from seeking the relief it afforded from the constant dry heat.

Mrs. Holley did everything she could to make the three young men comfortable. She was an excellent cook and fed them well. Moreover, she handled all her responsibilities, including the rearing of the seven Holley children, with one arm gone at the elbow. But Kidder noted that Mr. Holley was no worker and, as far as he could see, the whole family income came from a few acres of alfalfa and a small herd of cattle. Mr. Holley liked to dig for pots in the rubbish heaps and burial mounds of the older ruins near his ranch (AVK III:44). Kidder "got him the nickname 'Moki Jim', Moqui, 'The Dead Ones', being the derisive Navajo name for the Hopi Indians, which was used by Jim Holley and many other Whites for the ancient cliff-dwellers and Pueblos" (AVK III:35).[4]

On 7 July, their first Sunday in the field, Fletcher took a bad fall, suffering cuts, bruises, and a broken tooth. That same evening he got hurt again, when a mule he was leading into their corral broke away from him, leaving him with a nasty rope burn on his hands. Thereafter, the men decided to slacken their pace, and set aside Sundays for rest and recuperation. But for Fletcher the damage had been done, and from then on he became increasingly demoralized.

As their survey progressed, the men became more efficient workers and more astute observers. They found that Hewett's hint about finding ruins near the junctions of important drainages was correct. Kidder began to notice variations in the style and color of the pottery they found, noting that the most common type was black-on-white, but that red and gray wares were also present. Thus was born the interest in ceramics that spanned Kidder's long career.

Kidder found himself admiring the ingenuity of ancient Anasazi and their skill in stonemasonry. Recalling the many round and square towers perched along the rim of Ruin Canyon (now a major attraction at Hovenweep), he observed that "They had good eyes, these old fellows, to pick the strategic positions, for along this upper end of the canyon there is not a cliff or turn of the cliffs which is not guarded or at least overlooked and raked by some structure or other" (AVK III:45–48).

Despite their best efforts, the three students were not seasoned fieldworkers. Some details inevitably escaped them. Being preoccupied with the more prominent canyon-head pueblos of Mesa Verdean date, they failed to notice numerous earlier ruins, farther back on the mesa tops. Kidder did not even learn of their existence until the following summer (AVK II:50–51).

The McElmo survey continued until Hewett returned, on 25 July. He spent the rest of that day with his three novices, going over their field notes and maps, discussing the work accomplished there. Then he announced that the following day they would leave for Cortez, Colorado, and further survey work at the newly created Mesa Verde National Park. After that, he told them, their next project would take them to New Mexico (AVK II:56).[5]

MESA VERDE

On the morning of 26 July, after fond good-byes to their hosts, the Holleys, the party set out for Cortez. They arrived that evening, tired and hungry. The horses were fed, and the foursome walked to the local hotel for a beefsteak dinner, which lifted their spirits tremendously (AVK II:57).

After spending one day in Cortez, the party made the steep ascent to the high, sloping tableland of the Mesa Verde. Here they spent the next two and a half weeks, mapping the large, multistoried ruins using only the rudimentary equipment Hewett had given them. They began their survey with the large pueblo known as Spruce Tree House. It took five days for Fletcher and Kidder to do their part of the work, and two more for Morley to wind up his notetaking. Fletcher was feeling ill, so while Morley worked on his notes, Kidder began the mapping of the next structure, Cliff Palace, alone (AVK II:60). It was here that Kidder made his first discovery of human skeletal remains. He went into a cave looking for water when something made him glance up. Suddenly he found himself looking into the empty eye sockets of a skull, upright against a rock not ten feet away. Nearby he found a shoulder blade and part of a pelvis (AVK II:65).

Kidder later sent his find to the Peabody Museum at Harvard, where it could be properly studied. But the experience forced him to reflect again on the deficiencies of his education. He was able to identify the remains as human, but beyond that he could say no more about them. He knew nothing of the criteria for determining age or sex, not to mention diet, lifestyle, cause of death, or any of the other subtle information about the life of an individual that bones sometimes reveal.

Kidder, later recalling his first skeletal find, thought of Aleš Hrdlička and his earlier complaints that the anthropological community in Washington, D.C., at the National Museum already had too much in the way of skeletal material:

> Aleš Hrdlička, known in Washington as 'Ales and Hardliquor', that extraordinary man, who always anxious to build up the collections of his department in the National Museum, especially of the so-called soft parts of the human body, complained in one of his annual reports, 'We have more than 15,000 skulls, but no brains'. On reading which, W. H. Holmes, the Director, pencilled on the margin, Neil Judd once told me, 'Of this, I've regretfully been aware for many years'. (AVK II:67)

At Mesa Verde, as at Hovenweep, it appears that Hewett had again overlooked an earlier survey of the area. Gustav Nordenskiöld had carried out excavations at Mesa Verde and had published (in 1893) maps and descriptions of the ruins. Kidder must not have been aware of Nordenskiöld's work either, for he makes no reference to it in his field notes. Three years later, however, he cited Nordenskiöld in "Explorations in Southern Utah in 1908" (Kidder 1910).

For Kidder the two and a half weeks spent at Mesa Verde were also memorable because it was there that he and Morley cemented what was to be a lifelong friendship, and that he first met another lifelong friend, Jesse Nusbaum. Nusbaum, then only twenty years old, just out of normal school at Greeley, Colorado, and already a notable photographer, joined the Hewett party there and spent the rest of the summer with them. It was his first visit to Mesa Verde. Later he became park superintendent and "did so much for it in so many different ways that he deserves to be called 'Mr. Mesa Verde' " (AVK II:61).

Meanwhile Fletcher's situation was going from bad to worse. Morley wrote in his diary that Fletcher's constant complaining led to repeated confrontations with both Kidder and himself (Morley 1907a:7, 12; 1907b:19). Finally, on 5 August, Fletcher quit the party in disgust, with the remark that he was "tired . . . of being Morley's nigger" (Morley 1907b:30). Apparently he did not leave the group immediately, though, since Kidder noted in his diary that he was still with them a week later, when they left the Mesa Verde (Kidder 1907b:21).

PUYÉ

The next destination of the survey party—which now included Nusbaum as replacement for Fletcher—was the Puyé cliff dwellings, near Española, New Mexico. They traveled east to Antonito, Colorado, arriving there on 16 August, then south into New Mexico on a little, narrow-gauge railroad. At Española they met Ivan Gonzales, governor of Santa Clara Pueblo, who loaded the students and their baggage into his wagon and drove them to Santa Clara Canyon, where they set up camp. Hewett, meanwhile, went into Santa Fe to buy supplies (AVK II:68–69).

Kidder's diaries for the period spent at Puyé are incomplete. In writing his memoirs years later, he was obliged to rely more on Morley's diaries than his own.[6]

Santa Clara Canyon, where they made camp, is one of the many narrow canyons cut into the steep escarpment of the Pajarito Plateau, which itself forms the eastern flank of the Jemez Mountains. The Pajarito is a tableland of hard, dark basaltic rock, overlain by a layer of pure white tufa several hundred feet thick. Piñon, juniper, and some ponderosa pine dot the mesa tops. It is an area rich in archaeological sites, notably those in

Frijoles Canyon—now part of Bandelier National Monument—and at Puyé. It reminded Kidder of the Mesa Verde (AVK II:71).

From their camp in Santa Clara Canyon to the top of the mesa was a long climb, but it yielded a magnificent view in all directions. The ruin lay close to the edge of the canyon. Into the soft tufa of the canyon walls the old people had dug many rooms (AVK II:74).

Kidder's first experience with archaeological excavation came at Puyé.

{Puyé} {k}ept us very busy for it was the first piece of digging for either Morley {although Morley noted in his diary of 1907 that his first excavation experience was at Mesa Verde} or me and we'd had no training whatever. Nowadays most budding archaeologists go to one or another of the summer field schools that are held by several universities which possess a department of anthropology; or, as graduate students, one or two may accompany a seasoned investigator on an expedition. In either case, they receive a thorough practical grounding in all important techniques called for in excavation and they generally have course work or trenchside instruction on the theoretical aspects of stratigraphy, chronology, artifact classification, and site patterns. Hewett has written that he threw us on our own, both to try us out and to make us learn for ourselves. It may have been, probably was, very good for us although it may have been hard on the ruin. But, thanks again to Morley, we did a pretty good job . . . (AVK II:76–77)

Not everyone shared Kidder's enthusiasm about the dig. In the McElmo country and at Mesa Verde, the survey party had been working far away from any living descendants of the Anasazi. But here two modern pueblos, the Tewa towns of Santa Clara and San Ildefonso, lay nearby. The Puyé ruin was—and still is—located on Santa Clara land. From time to time, Morley noted in his diary, the Santa Claras sent delegations to protest the excavation of their land. Hewett had evidently not bothered to consult them or ask their permission to dig there. But Hewett, as usual, was never in camp to meet with them, so their objections were disregarded and the digging continued (Morley 1907b:22).

Kidder thought the fireplaces were one of the most interesting features encountered at Puyé, and they presented him with two puzzles that tested his skill as an investigator. The fireplaces were rectangular basins dug into the floor against a wall. If near a door, they were often screened from drafts by a slab or low masonry wall. Each one was lined with stone or neatly edged with adobe and set with two or three hard stones that evidently supported one edge of a cooking slab, whose other edge rested on an upright slab at the back. But Kidder found none of the cooking slabs in place, nor did any loose ones come to light. This was an oddity for which he could offer no explanation.

Years later after watching Pueblo women cooking *piki* (a thin, wafer-like cornbread) on highly polished and carefully seasoned stone griddles, Kidder realized that the missing cooking slabs must have been piki stones. The piki stone being one of the most valued possessions of a Pueblo housewife, and the proper type of rock for making them not available locally, the departing inhabitants of Puyé must have taken their piki stones with them when they left. His discovery of similar stone griddles at Pecos confirmed that piki making was an ancient practice, not one recently introduced, which further strengthened the argument. Mystery solved—but as often happens in archaeology, the solution was years in cóming (AVK II:77–79).

The second mystery was even more bizarre. Underneath one fireplace, Kidder found the skeleton of an infant, apparently stillborn. Puzzled by this discovery, he asked Hewett about it and learned that similar burials had been unearthed there and at the nearby site of Tschirege. No grave offerings accompanied the tiny skeletons (AVK II:79).

It was not until thirty years later that Kidder learned from various ethnographers that it was the custom among certain living Pueblo groups to bury stillborn infants, or babies dying shortly after birth, under the floor of the house. One explanation of this practice—suggested to Kidder by Mischa Titiev, who was familiar with a similar practice among the Hopi—was that it kept the soul of the infant within the home so that it might be reborn to the same mother, or at least to the same family, at some future time (AVK II:80).

Although Kidder did not publish these findings until 1937, it demonstrates that he was one of the first American archaeologists—apart from Frank Hamilton Cushing—to attempt to explain a puzzling discovery by drawing on ethnological research.

While at Puyé Kidder continued to collect potsherds, as he had during the McElmo survey, and began to organize and classify them by type. Out of this grew an interest in ceramics as an indicator of cultural similarity (or dissimilarity) that spanned his career.[7] Recalling this in his memoirs years later, Kidder wrote:

> *I, having incurably been infected by the ceramic bacillus, on my first exposure in the McElmo country, took the greatest pleasure in the several new types I saw at Puyé. There, that summer, I gave one of them a specific designation; a thick gray ware, it was, with decorations in dull black. I called it Biscuit, and it became, I believe the first of the countless hundreds of named ceramic types resulting from the taxonomic orgy that has spread, like the Black Death in the Middle Ages, over both the Americas and has resulted in so hopeless a situation that only recently have attempts been made to haul our archaeological heads out of the still rising flood of nomenclature that threatens to engulf us. I must have said, or maybe written somewhere, anyhow I've recently been quoted as remarking that when I came back to Southwestern archaeology I felt like an elderly rabbit returning to his native briar patch to find it overrun by a thousand descendants. (AVK II:82)*

His statement about a "taxonomic orgy" was a reference to the uncoordinated efforts of various scholars to construct cultural and chronological frameworks for the Southwest, based largely on pottery types, during the first decades of the twentieth century. The Pecos Classification (proposed by Kidder and others, in 1927) was an attempt to impose some order on this chaotic situation. In this he was at least partially successful, for the Pecos Classification became the standard that, in modified form, continues in use today.

Altogether the three-week period at Puyé was a great success for Kidder. It left him "more than ever sure that [he] didn't want to be a doctor" (AVK I:105).

> *The excavation there had climaxed that summer's three undertakings, each very different, each keenly interesting and each in a new and unforgetable environment. They were such as almost inevitably to make an archaeologist of a youngster who loved the outdoors {and} was naturally a close observer . . . (AVK I:106)*

Even though Kidder encountered problems with Hewett's hands-off approach to field training, he still thought of him as a good teacher

(Givens 1989; see AVK I:120). He recognized that Hewett's field school was giving him beneficial exposure to various archaeological problems. With this in mind, Kidder wrote to Hewett on 28 September 1907, after returning to Cambridge, about the possibility of attending the second field school, in 1908:

> *Dear Mr. Hewitt {sic}*
>
> *Since returning to Cambridge I have not written to you because I did not know just where you might be, and also because I had not had time to discuss things fully with my family. I have talked matters over with my father and was of course delighted to find that he was entirely in sympathy with my desire to take up archaeology as a life-work.*
>
> *Is there a possibility of my working for the early part of next summer in Utah? (Letter from Kidder to Hewett, 28 September 1907, ELH)*

Under the auspices of the Archaeological Institute of America, Edgar Lee Hewett founded the School of American Archaeology (later the School of American Research) in Santa Fe, New Mexico. The charge of the school was to train students in archaeology and ethnology. He conducted his first field school session during the summer of 1907, when he "trained" both Alfred Kidder and Sylvanus Morley. At about the same time, he was working on his doctorate in education at the University of Geneva. Hewett was a leading coordinator of archaeological efforts in the American Southwest and was instrumental in pushing through the Antiquities Act of 1906 for the protection of archaeological resources.

Despite Hewett's sometimes slapdash approach to fieldwork, Kidder and his colleagues held him in high esteem. In reminiscences written years afterward, Kidder described that summer's beginning of his long association with Hewett and discussed his impact on the development of archaeology in the Southwest:

> *He was thirty-nine in 1907, a tireless rugged man whom Morley and I, during those two summers, devotedly admired, for he was, and continued all his life to be, an inspiring teacher. His early archaeological work was good; he was effectively active in lobbying for the Antiquities Act of 1906 as well as in urging successfully the creation, the same year, of the Mesa Verde National Park. That*

*Santa Fe became a leading center for archaeological research was en-
tirely due to his efforts. The Art Museum, so significant an element
in the development of painting and sculpture in the Southwest, is a
monument to his leadership. These accomplishments and many others
have failed to bring him well deserved credit in the profession because
of certain unfortunate moves in anthropological politics, but even
more because he failed completely to keep abreast of the rapid growth
of archaeological practice, especially with the results of stratigraphic
and technological studies, which from about 1910 on have brought
increasingly clear understanding of the cultural and, by extension,
the social history of the greater Southwest. However, he inspired and
gave their first opportunities for research to many young people, including Morley and myself, which makes me especially anxious that
the errors, in great part negative, of which he was guilty should not
result in forgetfulness of his importance as a constructive force in
American anthropology. (AVK I:120)*

GRADUATE SCHOOL—AND A BRIDE

In 1908 Kidder graduated from Harvard with a bachelor's degree in
anthropology. That summer he spent another field season in the Southwest, again under the direction of Hewett, who had just been made
director of the newly formed School of American Archaeology, in Santa
Fe. The school's parent organization, the Archaeological Institute of
America, cosponsored the work, in association with the University of
Utah (Woodbury 1973:17). Sylvanus Morley also participated in the
project, which involved the same areas surveyed the previous year. Kidder later (1910) published a report of their findings, in "Explorations in
Southeastern Utah in 1908."

The following winter (1908–1909), Kidder became acquainted with
a type of archaeology far different from what he had been exposed to in the
American Southwest, when he traveled with his parents to Greece and
Egypt. It was during this trip that he met Madeleine Appleton, his future
wife. Ted and Madeleine became engaged shortly thereafter and were
married in 1910.[8]

In the fall of 1909 Kidder entered graduate school at Harvard to begin work on his doctorate in anthropology. There he had the opportunity to study under two men who were outstanding in their respective fields: the Egyptologist George Reisner and the art historian George Chase, a specialist in the study of classical Greek ceramics. From Reisner Kidder finally received his first formal training in field methodology (reversing the usual academic order of things, in which theory precedes practice). Kidder had heard much about Reisner while in Egypt and was eager to enroll in his class at Harvard. He later told a friend that he had never enjoyed a course so much. In a posthumous tribute to Kidder, Robert Wauchope summed up Reisner's influence:

> Reisner explained the aims of archaeology and how to attack a problem, how to determine a culture's chronological relations to other cultures and its trade contacts with its contemporaries, gave a lot of stratigraphic theory, recommended leaving test columns or sections for later checking, explained the proper disposal of backdirt, taught a classification of various kinds of debris, described details of cataloging, and discussed 'the organization and house-keeping problems of an expedition'. . . . One of the things that Kidder is important for in the history of archaeology is that he introduced Reisner's methods to the New World. (Wauchope 1965:151)

From George Chase, the art historian, Kidder received further confirmation of his belief that ceramics are worthy of careful study and analysis by archaeologists. The influence of Chase's course on Greek vase painting can be seen in Kidder's doctoral dissertation, in which the style and decorative motifs of Pueblo pottery are treated in detail (Wauchope 1965:152).

Kidder also had the opportunity to study under the eminent ethnographer Frank Boas, who was a visiting professor for a term. Kidder seems to have tolerated Boas's particularistic methods in the field, but did not embrace them as some of Boas's other students did.

Kidder's summers during graduate school were taken up with more fieldwork. In 1910 he participated in digs in Newfoundland and Labrador. In 1912 he returned to New Mexico, where he took part in the excavation of historic Pueblo ruins in Gobernador and Largo canyons, east of Bloomfield (Woodbury 1973:21).

In 1914 Kidder received his Ph.D. in anthropology. His doctoral dissertation was entitled "Southwestern Ceramics: Their Value in Reconstructing the History of the Ancient Cliff Dwelling and Pueblo Tribes: An Exposition from the Point of View of Type Distinctions." A portion of it, dealing with the pottery of the Pajarito Plateau, was published by the American Anthropological Association, in 1915. In his dissertation, Kidder tried to demonstrate that the pottery of the American Southwest could be used as a yardstick of cultural development, as was already being done in the Old World by archaeologists there. Two lines of evidence may be derived from a study of ceramics, Kidder noted in his dissertation: "the one technological, concerning itself with the quality of clay and methods of manufacture and burning; the other artistic, treating of the life-histories of design and their possible growth, changes and decadence" (Kidder 1914:17).

Thus by 1914 Kidder's expertise in the study of ceramics was firmly established. The next step was the integration of his detailed knowledge of pottery styles with the then-novel concept of stratigraphic analysis, to work out a system for assigning relative dates to sites all over the Four Corners region. That step was taken the following year, when Kidder began work on the project with which his name has ever after been associated: the excavation of Pecos Pueblo.

NOTES

1. See appendix 1 for a description of this trip from Kidder's 1907 diary.
2. John Fletcher also provides a glimpse into Hewett's method of training field archaeologists in his autobiography (1937), *Life is my Song*.
3. Morley's diaries (1907a, 1907b) are a valuable record of the 1907 surveys, although they do not mention any specific plans that Morley or Kidder had for their activities in the McElmo area. They were merely following the instructions of Hewett. Kidder's diaries of that period do not discuss this topic either. If they did record their own survey plans, they may be filed with the archives of the Archaeological Institute of America. Currently, the Institute has moved to newer quarters, and their archival materials are not available for study.
4. J. W. Fewkes noted the Hopis' natural dislike for the Navajo term and called them by their own name in his many papers. "It is now universally used, as is Kiva, another Hopi word, that J. W. Powell suggested be employed instead of

the Spanish *estufa* for the specialized ceremonial chamber of the Pueblo. Victor Mindeleff was, I think the first to put it into the literature" (AVK III:35).

5. Further details of the three-week survey of the McElmo region can be found in the extracts from Kidder's diary in appendix 1.

6. He does recall, however, that it later became the site of the famous Los Alamos research center. He writes (AVK II:71): "When Los Alamos was being made ready to lay those hellish eggs, whose hatching knew an awful peril for all mankind, I happened to run into Robert Milliken in Washington. 'In a letter I got the other day,' he said, 'a Santa Fe friend mentioned he'd seen you there. What were you doing in those parts?' I innocently inquired. The great physicist looked me squarely in the eye. 'Your correspondent was mistaken, I've not been in Santa Fe', he replied and asked me some question about Andover, where his son was, or had recently been, at the Phillips Academy. That was the first hint I had that something 'hush' must be going on out there."

The location for the Los Alamos research center was selected by Oppenheimer and General Leslie Groves because of the necessity for isolation. The mesa, because of its cottonwoods, was called Los Alamos.

7. Kidder's early interest in the value of ceramics for the archaeologist is reflected in his 1915 paper, "Pottery of the Pajarito Plateau and Some Adjacent Regions in New Mexico." He believed that ceramic material from a variety of Pajaritian sites, when collected together, could serve as an indicator of cultural similarity or dissimilarity. He also recognized that knowledge of ceramic material for that region was not generally known to other investigators, so he wrote his 1915 paper to satisfy that need. In it, he observed that "each new investigator has been without any hint as to what sort of pottery he might find in his region, or what he might reasonably infer from what he did find. The finding, for example, of sherds of a certain type in a certain section of a ruin might be a discovery of the last importance, but it would hardly be recognized as such, and therefore not properly recorded, unless the investigator had a general knowledge of the distribution of wares outside the immediate zone of his activity" (Kidder 1915:411).

8. Over the years that followed, the family grew to include five children: Alfred II (now deceased), Randolph, Barbara (now deceased), Faith, and James. Alfred II, the eldest, himself became an archaeologist, specializing in the prehistory of Peru; he was a faculty member of both Harvard University and the University of Pennsylvania. He also served as an associate director of the University Museum at the latter institution (Woodbury 1973:20). Randolph Kidder was employed by the United States Foreign Service and retired in 1968 with the diplomatic rank of ambassador. Barbara Kidder Aldana was married to a Guatemalan

physician and died in 1983 in Philadelphia, after a long illness. Faith Kidder Fuller "was for many years in charge of the girls at the Verde Valley School in Arizona, well known for its pioneering introduction of anthropology into its curriculum as well as first hand experience for its students among many ethnic groups of the Southwest and Mexico" (Woodbury 1973:20). James Kidder, the youngest of the children, followed a career in the United States Air Force, in the United States Foreign Service, and later went into private business.

THE PECOS EXCAVATIONS

The Southwest has been an archaeological paradise for American archaeologists since the 1880s; it was here that the earliest concentrated efforts were made in American archaeology. Before examining the role of A. V. Kidder in these endeavors, let us turn to a brief overview of the intellectual background for this flowering.

Much of the Southwest belonged to Spain and then Mexico until the middle of the nineteenth century. Rohn (1973:188) suggests that

although the Spaniards were remarkable explorers and colonizers, their chronicles deal mostly with descriptions of the lands and the peoples inhabiting them. Even when they exhibited a humanistic interest in alien customs, any historical curiosity probed only oral traditions. The Mexicans were too busy with domestic affairs and the administration of their outlying provinces to devote scientific energies to historical questions other than their own. Only on occasion did Spanish travelers, such as Kino, report the presence of old ruins, and then often as temporary shelter for themselves.

After the Treaty of Guadalupe Hidalgo, in 1848, many of the early explorers were American military. Examples of early accounts are those by Lieutenant James Simpson (1850), who described the ruins in Chaco Canyon and Canyon de Chelly while on a military campaign against the Navajos, in 1849.

"Knowledge about the prehistory of any area develops within the context of the questions researchers bring with them to the field" (Cordell 1984:50). The intellectual climate of early archaeological work in the American Southwest can best be described as one of exploring, description of ruins, and collecting artifacts for individuals and private institutions, that is, not at all problem oriented. The workers of this period were on a sort of "window-shopping spree" (Haury 1987:personal communication). This descriptive/collecting approach remained in vogue until A. V. Kidder began his professional career, in 1915.

The first description of an archaeological site in this area was made by William H. Emory (1848). Later exploration of the region continued with the survey work of F. V. Hayden, under the auspices of the United States Geological and Geographical Survey of the Territories. Contained in some of Hayden's survey reports of the American Southwest are descriptions of both ruins and artifacts from Colorado and New Mexico by William H. Jackson and W. H. Holmes (Jackson 1876, 1878; Holmes, 1878, 1886; Hough 1933:752–64); Mark 1980:135–36). In 1872 the Hayden Survey returned to Yellowstone, where W. H. Holmes painted and sketched the mountains and studied the geological strata (Holmes 1876:61). Additional collections were made from southern California and the New Mexico Pueblos by the United States Geographical Surveys under Lieutenant George M. Wheeler; these were analyzed and published by Frederick Ward Putnam (1879) of Harvard's Peabody Museum. During the summer of 1878, both Putnam and John Wesley Powell worked for the United States Geological Survey, making extensive explorations of earth mounds and burial sites in Tennessee. For two weeks, both men worked together. Later Putnam's Peabody Museum of Archaeology and Ethnology and Powell's Bureau of Ethnology would be rivals, but at this "early date they were more interested in the seemingly unlimited possibilities which lay ahead of them" (Mark 1980:23).

In 1879 Major John Wesley Powell became the first chief of the United States Bureau of American Ethnology. In this position he

encouraged and supervised such early archaeological works as Victor Mindeleff's Study of Pueblo Architecture (V. Mindeleff 1891) and Cosmos Mindeleff's works on Casa Grande Ruin (C. Mindeleff 1896), in addition to the invaluable record of American Indian cultures and languages (Rohn 1973:189).

Much of the earlier work in the American Southwest was privately financed, with both positive and negative influences on the archaeology of the Southwest (Hewett 1909, Kidder 1924). On the plus side, considerable impetus was provided by the scientifically untrained but remarkably astute Wetherill brothers of Mancos, Colorado (McNitt 1957). Under the sponsorship of the Hyde Exploring Expedition, the Wetherills conducted extensive surveys and excavations from 1893 through 1903 in Grand Gulch, Utah; Tsegi Canyon, Arizona; and Chaco Canyon, New Mexico, where important work was done in Pueblo Bonito (Pepper 1920:16).

In September 1880 Adolf F. Bandelier went to Pecos Pueblo and collected material for a report published by the Archaeological Institute of America, in 1881. Bandelier described the ruins as they were at that time; his discussion included a valuable series of measurements of house mounds, the Spanish mission church, and the surrounding defense wall (Kidder 1924:16). Bandelier also prepared tentative elevations of parts of the pueblo, upon which he based his conclusions about the size of the buildings and the number of rooms they contained (Bandelier 1881:37–135). He did not excavate there because neither he nor the Archaeological Institute of America was prepared to do so. He suggested that, since he was working alone there, his labors might be employed better in a survey of the site, leaving "the exhaustive labors [of excavation to] better situated archaeologists" (Bandelier 1881:64). While his work was not accompanied by excavation, "which would, of course, have solved many of the problems that puzzled him, Bandelier arrived at remarkably accurate conclusions" (Kidder 1924:16). Bandelier outlined a history of the pueblo, obtaining much of his historical material from Mariano Ruiz, a Mexican national adopted by the remaining Pecos inhabitants.

In central Arizona the Hemenway Southwestern Expedition drew attention to sites from the Verde Valley to Casa Grande (see Bandelier 1890, Fewkes 1898). This expedition ushered in the Cushing/Fewkes era; besides the emphasis on collecting and describing archaeological sites, its main goal was to connect "the living Indian cultures with their archaeological descendents" (Taylor 1954:561). Jesse Walter Fewkes excavated at Mesa Verde in a haphazard manner, collecting numerous artifacts without discussion of site context or provenance. Much of his work was undertaken after Nels Nelson and A. V. Kidder had applied their stratigraphic techniques in the Rio Grande valley, yet he virtually ignored the improved field methods of others (Brew 1946:24).

In New Mexico Frank Hamilton Cushing was interested in the archaeology and ethnology of the Zuni. He was also led into archaeology by his ethnographic interests (Taylor 1954:561). Cushing especially helped to pioneer the direct historical approach in the Southwest by combining archaeology and ethnology in his work (Cushing 1890, Mark 1980:96–130, Willey and Sabloff 1980:51).

During this period the multiphyletic nature of archaeological materials in the Southwest was not recognized (Taylor 1954:561). And it was probably influenced by E. B. Tylor's notion of culture as a singular item, "consisting of the amount or degree of civilization, measured on a universal scale" (Mark 1980:109). Chaco Canyon, Mesa Verde, Kayenta, and sites along the Little Colorado and Verde Valleys were attributed to some single source (Taylor 1954:561). There was also a general lack of concern for temporal distinctions of cultural materials and their deposition at sites, in favor of describing sites and collecting rare and beautiful artifacts for museums. In the Southwest this, of course, meant the collection of whole pieces of pottery and a concentration upon architecture. Taylor (1954:562) has noted that most effort was expended on large sites of relatively recent date, which held the promise of loot and more beautiful remains; this meant that smaller sites were neglected. The continuing choice of larger ruins over smaller ones may have reinforced the one-culture concept and further muddled any notion of a multiphyletic origin of Southwestern cultures.

An archaeological context at this period could not be compared with the ethnographic data; only material objects could. The find was the key item. Archaeological sites were dug for their material remains, not for information. Comparison of materials from the archaeological past and the ethnographic present were thus direct and "objective" (Taylor 1954: 562).

Cushing and Fewkes regarded culture change as indicative of the movement of a single people through varying environments, not as arising from cross-cultural relationships between peoples of distinct cultural traditions (Taylor 1954:563). It is quite possible that Cushing's disregard of human skeletal remains can be traced to his single-culture model, whereby physical characteristics of ancient Pueblo people could easily be seen and understood from their living descendants.

Financing himself, Gustav Nordenskiöld came from Sweden to the United States in 1891 to work on the Mesa Verde, producing one of the finest monographs on the subject (Nordenskiöld 1893). A decade later

T. Mitchell Prudden began his work in the Southwest with a superficial survey of the San Juan drainage, in 1903, and continued with years of smaller-scale excavations of Pueblo archaeological sites in the northern San Juan region (Prudden 1903).

An unavoidable presence during this period was Jesse Walter Fewkes, already sixty-five years old when Kidder first met him. In both appearance and philosophy, Fewkes

> *was an anachronism. . . . Looking distinguished with a clipped white beard and broad forehead, clad in a belted coat and knee britches, he bounced from one bit of research to another with the enthusiasm of a child, which totally belied his sixty-five years. (Lister and Lister 1968:11)*

With the establishment of Mesa Verde National Park, in 1906, Fewkes was assigned the task of opening many of the ruins for public visitation. Intellectually he belonged to the school of romanticists who popularized southwestern Indians and attempted to explain their prehistoric existence through legendary evidence. Fewkes saw his mission at Mesa Verde as one of making "mystical red man known to the literate public" (Lister and Lister 1968:11). He excavated many of the major cliff dwellings—Cliff Palace, Spruce Tree House, Square Tower House, Oak Tree House, and Fire Temple—and began intensive work in sites on the mesa top, such as Far View House, Pipe Shrine House, Sun Temple, and the first Basketmaker III pithouse (actually excavated by his assistant Ralph Linton). In addition to his work at Mesa Verde, Fewkes could be seen season after season at Zuni Pueblo, in New Mexico, or at the Hopi towns of northern Arizona, where he observed and wrote about their "ritualistic lifeway . . ." (Lister and Lister 1968:11).

Another figure who represented the collecting/descriptive period of southwestern archaeology, before the entrance of Kidder into the field, was F. W. Hodge. Hodge's field experience began when he became field secretary to Frank Hamilton Cushing, during Cushing's early excavations in southern Arizona. His contemporaries were Leslie Spier, just completing his B.A. at Columbia University, and Nels C. Nelson, who had changed his course of study from philosophy to anthropology, and who had recently joined the American Museum of Natural History, in New York (Woodbury 1973:30).

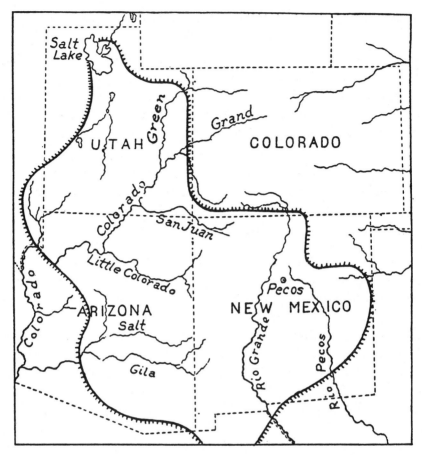

Map 1. Approximate extent of the Southwestern Culture Area. (Kidder 1924)

From 1915 through 1923, the United States National Museum engaged Neil M. Judd to survey and excavate sites from the Great Salt Lake, in Utah, to the Grand Canyon, in Arizona, and to prepare the large cliff dwelling, Betatakin, in Navajo National Monument, for public visits.

While much archaeological work in the early twentieth century was sponsored by the U.S. government, nongovernment survey projects also flourished. Primary among these was work sponsored by the Archaeological Institute of America, under the direction of Edgar Lee Hewett. Hewett's overwhelming project was a broad survey of archaeological sites from Utah to Arizona; it was on parts of this grand undertaking that

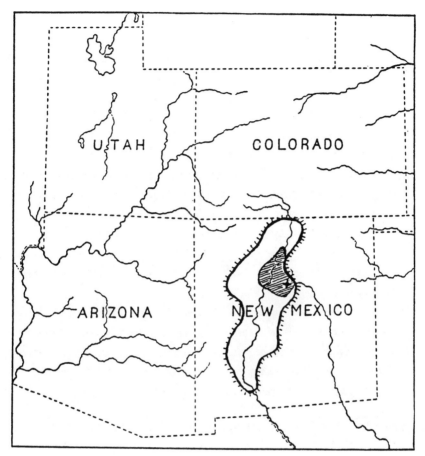

Map 2. The Rio Grande Area, the Santa Fe region, and Pecos. (Kidder 1924)

Kidder, Morley, and Fletcher had worked. Kidder's experiences in 1907 and 1908 would ultimately result in two papers, "Explorations in Southeastern Utah" (1910) and "Some Undescribed Ruins of the Historic Period from the Upper San Juan" (1913). From 1914 through 1917, Kidder and Samuel Guernsey surveyed the general vicinity of Kayenta; their collaboration produced, in 1919, a fine paper titled "Archaeological Exploration of Northeastern Arizona," which was published by the Bureau of American Ethnology. Guernsey continued to investigate the Kayenta region through 1923 (Guernsey 1931), but by 1915 Kidder had focused his attention on Pecos Pueblo.

Hewett's association with the Archaeological Institute of America and his direction of their activities in the United States has been concisely reviewed by Hinsley (1986:217–33). Alfred Tozzer (letter to Gardner M. Lane, 28 October 1910, ATM) wrote of Hewett's archaeology that the main criticism

> *in all {of his} excavations . . . is the lack of any well-defined plan of work which would settle once and for all certain broad questions still remaining . . . concerning the archaeology of the Pueblo region. His work is seemingly done where it will yield the best results from the point of view of collections and spectacular plans and restorations. There has been, as far as I know, little correlation in the many small bits of digging here and there undertaken by Hewett but in almost every case there has resulted a good pottery collection while the work has thrown very little light upon the more important questions of migration, etc., etc.*
>
> *. . . I feel strongly the evil effect of Hewett's work not only upon the good name of the Institute and of Archaeology in general but more especially on that of American Archaeology which has been endeavoring slowly to emerge from the rather forlorn state resulting from unscientific methods and untrained investigators.*

In 1904 Hewett had published a paper titled "Studies on the Extinct Pueblo of Pecos." To his credit, Hewett was the first investigator to recognize the importance of ethnographic fieldwork among the Pecos descendants at Jemez Pueblo, by using informants there to gain insight into Pecos culture. This approach was further developed by Kidder during his years of work at Pecos, but it is worth noting that the idea originated with his early mentor, Hewett. Hewett also surveyed the Rio Grande valley of New Mexico, in 1913 (Hewett 1913:11–22).

Although Rohn (1973:190) credits Neil Judd with being the first archaeologist to construct a systematic approach to southwestern archaeology, during his investigations of Pueblo Bonito (1915–23), A. V. Kidder was the first archaeologist to stress the need for explanation and synthesis in southwest archaeology. A long-time friend of Kidder, Judd's field method was similar to Kidder's: he recognized the importance of stratigraphy and ceramics for ascertaining cultural chronology and growth. And yet Judd's published papers of 1917a, 1917b, 1918, 1920, and 1922 are not explicit with regard to his field methods, as they contain only detailed descriptions of his field work in Utah, Arizona, and much later, Pueblo Bonito. His first explicit reference to stratigraphy can be found in his 1954 book, *The Material Culture of Pueblo Bonito*:

> *When our Pueblo Bonito investigations were inaugurated, in the spring of 1912, most archeologists working in the Southwest depended upon fragments of pottery to suggest the degree of development at any one site. Pueblo I pottery had a certain sameness, no matter where found; it could never be mistaken for P.III {(Pueblo III)} pottery. Therefore potsherds served as evidence of both material progress and passing time. Stratigraphy was the means by which that evidence was acquired.*
>
> *Hence our first desire, as soon as camp had been organized, was a good look at the Bonito dump. Two conspicuous rubbish piles stand just south of the ruin. Because floor sweepings at the bottom of these piles would be older than sweepings at the top, a cross section should reveal every major change in the material culture of the villages during the period that trash was accumulating.*
>
> *Previous experience in Utah and Arizona had taught me that certain types of earthenware were associated with early dwellings; other types, with later. (Judd 1954:16)*

The intellectual climate of the American Southwest before Kidder's professional career there is best summed up by Brew (1946:30) in the following manner:

1. *The eighteenth-century Spanish explorers established the fact that ancient ruins existed in the Southwest.*

2. *The nineteenth-century traders, cattlemen, and Mormon settlers added little more than was known in the previous century.*

3. *The railroad and the United States government surveys of the Southwest consisted only of reconnaissance.*

4. *The archaeological excavations of the 1880s and the 1890s were either very localized or superficial; results were not described in published reports.*

5. *Between 1900 and 1910 excavations of a few small sites were undertaken. All activities remained unpublished except for a short report by A. V. Kidder on his work on Alkali Ridge. At the time there was no understanding of stratigraphy.*

6. *The large amount of work done by Jesse Walter Fewkes in the second decade of the twentieth century is virtually useless, as Fewkes never kept up with newer field techniques.*

7. *Both Fewkes and Cushing took a singular view of culture and ignored the multiphyletic origins of culture in the Southwest. Both approached their analysis of Hopi and Zuni culture through an early form of the direct historical approach.*

In 1932 Kidder (1932a:6) wrote of the close association of early archaeological endeavors with museums, which he saw as "an expression of the innate human desire to collect." Museums at that time controlled almost the entire field, with "nine-tenths of all field-work being done by museums and practically all archaeologists being museum employees" (Kidder 1932a:6). The museum's relish of objects "instead of what [the object tells] has been a most serious brake upon the wheels of archaeological progress" (Kidder 1932a:6). Influenced profoundly by his training in Old World archaeology, Kidder saw the discipline as a historical one that seeks to reconstruct the lives of peoples who have left no written records. To select a few artifacts of outstanding or unusual appearance and to "neglect . . . everything which is not handsome . . . is therefore a perfectly fatal perversion of emphasis" (Kidder 1932a:6).

With the entrance of Kidder the direction of southwestern archaeology and, indeed, of American archaeology in general, was to change radically from the rather narrow objectives sketched by Judd. His Pecos excavations began emphasizing the behavioral explanation of prehistoric artifacts that heralded a new era in southwestern archaeology.

In 1915 the Trustees of the Phillips Academy, at the suggestion of Dr. Roland B. Dixon of Harvard University, and Dr. Hiram Bingham of Yale University, acting as Advisory Committee to the Trustees, for the Department of Archaeology of the Academy, on the foundation of the late Robert Singleton Peabody, determined to undertake excavations in the Pueblo area. It was desired to select a

field of operations large enough, and of sufficient scientific impor-
tance, to justify work upon it for a number of years. After the con-
sideration of a number of ruins, Pecos was recommended. (Kidder
1924:1)

Woodbury (1973:30) notes that "the selection of Kidder was a vigorous
expression of support for the new kind of archaeology he represented, in
contrast to the traditional excavation for the sake of collection."

Kidder, however, had been thinking seriously about working at the
Aztec Ruin instead of Pecos.

When Roland Dixon and Hiram Bingham offered me a job at An-
dover with the selection of a ruin in the Southwest that would last
several years, my first thought was Aztec. It's a very large ruin,
and is right in the heart of the Mesa Verde–Chaco area. It was
built by Chaco people, then abandoned, . . . and then briefly oc-
cupied by degenerate Mesa Verde people. . . . I was interested in the
San Juan because I had been working with Hewett. It was very very
lucky that I didn't take Aztec . . . Earl Morris took it over and
worked over there for a number of years and did a much finer job
than I possibly could have done . . .

While I was considering Aztec I went over to Pecos one day with
Kenneth Chapman. I happened to find two or three sherds of Little
Colorado Pottery as well as one or two Hopi sherds, plus every
known form of pottery of the upper Rio Grande. . . . the rubbish
heaps were large, very much larger than I had thought. So it was
very fortunate that I did take Pecos. (AVK II:1)

The abundance and variety of Rio Grande pottery types at Pecos was
the deciding factor for Kidder (AVK II:3); it had deep middens and
would permit large-scale excavation by the newly developed stratigraphic
method (Mason 1963:169).

Pecos was, indeed, chosen for investigation in preference to several
other ruins that were considered, because of the presence on the surface
there of fragments of all wares then known to occur in the Upper Rio
Grande, as well as certain of those of the Little Colorado and from

about the Hopi towns. This, of course, suggested both long occupancy and wide trade relations. Furthermore, Pecos' strategic position athwart the most favorable route between the interior of the Pueblo country and the buffalo plains, gave hope that excavation would produce imported pottery and other objects to link a sequence of stratigraphically determined phases of local culture with those of cultures both to the east and the west, thus providing the wide archaeological hookups which were so urgently needed for the preliminary blocking out of the then very imperfectly understood course of Southwestern prehistory. These expectations were in considerable measure realized (Kidder 1958:xii).

Although Kidder's assumption that he would find the earliest evidences of Pueblo culture at Pecos was mistaken, very little was known of the archaeological connections between Mesoamerica and the American Southwest at that time.

All my work had been in the east or easterly {area of the Southwest}. I knew nothing about the Hohokam and nobody else did really either. Fewkes had published on the ruins of the Little Colorado and the Hopi country but there was very, very little known, particularly about the far south {southern area of the Southwest}. Of course, the Mogollon hadn't been heard of in those days. That was one of several reasons we {settled on} . . . Pecos. (AVK II:3)

In addition to signs of long occupation, the site had no evidence of being violently destroyed or suddenly abandoned (Kidder 1932a:6).

The Cushing/Fewkes tasks of exploring and collecting were replaced by Kidder with a new set of problems—temporal and spatial variability in archaeological analysis, or tracing changes in time and space. Stratigraphic excavation, ceramic analysis, and the beginnings of a multidisciplinary approach to archaeological problems were the new additions to the tool kit of the field archaeologist.

During the summer of 1911, the intellectual climate of Southwestern archaeology began to change. During that summer Kidder inaugurated his sherd survey, collecting surface ceramic material from as many sites as possible. His limits for collecting data were geographic, rather than influenced by the "traditional range of a particular modern Pueblo" (Taylor 1954:564).

A few years later Kroeber and Spier extended and verified the sherd-survey method. Their goal, "that of tying the archaeological to the ethnographic record reflected the aims of the days of Cushing and Fewkes" (Taylor 1954:564). However, Kroeber and Spier brought to their problems the additional methods of quantitative analysis and seriation.

About the same time, Nels C. Nelson, of the American Museum of Natural History, made an extensive survey of the Rio Grande valley in New Mexico (Woodbury 1960:400–401). Although Nelson was to work in the Southwest for only four years, his famous work at San Cristobal (Galisteo Basin), led the way for the further application of stratigraphic excavation by Kidder at Pecos. Nelson dug by arbitrary layers and then classified and recorded the sherds by levels. Thus began the marriage of the potsherd with stratigraphic excavation that so marked Kidder's work at Pecos Pueblo. At this early stage, Nelson's emphasis on stratigraphy and ceramics was criticized by Hewett:

It would be hard to find a student of Southwestern archaeology of the last twenty years who has not been carried away, more or less, with the study of pottery; there are those who apparently look upon cultural stratification as embracing the entire science of archaeology and who regard the pottery record as the key that is to unlock the doors of antiquity. Just why chronology should be considered of such vast importance is difficult to understand. (Hewett 1930:156–57)

Although it was Kidder, not Nelson, who carried out intensive excavations in the Rio Grande, it was Nelson, Taylor (1954:564) suggests, through his theoretical principles and direct suggestion that led Kidder to excavate Pecos. Attention was being paid to the larger picture of cultural development in the American Southwest; "we are looking for someone to correlate all of this vast accumulation of data and to tell us what it really means" (Nelson 1919a:133).

As a method of establishing cultural chronology in the Americas, stratigraphy did not become an established tool of analysis until after 1920. This technique was born in Europe, out of geology, where great time gaps were perceived in both the geological and cultural records. In the Americas attempts (by, e.g., Holmes and Hrdlička) to demonstrate the early existence of humankind had not proved successful; as a result, the stratigraphic method of excavation was discredited in Americanist archaeology (Willey 1968:38). American archaeologists did not think of studying change over time in prehistoric deposits later than those in Europe, without corresponding geological strata.

Another part of the intellectual climate of Kidder's time in the Southwest was the so-called expedition attitude, by which eastern institutions defined the direction and procedures of archaeological excavations in the Southwest.

An additional influence was the culture-area concept, then in the forefront of anthropological thought. This concept involved distributional studies and descriptions of culture areas.

PECOS PUEBLO

Pecos Pueblo is situated in the San Juan drainage of San Miguel County, New Mexico. The environment can best be described as arid, with a parched land surface broken only by mesas dotting the landscape. The Pecos ruins occupy the top of a long rock ridge. At the north end the site occupies a narrow band of bare sandstone; to the south the ground widens and then again becomes constricted and falls away until it merges with the uplands that stretch off toward the river.

At the extreme southern end of the site lie the ruins of a mission church and *convento*. Directly north of the church is the pile of pueblo ruins, four hundred feet long by sixty-five or seventy feet wide (Kidder 1924:17).

FIRST FIELD SEASON—1915

Before Kidder could begin his work at Pecos, he had to solicit the final approval of Edgar Lee Hewett. He had probably read Hewett's (1913:13–22) "Rio Grande Valley, New Mexico," in preparation for their meeting, as Kidder was extremely interested in the entire area. Hewett at the time was a self-styled archaeological liaison between the State Museum of New Mexico and investigators who wished to excavate selected sites in that state. The museum wanted the Pecos mission church reconstructed and stabilized, to prevent further deterioration; as part of their agreement to allow Kidder to excavate the pueblo, he would have to reconstruct and stabilize the church. Through Hewett, Kidder and the museum agreed, and the work began. Kidder must have sensed that Hewett had the power to cause the museum to refuse its permission if he were not consulted. [1]

With Hewett's approval and any internal politics behind him, Kidder selected his field assistants and began a detailed survey of the site. One of the field assistants was his wife, Madeleine Kidder. After their marriage, in 1910, she remained his companion in the field. She was charged with cleaning and sorting thousands of potsherds recovered from the first season's excavations (Kidder 1924:100). There is no record of possible earlier experiences Madeleine may have had with ceramic analysis. Thus it is not known if she worked with her husband on the ceramic studies for his doctoral dissertation on Southwestern pottery. Although Kidder's personal papers do not mention the influence of Madeleine on his ideas about how to handle ceramic analysis, it is probable that she contributed greatly to their development. In 1917 a detailed paper, "Notes on the Pottery of Pecos," appeared, coauthored by Madeleine and A. V. Kidder. The paper is largely descriptive, but also contains a cogent discussion of the ceramic findings of the Kidder's first season at Pecos. There is no doubt that Madeleine contributed greatly to the final product.

His other field assistants included Samuel K. Lothrop, his wife, Rachel, J. P. Adams (as surveyor), and a long-time friend, Jesse L. Nusbaum, who took charge of the repairs of the Spanish mission church that had been built upon the ruins of the pueblo. Although Kidder writes in his memoirs (AVK II:4) that the request for repairs of the church was Hewett's, other letters and references make it clear that church repairs were required by the State Museum of New Mexico. Kidder (AVK II:4) mentions Nusbaum as the logical candidate to undertake the reconstruction, because of his experience with similar projects at Mesa Verde.

In his unpublished papers, Kidder virtually ignores Hewett's interest in Pecos. It is possible that Kidder's concern about Hewett's failure to keep abreast of archaeological endeavors in the Mesa Verde region caused him to ignore Hewett. Hewett seems to have been satisfied with the selection of field personnel, provided nothing in the way of aid, and then retreated from all the Phillips Academy endeavors at Pecos Pueblo.

During the early work of midden excavation at Pecos, Kidder modified Nelson's stratigraphic approach to San Cristobal by formulating detailed descriptions of the nature of the refuse found in Pecos middens, the probable history of refuse deposition, and methods employed in the excavation of middens. According to Mason (1963:169), Kidder chose to excavate Pecos largely on account of its deep middens, which "would permit large-scale investigation by the newly developed stratigraphic method."

Kidder's improvement upon Nelson's stratigraphic method involved deep profile exposures of middens at Pecos, providing the first test of stratigraphy in a large-scale excavation in the American Southwest. Of the profiles made at the Pecos excavations only selected sherds were saved and noted from the trenches. With the deep profile exposures as a guide, a more thorough excavation was done by natural strata, and potsherds were given provenances according to their strata units. Each profile was examined by Kidder for signs of disturbance; if intrusions were found, that location was not stratigraphically tested. He also marked with pegs and string the physical strata of the site to allow for ready recognition of varying strata during the period of ongoing excavation (Willey and Sabloff 1980:90). Kidder's controlled provenances contained potsherds that were classified and tabulated; in his ceramic report on Pecos (1931a) he gave these tabulations both as raw numbers and as percentages. Kidder (1931a:7) also employed seriation, where Nelson did not. He wanted to obtain as much information as possible on the distribution of ceramic types in time and space.

As originally planned, "the work of the Pecos expedition was to be first intensive then extensive" (Kidder 1924:31). The intensive phase was to consist of the excavation of the pueblo and the determination by stratigraphic methods of the sequence of the pottery types found at the site. During the second, or extensive, phase Kidder was able to use his knowledge of the sequence of pottery types to arrange in their proper chronological order all other ruins that contained those types. This work was aided by a thorough archaeological reconnaissance of the Rio Grande drainage (Kidder 1924:31). Kidder identified various excavation levels at Pecos by the ceramic variability found at each level. It was his hope not only to construct a cultural chronology at Pecos, but also to link ceramic evidence at Pecos with similar chronologies throughout the Southwest. At the beginning of his work at Pecos, he wanted to use what he knew of European archaeology as well as his own ideas, developed in his doctoral dissertation on southwestern ceramics (AVK III:3).

The excavation of the Pecos ruin began with the opening of a trench on the east side of the pueblo, to determine the extent of the site's eastern boundary. The various types of pottery that Kidder found in this trenching operation were later to yield information about the antiquity of the various groups who lived at Pecos, representing occupations of the pueblo from its earliest inception through the period in which the pueblo attained its greatest size. Kidder determined that the Black-on-White pottery found at Pecos represented the oldest habitation, while the later Biscuit ware and still later Glaze ware represented later occupations.

At that time, I also didn't know the various types of Black-on-White ware—the first ware. I had distinguished, by that time, Black-on-White from Biscuit but that was as far as it went. Of course, now they have got four or five or six stages in the Black-on-White even of the Rio Grande. They were mostly worked out by Harry Nearer. Stanley Stubbs of the Laboratory of Anthropology is conversant with all those types. I didn't have savvy enough about pottery to realize that the fragments of pottery that I picked up at this old ruin across the crick were different than those at Pecos. (AVK II:4–5)

The trenching operations on the periphery continued through the first year, with no formal excavations of the ruin (with the exception of two test pits) during this season. As the trenching continued, Kidder and his field crew began to encounter burials that seemed to have been interred originally in a haphazard manner. Mention of the initial burial discoveries is found in Kidder's 1924 work and in his unpublished memoirs of 1957. Kidder was anxious to locate burials at Pecos; a reward of twenty-five cents was offered to the workmen for every skeleton uncovered.

The next day one appeared, the following day six; the reward was reduced to ten cents; this brought fifteen more, and in the course of a week or so we were forced to discontinue the bonus or go into bankruptcy. (Kidder 1924:18)

The higher his field crew worked uphill, the deeper the rubbish grew, and more numerous became the skeletons. It was obvious that Kidder and his field crew were digging in the greatest rubbish heap and cemetery that had ever been found in the Pueblo region up to that time.

That rubbish heap was literally full of skeletons, and it turned out to be far deeper than I ever expected. I figured that probably it was about ten feet deep and it turned out to be over twenty feet deep against this original cliff. (AVK II:6)

Kidder notes that he and his field assistants, Sam and Rachel Lothrop, ran a big trench with a fifty- or sixty-foot-long horizontal face. The deposit was very deep, and they cut three salient trenches through the midden. Kidder and his field crew took many stratigraphic tests, but they found no Black-on-White ware in the rubbish. The earliest ceramic evidence found was Glaze I, which they called Agua Fria. Sam and Rachel Lothrop ran two of the trenches, while Kidder ran the third one,

keeping track of the stratification and from time to time, taking what . . . {they} . . . called shovel tests, a rough test of looking over the stuff from given faces. When we got up into the very deep rubbish we isolated a very large test, between two of the salient trenches so that I could see it on three sides and mark out the stratification. (AVK II:6–7)

That 1915 test trench was important, as it yielded many thousands of sherds. Kidder worked on them the winter of 1915–16, which he spent in Santa Barbara, California, with his mother and father (AVK II:6–7).

The immense size of the midden forced Kidder to abandon any notion of excavation in the ruin itself that first field season. He was hoping that his excavation of the midden would disclose an undisturbed rubbish heap that would be stratified,

the earliest remains at the bottom, later ones above them, and so on up, so that by taking samples from the different levels, we should be able to get evidence as to the exact sequence of the various types of pottery that had been made at Pecos from the time of its foundation down to the beginning of the 19th century. (Kidder 1924:18)

The first field season at Pecos produced another problem for Kidder: that of disentangling the remains of complex building and rebuilding episodes as they appeared in the trench profiles.

I had worked with Fewkes on the Mesa Verde and Hewett was very
anxious to make a tourist attraction out of Pecos. Before I had only
worked on the cliff-dwellings of the San Juan—which are beau-
tifully built of course, and in the ruins up on the Pajarito Plateau
which were also extremely well built, and were built on flat bare
rock, out of soft tufa which could be cut into brick-like shape, so
those ruins were in good shape, and they weren't occupied for a very
long time so that there was no difficulty in doing those rooms. (AVK
II:7)

But as soon as he started digging in the rooms at Pecos, he found that they
had been built and rebuilt again out of very poor masonry.

In fact, Bandelier, in his report on Pecos, says 'This cannot be prop-
erly be described as masonry but rather as judicious piling'. And
sometimes it wasn't so darned judicious. The walls didn't even cor-
respond in many cases. The ruins were in terrible shape. (AVK
II:7–8)

STRATIGRAPHY VIA CERAMICS

In 1913 Roland Dixon (1913:577), a teacher and friend of Kidder's,
wrote that

[c]hronology is at the root of the matter, being the nerve electrifying
the dead body of history. It should be incumbent upon the American
archaeologists to establish a chronological basis of the precolumbian
cultures, and the American ethnologist should make it a point to
bring chronology into the life and history of the postcolumbian In-
dians.

This was one of the tasks that Kidder set for himself during his
professional life.

The stratigraphic revolution, in which Kidder was a leading figure,
heralded a new era in the determination of chronology for the prehistoric
Southwest. By stratigraphic ceramic sequencing, Kidder was able to
determine not only chronology but also the cultural development of the
pueblo. It is interesting to note that Kidder's experiments with Pecos

stratigraphy in 1915 occurred at about the same time as Nels C. Nelson's stratigraphic work at San Cristobal. Kidder's unpublished memoirs (AVK II:50–90) mention Nelson's introduction of stratigraphy to the Southwest. In his "Pottery of the Pajarito Plateau and Some Adjacent Regions in New Mexico" (1915:461), Kidder wrote that he was aware of Nelson's work at San Cristobal. During Kidder's early days (1910–15) Nelson, Alfred Kroeber, and Leslie Spier all used stratigraphic dating of artifactual materials. The parallel stratigraphic activities of these four men pose the interesting question of whether any of them knew of the work of the others, including their preliminary results. Kidder unfortunately makes no mention of correspondence with these colleagues at that time, but the stratigraphic method of excavation he employed at Pecos Pueblo must have derived from his knowledge of Nelson's work at San Cristobal.

> *if similar deposits could be found at Pecos, they would serve not only to complement and, so to speak, cross-reference the finds of Mr. Nelson, but also to carry the story of Pueblo arts from 1680, the date of the abandonment of San Cristobal, down through the very little known eighteenth century to the middle of the nineteenth, from which time to the present day it may still be recovered by studies among the living tribes. These were the chief reasons for the choice of Pecos. (Kidder 1916b:120)*

Kidder concluded that the stratigraphy of the site gave clues to the growth of the local culture that could also provide information regarding external relations with other cultures. But first he had to recognize and chronologically arrange the successive culture stages at Pecos. He wanted to extend that knowledge and thus fit into their proper chronological order the single-culture ruins that are found throughout the Rio Grande area. He also hoped to learn, from trade objects found at Pecos and in the "chronologically arranged one-culture ruins, the relative age of many other groups, not only in the Southwest but even well beyond its borders" (Kidder 1916b:123).

Nelson made several references to Kidder's stratigraphic work in the Southwest by contrasting the latter's direct comparison approach with his own system of tabulation (1916:161, 1919a:134, 1919b:117). It seems highly probable that the two men were communicating informally about the analytical benefits of stratigraphy for chronology. Nelson wrote in 1919 that

> {c}eramics, or pottery, {is} . . . selected {for chronological analysis} partly because of its universal distribution and ready accessibility, but mainly because of its variability. (Nelson 1919b:134)

He also noted that

> {p}ottery—an ever present accompaniment of the ruins—is on the other hand, an exceedingly plastic phenomenon, varying from place to place and from time to time, in response to the inventive faculty, far more readily than does architecture. We may therefore decide the relative age of any given ruin by determining the age of the particular style of pottery which it exhibits; and this latter feat is easily accomplished. We have but to find the stratigraphic position of this particular style in the total series of styles as they occur in refuse heaps or in actually superposed ruins. Sometimes the stratigraphic position has to be determined without digging into the refuse heaps—there being none, but the principle involved is the same: we have to begin with the style of ware laying on top or still in use and must work back or down through the series until we arrive at the bottom most style, which is the oldest. (Nelson 1919a:118)

During their work in northeastern Arizona, both Kidder and Samuel Guernsey recognized the superposition of remains at various locations in this area. Marsh Pass and Hagoe Canyon are mentioned in their report, "Archaeological Explorations in Northeastern Arizona," as having layered depositions of remains (Kidder and Guernsey 1919).

Before Nelson's San Cristobal work, he had had experience with stratigraphic digging in the California shell mounds under the direction of A. L. Kroeber and under the influence of Max Uhle (Nelson 1909, 1910). Uhle had focused his attention on the problems of sequence for the Emeryville Shell Mound, in 1902, and roughly divided its strata into two main groups, the latter neolithic in character, and the former perhaps intermediate between paleolithic and neolithic (Steward 1973:39). Kroeber was skeptical about any new proposals that would violate the general notion that North American archaeology lacked any significant, distinguishable time dimension. Perhaps his stance was a reflection of his contemporaries' notion that the neolithic period, as distinct from the paleolithic, could not be recognized in North America (Steward 1973: 39–40).

Nelson visited the French and Spanish caves in 1913, where Obermeier and Breuil were conducting stratigraphic excavations (Willey and Sabloff 1980:87). This experience had a profound influence on him. His own approach to stratigraphy involved keeping potsherds from arbitrary levels of his excavations separately, and classifying and counting them by level. Nelson did not compute percentages, but provided numerical results in the form of small tables (Willey and Sabloff 1980:88). He was concerned with the numerical tabulations of potsherds at certain depths: each type of potsherd represented a relative age for the people who made them. Obviously "he was thinking very much in terms of the unimodal life-curves of pottery styles and types that are today the stock-in-trade of the archaeologist" (Willey and Sabloff 1980:88). Kidder must have had many occasions for direct contact with Nelson and for discussions about stratigraphy and its importance in southwestern archaeology. Unfortunately, Nelson never finished his work in the Southwest, but went on to work in Mongolia and later was employed by the American Museum.

A. L. Kroeber mentions the stratigraphic work of Kidder and Nelson, citing Kidder's 1915 paper, "Pottery of the Pajarito Plateau and of Some Adjacent Regions in New Mexico."

> *A. V. Kidder's recent 'Pottery of the Pajarito Plateau,' in volume 2 of the* Memoirs of the American Anthropological Association, *presents analogous results, obtained by a method differing in some details, for another region of New Mexico; and at San Cristobal in still another part of the state, N. C. Nelson has excavated a stratified deposit showing four successive layers of different type. (Kroeber 1916:45)*

Although Nelson must have been the primary influence on Kidder concerning stratigraphy, Kroeber and Leslie Spier influenced him as well. Kidder (AVK II:11) mentions that he visited Kroeber and Spier at Zuni (without saying exactly when the visit took place), but provides no comments on their discussions. Surely Kroeber and Spier's field method for chronology must have been discussed during that meeting. Spier's published works make reference to the work of Kidder and Nelson (1918: 341, 1919:385, 1931:275–83), but Spier does not discuss Kidder's work in detail, making only footnote references to him and his wife Madeleine. Spier's 1931 paper, "N. C. Nelson's Stratigraphic Technique in the Reconstruction of Prehistoric Sequences in Southwestern America," is an evaluation of Nelson's 1916 paper, "The Chronology of the Tano Ruins."

Kroeber and Spier were engaged in a different type of stratigraphic analysis than was Nelson. Their technique was seriation, and has been referred to in archaeological literature as "occurrence seriation" (Steward 1973:93; Willey and Sabloff 1980:95). They were concerned with "frequency counts" of discernible diagnostic pottery types.

Petrie's form of seriation must have made some impact upon Kidder at Harvard, through the teaching of George Reisner. His course required the seriational techniques then recently proposed by Petrie for Egypt.

His course, I think, was the best single course that I ever took. I think I have covered the principal elements of it {ceramic analysis} in recording and chronological correlation with cultures through traded material or introduced material. I came back from the field (1907–1908) all het up about pottery and I was delighted to find in my reading and in Reisner's course . . . that pottery was an important element in archaeology and which I didn't know anything about before at all. So I felt that it was a respectable and useful branch of research to pursue. (AVK II:4–5)

From Reisner, Kidder learned of the different types of debris likely to be found at a site (debris of occupancy and clearing), and a cataloging system for recording artifact finds. He also learned that traded objects from one culture to another are evidence of culture contact (AVK III:2).

The first field season at Pecos provided Kidder with invaluable experience in establishing cultural chronology by the use of stratigraphy (see fig. 1).

We must here consider briefly the application of such stratigraphic data. In the Rio Grande, as in other parts of the Southwest, there are great numbers of prehistoric ruins. Some of these contain one type

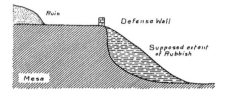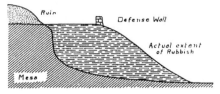

Figure 1. Midden cross section at Pecos, excavated during first field season.

of pottery, some another, still others show two or more types. It has been inferred that these differences represented differences in age, but there was no sure method for arranging the types in their proper chronological order, though such an arrangement was of course necessary as a first step toward a study of the history of the region. With the discovery of the stratified deposits at the Galisteo basin ruins and at Pecos we were at once provided with a key to the whole problem; for they disclosed, as has been explained, an orderly superposition of all these types, the oldest naturally lying at the bottom, later ones above, and the latest at the top. With the sequence of the pottery types thus established, it became a perfectly simple matter to arrange all sites containing one or more of them in their true chronological order. The same principle is also used in the local work at Pecos. (1924:19–20)

The first field season at Pecos for Kidder was a time not only for initial investigation of the ruin, but also for the development of analytical and excavation techniques to interpret this site (see fig. 2). Kidder was the first southwestern archaeologist to make use of the stratigraphic method on a large scale, trenching and selecting sherds from various levels representing differing cultural periods. Such profile trenching was done to reveal signs of intrusion or disturbance of material remains. In some instances columns of refuse were isolated on two, three, or four sides, to allow for careful examination of intrusive influences. For Kidder the only really safe way of ensuring the original order of deposition was the use of a column of material intentionally left undisturbed. His method consisted of exposing a

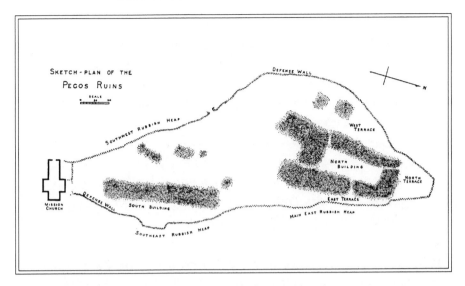

Figure 2. Sketch of the Pecos ruins. (After Kidder 1924:20a)

column on . . . four {sides}. One should mark off on the column one's cuts, to correspond to the observable trend of the midden, basing them as far as possible on actual ash or sand layers. The column should then be allowed to stand awhile, for drying will often bring about changes of color that reveal strata not before distinguishable. (Kidder 1958a:338)

The potsherds from these controlled provenances were classified and tabulated with the intention of noting the numbers of potsherds per type per provenance unit with corresponding percentages. The relationship between known types of pottery and their deposition in the ground provided a reasonable way to chart the growth of a specific culture.

Kidder's stratigraphic method was the means by which to implement a plan of regional cultural chronological research. His plan consisted of five steps:

1. *A preliminary archaeological survey of the region to be studied.*
2. *Development of criteria for chronologically ranking the known sites of the region.*

3. *A study of the manifestations of the criteria, to arrive at a tentative chronological ranking of the sites containing them.*

4. *The search for and excavation of sites in which material remains might be found in a stratigraphic relationship, in order to validate the tentative ranking and also to obtain a large number of specimens for morphological and genetic studies.*

5. *To perform a thorough resurvey of the area in the light of the fuller knowledge now at hand, in order definitely to rank all sites, and if necessary, "to select for excavation new sites which may be expected to elucidate problems raised during the course of the research." (Willey and Sabloff 1980:91)*

Although Nelson, Kroeber, Spier, and Kidder were each working with stratigraphy about the same time in the Southwest, it was Kidder who combined the features of Nelson's method with Kroeber and Spier's work into a workable dating approach.

SECOND SEASON—1916

During the winter of 1915–16, Kidder and Madeleine spent much of their time sorting and analyzing the pottery recovered from the stratigraphic tests carried out during the 1915 field season. When the analysis of the ceramic material was completed, it was found that very little in the way of early types was present, while disproportionately large quantities of later types were in evidence. Kidder decided that this was due to the fact that his tests had been made too far down from the top of the mesa. He reasoned that the thickest deposits of early material must lie at the base of the heavy rubbish, close against the mesa; he felt that several deep tests must be made (Kidder 1924:20). Not having a firm idea as to the extent of various middens at Pecos, Kidder would continue to open narrow trenches at other locations on the mesa, to define the areas of such rubbish deposits.

During the second season of field activity, Kidder directed the investigation of the "north terrace" portion of the Pecos site, a smooth, gently sloping surface running from where the defense wall cuts across the narrowing neck of the ridge up to the foundations of the north wall of the main north quadrangle. There are no signs of house structures except for a single low mound. This part of the site contained nothing but shallow rubbish and material "washed down from the decaying pueblo" (Kidder 1924:21).

The trenching of the north terrace continued and disclosed house walls. Once excavation was undertaken inside these walls, forty rooms were discerned, and a kiva and more than two hundred burials were exposed. Because of a "piling" of Black-on-White pottery within the rubbish of the house structure, the discovery was dated from the first occupation of the Pecos mesa. This was Kidder's initial discovery of evidence relating to the earliest occupations of the mesa. He found debris of the Black-on-White period to be scanty at the bottom of most parts of the rubbish deposits throughout the rest of the Pecos Mesa; however, this early period was well represented on the north terrace, both on the east and west sides. Kidder concluded that the nucleus of Pecos Pueblo lay on the north terrace (Kidder 1924:21).

Kidder was also able to delineate a later occupation, characterized by Glaze I ceramics, to the south of the north terrace. Although not excavated at the time, the southern area of the site, including the great quadrangle, Kidder believed, contained the nucleus of Glaze I development.

Its approximate position may nevertheless be guessed at from the quantities of Glaze I rubbish that encumber the eastern mesa slopes below the quadrangle, and which are also heaped along the southern part of the North Terrace itself. (Kidder 1924:21–22)

Kidder continued his investigations of the north terrace while examining the eastern wing of the pueblo. Here he found evidence of younger occupations, characterized by Glaze II, Glaze III, Glaze IV, Glaze V, and Glaze VI pottery. Ceramic evidences of Glaze ware II through VI were oriented in a southerly direction in their deposition. Investigations then in the southern end of the site confirmed the gradual abandonment of the northern part of the mesa in favor of the southern end, as occupations of later times continued to populate the site (see fig. 3). From these investigations Kidder inferred that during these periods the pueblo was spreading to the south and that the great quadrangle, and perhaps also the long, narrow south house, were gradually assuming their final form. It was not

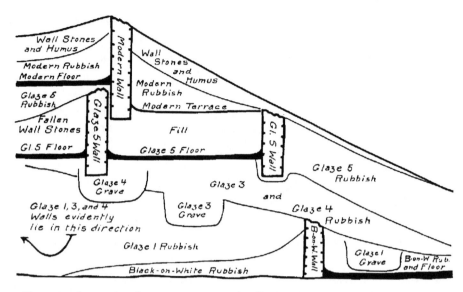

Figure 3. Cross section showing superposition of walls, burials, and other details on the north terrace at Pecos. (After Kidder 1914:22)

until growth of the southern end of the site was completed, or at least well under way, that the inhabitants turned again to the north terrace, "the neglected site of what we supposed to have been their earliest homes" (Kidder 1924:22).

The most important contribution of this second season of fieldwork at Pecos (1916) was the application of stratigraphic information to the chronological analysis of the site. Nels Nelson visited Kidder that season and mentioned Kidder's stratigraphic work there in his 1916 paper, "The Chronology of the Tano Ruins." Kidder discussed the importance of stratigraphy in many publications on southwestern archaeology, notably his 1916 papers, "Archaeological Explorations at Pecos, New Mexico" and "The Pueblo of Pecos," as well as in his *An Introduction to Southwestern Archaeology with a Preliminary Account of the Excavations at Pecos* (1924).

That summer Kidder took on other field assistants. Two of these were Carl Guthe and George Vaillant. Vaillant remained longer than any of the other young archaeologists and, as Kidder (AVK II:8) noted, cut "his archaeological teeth with me and . . . turned out to be [one] of the leading men in the profession."

After Nelson's and Kidder's work with stratigraphy at the San Cristobal and Pecos sites, respectively, this method of establishing relative chronology began to be used by other archaeologists. In 1917 Kidder appeared to take an active role in communicating the importance of stratigraphy as a chronological tool (1917a:369–70). His article, "A Design Sequence from New Mexico," argued that design motifs on ceramics can only be arranged in chronological order based upon stratigraphic means. Articles by Alfred Tozzer (1926) and others appeared, extolling the value of stratigraphy in archaeology.

Yet Kidder felt that his concern with stratigraphy gave him less time to interpret excavated cultural remains effectively. Much of his second field season at Pecos was indeed spent in stratigraphic work at the expense of other field duties. Although there is no relevant documentation, it is probable that Edgar Lee Hewett might also have been demanding much of Kidder's time for the reconstruction of the mission church on the site. Some accounts of Hewett (e.g., Chauvenet, 1983) suggest that he was somewhat hard to get along with, and it seems reasonable to assume that Kidder spent some of his time in satisfying him. Correspondence between Hewett and Kidder (1913–29) in the Edgar Lee Hewett Papers shows that Kidder was involved in helping Hewett in many areas: giving lectures, providing the Museum of New Mexico with artifacts from Pecos to exhibit, and in various lobbying efforts in the state legislature of New Mexico (ELHP).

THIRD SEASON—1917

During this field season no excavations were undertaken in the main Pecos ruins, but a number of other excavations were carried out. The United States had entered World War I, and Kidder joined the army. Before leaving for the Presidio, in San Francisco, California, he was able to spend a few weeks exploring the Hopi country, in northeastern Arizona, and examining the ruined pueblo of Awatovi. This pueblo resembled Pecos in that its occupancy embraced both the prehistoric and historic periods. Evidences of stratification were noted. This site was interesting to Kidder as a means of acquiring data from a more distant region to use in checking the Pecos finds (Kidder 1924:24).

While Kidder was serving his tour of duty in the United States Army,

Carl Guthe continued the work of the Phillips Academy in the Pecos area, exploring sites along the river below Pecos as well as sites to the west of it. He investigated many ruins on the upper Rio Grande and traced the northern limits of Pueblo culture by following it to its vanishing point, in the San Luis valley of southern Colorado (Kidder 1924:24). Guthe then returned to Pecos, where he excavated the main ruin at the nearby site of Rowe for six weeks.

Whether instructions were left for Guthe to investigate the Rowe ruins for ceramic evidence that could be linked to Pecos stratigraphically is not evident in Kidder's unpublished papers, but Guthe did find extensive evidence of Black-on-White pottery at the site. This was important for Kidder's work in two ways. Abundant Black-on-White materials from Rowe would enable him to work with a larger collection of these materials, since Black-on-White ceramics at Pecos were scanty. And Kidder considered the location of this ceramic material, thought to be the oldest pottery made by the inhabitants of the area, crucial in studying the origins of Rio Grande cultural sequences. One striking difference noted by Guthe between Rowe and Pecos was the quality of the masonry; the Rowe masonry was "infinitely superior to that of Pecos" (Guthe 1917:31, Kidder 1924:24).

During the later part of 1917, Kidder went to an army training center, where he was rejected for the first training camp in San Francisco. He was told that he had to have three people recommend him for the next training camp. He was determined to get into the second training camp, so he asked Theodore Roosevelt, President Lowell, of Harvard, and Charles Meyer (who was postmaster general) for recommendations. His connection with President Roosevelt was through his son, Teddy, who was a contemporary of Kidder's at college. Kidder was living in Santa Barbara at the time he was accepted for the second training camp. However, since it did not begin until August, he went out to the Hopi country, where he lived at First Mesa with a sculptor named Emory Kopta, "whom I hadn't known before but who very kindly asked me to stay with him" (AVK II:12).[2]

Kidder's stay in the Hopi country with Emory Kopta was a pleasant one. Kopta was doing a bust of 'Harry,' a Hopi Snake Priest, and gave Kidder information about sites in the area. There was a

nice sharp mesa not more than five or six miles away down to the
south, and I asked Harry about it, 'Is there anything down there?'
And he said 'Oh, there's nothing there, you don't want to go there.
It's not worth your while, and it's a lot of trouble getting down
there'. So, I thought maybe I better go. (AVK II:13)

The next day he started off in a different direction, then swung around
toward the mesa, where he found some beautiful Hopi shrines set on slabs
of stone. The shrines contained little ceremonial vessels with tadpoles,
dragonflies, toads, and "all sorts of rain-making critters painted on them
and offerings of turquoise and shell. I didn't touch a thing" (AVK II:13).

Kidder continued his explorations of the area. He traveled to Second
Mesa to see Piuteque, where a group of Rio Grande people had taken
refuge during the troublesome times of the 1690s.

I went over there, with my tongue hanging out, thinking that I was
going to find some Rio Grande pottery—{but} it was all Hopi pot-
tery, every bit of it. I couldn't find a single sherd. I have since found
that's true elsewhere. When a people move into a new place they take
over the local culture, at least, in ceramics. It is almost invariably
true. (AVK II:14)

But Kidder recognized that moving groups do not necessarily assimi-
late the totality of cultural traits upon contact with an indigenous population. The process of adoption of traits is based upon selection of the
most advantageous at any one time. It would be interesting to know
whether the subjects of culture contact and assimilation of culture traits
were covered by Franz Boas in the class Kidder took from him. Kidder,
however, did not accept Boas's form of historical particularism, and he
may have dismissed most of what Boas had to say in that class.

Although he learned a good bit about Hopi archaeology, Kidder came
to distrust Hopi historical tradition.

I learned a great deal about Hopi archaeology and among other
things discovered that {Robert} Lowie was quite right. Lowie
{said} 'Under no circumstances will I ever believe any historical
tradition told me by the Hopi'. Fewkes swallowed all those tradi-

tions whole. One of the traditions which he recorded was about Sikiacki (spelling used by Kidder), which lies down below the First Mesa. You would have to be a good thrower, but I think you could throw a stone into Sikiacki from the top of the mesa. He gives this long story about how a man in a pueblo, up on the mesa, just above Sikiacki, stole a girl out of this pueblo just above it on the First Mesa, which started war and Sikiacki was ruined by stones thrown down from the ruin on top. When I came to examine this pueblo it turned out to be a Basket-Maker III, and Sikiacki was, of course, 17th and 18th Century. This soured me on Hopi traditions. (AVK II:14–15)

Kidder goes on to suggest that the same might be true of other Puebloan groups:

A number of things have been wrecked. The Jemez people, for example, told Hewett that a certain ruin down below Pecos was the last of the outlying sites to be abandoned when they were at Pecos. It wasn't true, for it had been abandoned while two other sites had remained occupied. I believe the main thing is that they are not interested. When some one like Fewkes began pestering them, and asking them leading questions, they, of course, had to say something, so they just made these things up out of the whole cloth. I don't believe there is any truth in any of that stuff. This history of the development of the Hopi towns has to be worked out archaeologically, and it has been, Colton and the Museum of Northern Arizona people have done it very well. (AVK II:14–15)

Clearly Kidder did make productive use of ethnography, as evidenced by his recruitment of Elsie Clews Parsons and his assignment of Guthe to study the contemporary manufacture of pottery. Kidder raised the science of archaeology to a new interpretive level by melding ethnographic and excavation data into a workable whole; this was in fact, the methodological foundation of his approach to synthesis in Americanist archaeology.

Further work on the Pecos site had to await Kidder's return from the United States Army and the beginning of the fourth field season, in 1920. Kidder enlisted in the United States Army in 1916 while in Santa

Barbara, California working in Basket Maker artifacts. After going to Officer's Training School in 1917, he went to France as a lieutenant in the 91st Division. He was assigned to intelligence work, and his fluency in French greatly helped. Kidder saw combat on the battlefield and was later promoted to captain and made a Chevalier of the Legion d'Honneur (Woodbury 1973:39).

FOURTH SEASON—1920

The Pecos work was at a standstill from the autumn of 1917 until July 1919. Many of the routine matters of laboratory work were completed during this time, such as cataloging collections and bringing maps and field notes up to date. Upon his return Kidder spent the winter of 1919–20 studying specimens already on hand.

The analysis continued of artifactual remains unearthed during previous field seasons at Pecos, but Kidder felt a definite lack of expertise in the study of human skeletal remains and what could thereby be added to the knowledge of prehistoric culture. During the 1920 field season he arranged for Dr. Earnest A. Hooton to join his staff at Pecos; Hooton was then curator of physical anthropology at the Peabody Museum of Harvard University.

Hundreds of human burials had been found during previous field seasons. Kidder thought it might be a good idea for Hooton to see first-hand the conditions under which the material was found and also to assist in developing methods for caring for such material (1924:25). Kidder took advantage of Hooton's presence to run a number of new trenches into the refuse-heap cemeteries on the east slope of the Pecos site. Through the work of Hooton and his collaborator, T. Wingate Todd, the physical anthropology of the Pecos Pueblo would provide not only the criteria for sexing and aging human osteological remains, but would also be of interest in epidemiological concerns (Hooton 1930:13–32). Preliminary data were obtained for the following: population ratio of male and female, average life span of the pueblo residents, and evidence of diseases that had affected the population. Hooton's work there was one of the earlier examples of a physical anthropologist working alongside an archaeologist in the field, although Kidder had been aware of the importance of this discipline to fieldwork as early as 1908 (Kidder 1910).

FIFTH SEASON—1921

The field season of 1921 at Pecos led Kidder to conclude that the "surest archaeological results were to be derived from the study of pottery" (Kidder 1924:27). The wealth of ceramic discoveries was overwhelming, and Kidder confessed that such an abundance of material led at times to confusion.

{I was} being called upon to classify wares, make comparisons, and form judgements as to the relations between different ceramic groups. We found that in doing this we were severely handicapped by a lack of precise knowledge as to the technology of Pueblo pottery, a lack which could not be supplied by any printed work. (Kidder 1924:27)

In the spring of 1921, Kidder found that he would be unable to excavate at Pecos that summer because of his ailing mother. Although he was working for the Phillips Academy, he informed Hewett of the situation because Hewett's continuing support of the Pecos excavations was necessary for Kidder's work there. He wrote that his mother was not expected to live through the summer, and that he would stay in the east for an unspecified period of time (Kidder to Hewett, 9 May 1921, ELH) Hewett wrote back saying that he understood the situation and that "Pecos will wait for you just as long as may be necessary" (Hewett to Kidder, 14 May 1921, ELH). Kidder's mother died within a year (AVK I:30).

During the field season of 1921, Kidder sent Carl Guthe to undertake a thorough study of pottery making "as it is practiced among the Pueblo Indians . . ." in New Mexico (Kidder 1924:27–28). Guthe selected for his study the Tewa pueblo of San Ildefonso, a village on the Rio Grande north of Santa Fe, whose women have for years been recognized as the most skillful and versatile potters of that region (Kidder 1924:28). He spent several weeks there and recorded every step in the manufacture of pottery, from the digging of the clays to the firing of the completed vessels. The San Ildefonso study was the first of a series of investigations into the technical areas of pottery making, and was an early form of what is called today ethnoarchaeology. Later, in conjunction with Kidder's

work at Pecos, he asked Anna O. Shepard to analyze the physical properties of the paste, slips, and paints of the Pecos pottery (Shepard 1942,
Rohn 1973:195). Shepard's ceramic reputation began with Kidder's work
at Pecos, and she found herself examining petrographic sections of ceramic specimens from other archaeologists throughout the Southwest and
from around the world. Her work led to *Ceramics for the Archaeologist,*
which is a standard reference tool for all those interested in ceramic
analysis (Shepard 1956).

Kidder also wanted ethnographic work to be carried out among the
living descendants of the Pecos people. The Jemez and Pecos were closely
allied linguistically, and their common dialect was not spoken at any
other town. When Pecos was abandoned, "the surviving members of the
tribe naturally went to live with the Jemez" (Kidder 1924:28). Kidder
believed that such ethnographic fieldwork would tie the prehistory of
Pecos to its modern-day descendants. Since the beginning of the Pecos
work, Kidder realized that the investigation would not be complete until
an attempt had been made to recover from the descendants of the Pecos at
Jemez whatever knowledge they still had of their former home and of the
life their ancestors lived there. Also, he thought it desirable to learn
something of the ethnology of one of the modern Rio Grande pueblos,
because at that time, little was known of the social and religious organization of those towns, and such studies could hardly fail to throw light on
many of the problems raised by the Pecos excavations. No member of his
field staff was qualified to undertake this work, and no opportunity to
have it done by anyone else presented itself until Dr. Elsie Clews Parsons
decided to include Jemez in the intensive ethnological survey she had
been carrying on at the villages further west. She spent the seasons of
1921 and 1922 at the pueblo, where, in spite of great difficulties due to
the "conservatism and secretiveness of the pueblo, she has collected a
mass of most interesting and important data" (Kidder 1924:28).

Both Kidder and Parsons came to value what Steward (1942:337–44)
would later refer to as the "direct historical approach" of archaeological
analysis. Kidder (1930a:145) accepted the "principle that in any investigation one should proceed from the known to the unknown, which in
archaeology means that one should work from the known present back to
the unknown past." Parsons (1940:214) agreed with Kidder that there is

"no dispute that the living culture has light to throw upon the buried one" and that archaeological data might suffer from "ignorance of ethnological ambitions or of ethnographic details." However, Parsons (1940: 218) also believed that "[i]nformation from the other partner should not be used merely to support one's own hypothesis; the integrity of the other is to be considered if only to preserve one's own integrity."

Thus although Kidder did not excavate at Pecos during the 1921 field season, the technology of pottery making and the ethnology of the Pecos-Jemez Indians were documented by Carl Guthe and Elsie Clews Parsons. The activity of this period led to Kidder's notion of the direct historical approach for use in explaining archaeological remains. Included in appendix 3 is a verbatim transcription of Kidder's recollections of this period, which were set down in 1957.

SIXTH SEASON—1922

The Pecos season of 1922 saw the continuation of excavation of the main quadrangle of the site. Particular attention was devoted to architecture, town growth, and the stratigraphy of the beds of early rubbish next to the building on the west side of the site (Kidder 1924:28). During this field season, Ida Sanford, George Clapp Vaillant, and S. P. Moorehead were Kidder's field assistants. Madeleine Kidder continued with the classification and sorting of potsherds.

By the end of the summer of 1922, excavation of the Pecos site virtually ceased, and time was spent surveying and investigating other archaeological sites in the general area. A large site at Bandelier Bend, across the Arroyo de Pecos from the main ruin, was surveyed. Enough was done to get an idea of the nature of the pottery and to determine that the buildings had been low, rambling structures made of adobe. Pottery analysis indicated that Bandelier Bend was an ancient settlement that coalesced quite early in the Pueblo period, and that it had been inhabited for a long time. The pueblo was abandoned at about the time Pecos was founded, which makes it seem likely that its people merely moved across the arroyo to the more easily defended site on the Pecos mesa (Kidder 1924:30). Kidder's preliminary excavations revealed a round subterranean kiva, which was thought to be "the oldest example of such a structure so far reported from the Rio Grande" (Kidder 1924:30).

THE IMPORTANCE OF THE PECOS EXCAVATIONS

A. V. Kidder was a dedicated cultural historian of the prehistoric Southwest and a superlative field archaeologist. Using these interests and skills, he carried out the first long-term, multidisciplinary archaeological project in the Southwest. Because of the prominence of southwestern prehistory in North American archaeology and Kidder's personal prominence in the discipline, his work and his values have had a major influence on the whole of Americanist archaeology. Although Kidder had cut his archaeological teeth under Edgar Lee Hewett, nothing was provided by Hewett in the way of methodological or theoretical precedent. Analysis of Kidder's work at Pecos Pueblo has revealed a number of methodological contributions to southwestern Archaeology that show him to be an excellent field archaeologist, archaeological administrator, and dedicated cultural historian.

Being committed to building a cultural history of the prehistoric Southwest, Kidder viewed stratigraphic and ceramic analysis as major tools for delineating cultural growth through time and space. The relative chronology of prehistoric Pueblo ruins was virtually ignored by southwesternists until Kidder made popular the use of stratigraphic dating there.

Valid cultural histories . . . can only be compiled by studying series of specimens whose age, relative to each other, is known. Only from chronologically seriable specimens can dependable conclusions be drawn as to the origin and spread of culture traits and as to the improvement or decline of techniques; in other words, as to the genetics of culture. But the time sequence of archaeological materials is usually very hard to establish. They are found in all sorts of places and under all manner of conditions. Very often they come from widely separated sites. To bring these into sequence, there must be selected certain classes of specimens which more clearly and more easily than others, can be used as indicators of the passage of time, and which can serve as preliminary criteria for determining the relative age of less readily seriated remains with which they are associated. Any class of objects to be employed in this way must possess certain indispensable characteristics. The specimens which go to make it up must be imperishable, they must be abundant and widely disseminated, and they must be of such a nature as very sensitively to register culture change. Pottery admirably fulfils the requirements. (Kidder 1931a:3–4)

Although he did not initiate stratigraphic dating in the Southwest, Kidder was the first to call for its widespread implementation.

The ideal form of chronological evidence is provided by stratigraphy, i.e., when remains of one type are found lying below those of another. Such evidence is of course conclusive, and has provided us with sure data as to the relative age of several phases of Southwestern culture. If we could find in each district {in New Mexico} sites containing material running from the very earliest times down to the site period of abandonment, our task would be a comparatively simple one; but no such site has ever been discovered. Pecos presents the longest complete series so far known, but Pecos does not carry us back to really remote times. Even short series, covering two or three periods, are rare enough; but they do occur and can be made, by the principle of overlapping, to yield excellent results. (Kidder 1924:45)

Kidder wanted to determine the sequence of local ceramic types and to provide cross finds of contemporaneous nonlocal ceramic types for solving the "broader and more important problems of inter-area chronology" (Kidder 1924:45). It was by this method that Kidder hoped to piece together the story of Pueblo development through time (Kidder 1924: 135).

Kidder's field method at Pecos was a well-planned approach. He employed profiling as a means of exposing the chronological record of Pecos. His trench faces were cut clean for observation, and a record of the strata and the kinds of pottery appearing at various depths was made. Thus he gathered a preliminary body of data from which the succession of wares at Pecos could be developed. For more exact determinations and to collect material for typological and statistical study he relied upon stratigraphic tests.

He employed two types of tests at Pecos: the "look-over" and "bag" tests (Kidder 1931a:9). The look-over test consisted in taking down, little by little, a section of a trench face, beginning at the surface and working toward the bottom. The sherds from each level were examined and their morphology, style, and structure recorded. He saved representative specimens from each level before moving on to a lower level in the excavation. He made this test for every fifteen or twenty feet of forward progress; "and whenever there appeared any important new stratum or any representation of a ware not hitherto encountered" (Kidder 1931a:9).

In Kidder's bag test the specimens recovered were gathered and stored in paper sacks; this was a much more detailed analysis. This test was reserved for areas that had the promise of yielding unusually long sequences of material, as well as for areas where a deposit was unusually well stratified or for parts of a midden that might allow for the recovery of evidence of "special [cultural] periods" (Kidder 1931a:9).

Kidder considered these stratigraphic tests valuable only to the extent that they represented a true picture of prehistoric conditions at Pecos. He chose for testing only those areas that gave indication of being undisturbed from the time of deposition of the rubbish.

The suitability of an area for test purposes was determined by observation of a face as exposed by excavation. If it showed unbroken banding and generally even trend of strata, a column, its size determined by the extent of deposit, was isolated by exposing two, three, or even all four of its sides by trenching from surface to bottom. A horizontal base line was established toward the center of this column, for measuring purposes. The exposed faces were then carefully scraped to a vertical face to reveal every line and band in the column, and the limits of each cut to be made were fixed among such lines by placing pegs at frequent intervals to guide the workmen, who were instructed to cut each layer precisely down to the row of pegs. A drawing of the column was then made showing position and thickness of every layer. In dividing the column into layers care was taken to follow a natural division, such as a layer of ash or charcoal, a hard-packed living surface, etc., rather than an arbitrary line. (Kidder 1931a:9)

The results of his studies at Pecos were a classification and tabulation of ceramics, expressed in linear graphs, drawn for percentages of types per unit or level in the excavation (see fig. 3). In 1931, based upon the results

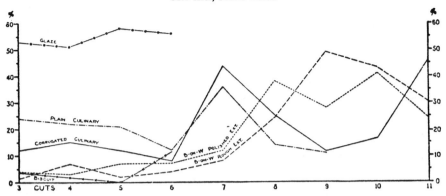

GRAPH VII
Test XIX, Pecos. Wares

TABLE IX
Test XIX, Pecos. Wares

Cut Number...	Number of Sherds									Approximate Percentages								
	3	4	5	6	7	8	9	10	11	3	4	5	6	7	8	9	10	11
Glaze	47	32	25	49	×	×	×	×	×	54	51	58	56	×	×	×	×	×
Biscuit	4	1	×	10	×	×	×	×	×	4	2	×	12	×	×	×	×	×
B.-on-w. polished ext. ..	4	2	3	6	10	8	13	13	10	4	3	7	7	12	38	28	41	24
B.-on-w. rough ext.....	2	4	1	4	7	5	23	14	12	2	7	2	4	8	24	49	43	30
Plain culinary	20	14	9	11	31	3	5	×	×	24	22	21	12	36	14	11	×	×
Corrugated culinary....	10	9	5	8	38	5	6	5	19	12	15	12	9	44	24	12	16	46
Totals...........	87	62	43	88	86	21	47	32	41	100	100	100	100	100	100	100	100	100

Figure 4. Example of linear graph and tabulation for Pecos ceramic types. (Kidder 1931a:38)

of the ceramic stratigraphic method, Kidder established the relative ages of the Forked Lightning Ruin and Pecos Pueblo: Pecos is the younger of the two.

Much of what Kidder envisioned for Southwestern archaeology, indeed for Americanist archaeology in general, can be found in shorter publications that appeared between 1910 and 1929. Kidder's favorite vehicle for reporting archaeological progress was the magazine *El Palacio*. Kidder also suggested, in "A Design Sequence from New Mexico," that

> {t}he only safe method for the working out of developments in decorative art is to build up one's sequences from chronologically sequent material, and so let one's theories form themselves from the sequences. (Kidder 1917a)

Preconceived notions about the design of ceramics or the cultural growth of Pecos must not color the evidence found in an excavation. "The specimen is no longer an isolated fact, but a bit of evidence for the solution of [a] historical problem" (Kidder 1926:223).

Kidder began the long process of establishing the cultural chronology of the Southwest. In particular, he wanted to work out the cultural growth of the Puebloan groups. As a cultural historian, he began to bring together knowledge of isolated archaeological sites into a workable whole. By tying this material together, he created a larger picture of cultural development in the prehistoric Southwest.

Where applicable Kidder incorporated the field methodologies of other investigators into his master plan for the Pecos site, so that he might benefit from their findings as well as their mistakes. A complete cultural history of a group, he suggested, would benefit from the work of earlier investigators. He incorporated Hewett's 1904 work into his overall scheme of research, made use of some of the material left by Spanish visitors to the area, and included the site survey of Pecos performed by Adolph Bandelier, in 1881. In his unpublished memoirs, he noted that Bandelier's 1880–81 survey provided much in the way of useful information for the analysis of the pueblo, especially concerning style of masonry employed by the Pecos inhabitants (AVK II:23). Thus, although not in so many words, Kidder was indicating that an investigator should survey all pertinent literature relating to his area of endeavor before going into the field, to benefit from the work of others and avoid their mistakes.

As an excellent archaeological administrator, Kidder believed that detailed, systematic study, not only of pottery but also of other artifacts and of architecture as well, is of the utmost necessity in determining the distribution of types through time and space (Woodbury 1973:32). In 1917 he wrote of the need for gathering data, and particularly for careful analytical and classificatory research. His interest in classificatory research can be traced back to his ornithological training as a youngster.

In an important paper published in 1915, he said that "what we need in the present state of our investigations in the Southwest is data rather than conclusions" (Kidder 1915:407–408). He wanted a system of classification that could handle massive amounts of data efficiently and accurately, since conclusions based upon scanty data do not provide an accurate foundation for the analysis of prehistoric human behavior (Kidder 1917c, 1929, 1924, AVK II). He called for increased effort by Southwesternists to obtain more evidence, so that more detailed analyses could be made and firmer conclusions drawn. Of particular importance is the phrase "analytical and classificatory research," which indicates that Kidder wanted to emulate the precise, analytical methods of the hard sciences (AVK II:48). What he advocated for the enhancement of method and theory in American archaeology between 1916 and 1929 can be found in his paper on "Prehistoric Cultures of the San Juan Drainage" (1917c). He advocated more data, both for a culture itself and for its area. In terms of the analysis of a culture's component parts, such as

> the weaves of its basketry, sandals, and bags: the technique of its wood, stone, and clay working, —we must prosecute a thorough search, both in the Southwest and in all directions beyond its limits, to ascertain the relationship of the cultural traits that our intensive study has established (Kidder 1917c:110–11).

Kidder was suggesting that the archaeologist should not restrict attention to narrow problems that produce little in the way of knowledge about an entire prehistoric culture or technology. Attention must be paid to the entirety of cultural development through time and space.

Kidder realized that analysis of prehistoric events must be a group effort, as seen in his multidisciplinary ("pan-scientific") approach to Southwestern archaeological problems. His borrowing of Nelson's stratigraphic method and utilization of the archaeological literature of his predecessors enabled him to construct a better plan for the excavation at Pecos, one based on improved field approaches to archaeological problems. He knew early on that the day of one-worker excavation would have to end; the archaeologist was simply not fully trained to carry out all the necessary work at an archaeological site.

> Much work has been done, but it has been erratic, and has not followed any well-ordered plan. What is needed is a series of careful intensive studies of the various phases of Archaeology, Ethnology and Somatology of the region (Kidder 1914:2).

Although Kidder was a central figure in the development of Southwestern archaeology, it is not clear from his unpublished papers and diaries whether he knew that he was setting methodological precedents. Emil Haury (1987:personal communication) indicted that Kidder was quite aware that he was breaking new ground. Believing that he could not competently undertake all the necessary investigations himself at Pecos, he had the foresight and logic to involve others who were appropriately qualified.

Kidder believed that all archaeological research should be organized with one goal in mind: contributing to the general understanding of American prehistory. Archaeological sites individually are fascinating, but they supply nothing to the knowledge of the Americas unless the archaeologist interprets and explains the development of the larger area. Without such interpretation the investigator remains nothing more than a relic hunter.

Kidder suggested that both detailed and general studies are essential, and that no simple rule can guide the choice between them in particular situations. Although one of the goals of communication among archaeologists is to provide commonality in field methods, he understood that no two sets of field circumstances are the same. He suggested that archaeologists must be careful to hold themselves to a proper balance between the detailed and general focuses of study; each problem must be attacked in its own way, and fieldworkers must decide where to place their energy (Kidder 1924:34).

As an archaeological administrator, Kidder always sought to upgrade field methodology in the Southwest, urging archaeologists to communicate their methodological improvements. He instituted the yearly Pecos Conferences to contribute to the development and dissemination of innovative methods. The first conference, held in 1927 at Pecos Pueblo, was a forum designed so that archaeologists, ethnologists, physical anthropologists, and linguists interested in the Southwest might be able to trade ideas and jointly seek to resolve various archaeological problems. It was during this conference that Kidder and the other participants put together the chronological framework later referred to as the Pecos Classification. "Details [were] added, names of time units [in the classification scheme] modified, but the basic scheme [was] only superseded in the last few years" (Woodbury 1973:113). Kidder's classification system was devised so that other southwesterners would be able to communicate in a common language. It organized vast amounts of data already compiled by other workers in the Southwest (Kidder 1927:489–91). The tradition of these conferences has continued to the present, and they still serve as a professional forum for discussion among archaeologists.

Kidder organized the 1927 conference as an informal gathering, without prepared papers, held in the field and attended by southwestern-ists actively involved in research. Students of Southwest archaeology have generally accepted the idea that the first Pecos Conference was also the first Southwest regional conference. However, Neil M. Judd provided an earlier example of a regional conference through gatherings he organized at Pueblo Bonito, during the summers of 1921, 1922, and 1925 (Woodbury 1983a:251).

> *Judd has written that he was delighted to give them up in favor of the Pecos Conference. Travel was difficult to Chaco Canyon and feeding even the small group he invited was a problem. In one way Judd's meetings were different—he invited specialists not just in archaeology and ethnology, but in agronomy, botany, geology, and physiography, to assist in interpreting the past of Chaco Canyon, rather than report on their recent research. But they all shared an interest in the archaeological research going on in the Southwest. (Woodbury 1983:251)*

The unpublished memoirs of A. V. Kidder (AVK II) do not refer to Judd's seminars as models for the 1927 Pecos Conference, but they may well have been.

A distinctive feature of the Pecos Conference is that there have never been officers, there are no by-laws, it has no headquarters, dues, or memberships, and for many years it had no formal programs at its meetings, only a series of informal reports on participants' recent field-work. Each year someone volunteers to host the next conference at their field headquarters, museum, or campus, and an ad hoc committee is appointed for program and arrangements (Woodbury 1982:5).

The genesis of the Pecos Classification provides a wonderful example of the creative potential of this informality. By the middle of the second day of the first Pecos Conference, some of the participants saw little progress in the discussions taking place. Kidder described the cure for the problem as well as the method of treatment:

> *we had got ourselves pretty talked out and had come to arguing about matters of relatively little moment. Along toward noon, Tom Waterman drew Alfred Kroeber and me aside. He said: 'We've been getting nowhere this morning. Let's hatch up something important*

enough to interest everybody'. So we went off by ourselves and sat down in the shade of a big piñon. Kroeber said: 'Why don't we work up a general statement about what's been learned to date of the whole cultural history of the Southwest? I'll bet that will give us plenty to wrestle with. There are people here who've worked on about every period'. So I produced my notebook and, in an hour, we roughed out what came to be known as the Pecos nomenclature. It's been pulled to pieces at one time or another by almost everybody. Nevertheless, it's still generally in use. As Watson Smith (1959) has written, 'The Pecos classification bends with the wind but does not break'. (AVK I:145)

Another innovation of the 1927 Pecos Conference was an interest in cultural resource management. Frank Pinkley led a discussion about problems encountered in working on public lands, the problem of unauthorized digging, and the relationships between the field archaeologist and the National Park Service (Woodbury 1983a:258).

The second Pecos Conference was held in 1929. One of the highlights of this conference was the discovery, by members of the National Geographic Society's Third Beam Expedition, of the now-famous Show Low Log. This beam enabled southwesternists to construct a continuous dendrochrological record going back to about 700 A.D. Southwest archaeologists could now replace their rough chronological estimates of a site's age with more accurate dates (Woodbury 1983a:259). A more complete discussion of the second Pecos Conference can be found in Charles Amsden's "The Second Pecos Conference" (1929:28–29).

Kidder was the driving force behind the Pecos Conferences throughout his lifetime, although he was frequently unable to attend because of ill health. In letters between Kidder and Harold Colton, discussions about the content of various Pecos Conferences were laid out (see Kidder-Colton correspondence at Museum of Northern Arizona). Kidder emphasized that Americanist archaeologists should always be alert for better field and analytical methods, at the same time they must be concerned with the creation of new theory. Yet he realized that such advances come only with time and additional experimentation in the field (Kidder 1924, 1925, 1927; AVK II).

Forty-five years later, James B. Griffin, in an appraisal of Southwestern archaeology, wrote:

> *If Kidder's conceptual approach were translated into modern archaeological jargon, with the correct sprinkling of terms taken over from the current social anthropological idiom, it would be regarded as a marvelous model for the next 20 years (Griffin 1959:386).*

Gordon Willey (1967:299) wrote of *An Introduction to Southwestern Archaeology With a Preliminary Account of the Excavations at Pecos* (Kidder 1924) that

> *it is a rarity in that it introduces systematics to a field previously unsystematized, and, at the same time, it is vitally alive and unpedantic. It might well be said that Kidder put the classification of potsherds into Southwestern archaeology without removing or obscuring the people who made the pottery. He wrote a book that was romantic but not ridiculous, scrupulously close to the facts but not a boring recital of them.*

In 1933 Kidder undertook his final work in the Southwest, before partially severing his ties with that region in favor of the Mayan area. With his close friends Harriet and Burton Cosgrove, he participated in the excavation of a Mimbres culture ruin near Silver City, New Mexico. This dig at the Pendelton Ruin saw no major finds, but Kidder's foreword to the 1949 report on the ruin reflects how hard the departure from the Southwest must have been in 1929.

> *The present paper, as a matter of fact, would probably never have been finished had it not been for a busman's holiday in the Southwest that my wife and I took in the summer of '47. We visited E. W. Haury's University of Arizona Point of Pines field school on the San Carlos Indian Reservation in Arizona and later were driven by J. L. Nusbaum up to the San Juan country. That was a memorable month. At Point of Pines we watched the gray curtains of the summer storms trailing far off across the Big Prairie, savored the unforgettable smell of the first rains on the parched Arizona soil. In the north we saw again the brown walls of Pueblo Bonito, Cliff Palace*

brooding under its vast sandstone arch, the strange rock-perched
towers of Hovenweep. It was all most unsettling, because for years I
had been struggling to get the Southwestern virus out of my system—
and here it was back again worse than ever. And at Haury's dig-
gings good honest Southwestern pottery—not fancy Maya stuff—
was coming out of the ground. I had a wonderful time with those
sherds, particularly the corrugated ones. Some of them seemed to be
like pieces I dimly remembered from the Pendelton site. So, back in
Cambridge, I asked Mrs. Cosgrove to go over the field notes, the
plans and photographs. The first thing I knew I had temporarily
ditched the Maya and was happily at work with Mrs. Cosgrove in
her room in the Peabody basement. (Kidder 1949:109)

Before turning attention to A. V. Kidder's Maya program and his
association with the Division of Historical Research–Carnegie Institution of Washington, one final comment must be made. Kidder wanted
Americanist archaeology to strive constantly for internal coordination
and cooperation. The task of the archaeologist is to collect small contributions into a larger scheme and thus to shed light upon the prehistory of
the American Indian. Kidder's work in 1924 ends with a paragraph that
is a reflection of what had been accomplished:

To understand the problems of Southwestern archaeology it is nec-
essary to consider the nature of our knowledge of man in America.
Historical information in regard to the American Indian runs back
at the farthest for only about four hundred years, and in most parts
of the New World the record is very much shorter. Furthermore,
where the historical record begins, there, as a rule, the history of the
Indian abruptly ceases. There are a few exceptions, such as those
provided by the datable monuments of the Maya; and certain in-
stances, as in Peru and Mexico, where native traditionists have set
down in European characters the more or less legendary histories of
their own particular peoples. At best, then, recorded history for the
aborigines of the New World is brief, and in the case of most areas it
is entirely lacking. The student has before him data as to the dis-
tribution of great numbers of tribes, infinitely diverse in language

and customs and ranging in culture from the lowest savagery to the relatively high civilization. This state of affairs must of course be the result of a very long sequence of historical events, and our problem, as Sapir has so admirably phrased it, 'may be metaphorically defined as the translation of a two-dimensional photographic picture of reality into the three-dimensional picture which lies back of it. Is it possible,' he asks, 'to read time perspective into the flat surface of a photograph?' {Sapir 1916:14}. Sapir proceeds to answer his question in the affirmative, basing his deductions largely on the inferential evidence provided by ethnology and linguistics; he emphasizes, however, the great potential importance of archaeological studies. Such studies had not, when Sapir wrote, been prosecuted with any great energy, but during the past decade archaeologists have been devoting more and more attention to the definite information bearing on the time-relations of remains of man in America. Nowhere has this search been more diligently prosecuted than in the Southwest, and the results so far obtained are extremely promising. (Kidder 1924:34–35)[3]

NOTES

1. The Edgar Lee Hewett papers, deposited with the Museum of New Mexico, contain correspondence between Hewett and Kidder about the Pecos work, August 1913 through July 1929.
2. A more complete discussion of Kidder's military career can be found in Woodbury's excellent book, *A. V. Kidder* (1973).
3. See appendix 2 for transcriptions of A. V. Kidder's unpublished memoirs concerning Pecos, the Southwest, and his goals and aims for southwestern archaeology.

Figure 5. Neil M. Judd, Alkali Ridge, 1908.

Figure 6. A. V. Kidder, Pajarito Plateau, 1911.

Figure 7. A. V. Kidder, Mesa Verde, 1912.

Figure 8. Samuel J. Guernsey, Marsh Pass, 1914.

Figure 9. Samuel J. Guernsey, location unknown, ca. 1914.

Figure 10. Clayton Wetherill (1) and Uncle Jett (Wade?) Wetherill, Kayenta, 1914.

Figure 11. Jesse L. Nusbaum with Kate Murray (Romero), Pecos Pueblo, 1915.

Figure 12. A. V. Kidder at Pecos mission church, excavation under the mission floor. Bodies in coffins are mission priests.

Figure 13. Trenching excavation, north terrace, Pecos Pueblo, ca. 1916.

Figure 14. Alfred and Madeleine Kidder at Pecos Pueblo, ca. 1916.

Figure 15. Pecos Pueblo, 1916. Left to right: Carl E. Guthe, Alfred Kidder II, A. V. Kidder, Nicolas Encimas.

Figure 16. Carl Guthe taking notes on stratigraphy. Pecos Pueblo, ca. 1916.

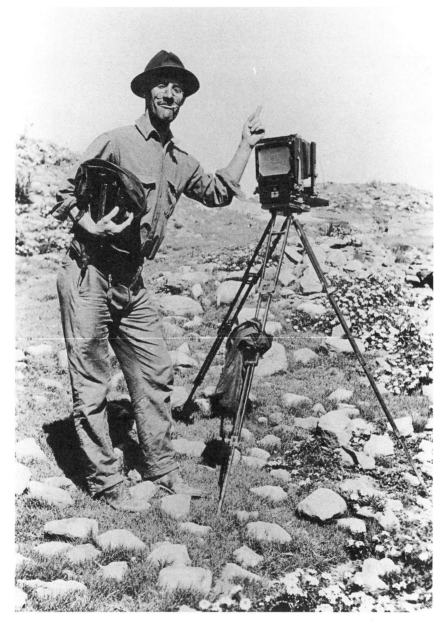

Figure 17. Jesse Nusbaum, Pecos Pueblo, ca. 1916.

Figure 18. Leslie Spier (1) and A. L. Kroeber, "Cora Mountain," Zuni, 1920.

Figure 19. Party in Chaco Canyon, 1920. Seated, left to right: Unknown, Mrs. Edgar Lee Hewett, Sylvanus Morley, Earl Morris. Standing, left to right: Neil Judd, unknown, Wesley Bradfield, Edgar Lee Hewett, A. V. Kidder, Jack Martin.

Figure 20. Camp of F. W. Hodge, Hawikuh, 1920. Seated, left to right: F. W. Hodge, A. V. Kidder. Standing, left to right: Sylvanus G. Morley, E. Coffin, Jesse Nusbaum, Eleanor Johnson, Deric Nusbaum, Neil Judd, Earl Morris.

Figure 21. A. V. Kidder holding effigy from Kiva 12, Pecos Pueblo, 1925.

Figure 22. Temple E-VII-Sub, Uaxactun, Guatemala, n.d.

Figure 23. Temple of the Wall Panels, Chichen Itza, Yucatan, n.d.

Figure 24. Group E, Uaxactun, 1928. Left to right: George C. Vaillant, A. L. Smith, Sylvanus Morley.

Figure 25. Charles Lindbergh helping Ann Morrow Lindbergh into plane. A. V. Kidder and his two young sons, Alfred II and Randolph, are on the left. Pecos Pueblo, 1929.

Figure 26. Yucatan, ca. 1930. Photograph taken from Charles Lindbergh's plane, probably by Ann Morrow Lindbergh.

Figure 27. Vannevar Bush at Awatovi, 1938. (Courtesy of Watson Smith)

Figure 28. Gustav Stromsvik in Norwegian Free Navy uniform, WWII.

Figure 29. Alfred Kidder (1) and Harold Colton, Pecos Conference, Point of Pines, Arizona, 1948.

Figure 30. Earl Morris at the 1948 Pecos Conference.

Figure 31. Emil Haury presenting the University of Arizona "Medal of Merit" to A. V. Kidder, Cambridge.

Figure 32. Alfred Vincent Kidder, 1960.

THE MAYA AND THE CARNEGIE INSTITUTION

In 1959 A. V. Kidder suggested that Middle American archaeologists trained in the United States received but little instruction in theory and its implications for field methods. His ideas about the development of Middle American archaeology may be found in "Middle American Archaeology Since 1906," read before a special symposium organized by the American Anthropological Association. Kidder (1959a:1) noted that Middle Americanists had devoted little time to the formulation of field methods designed to discern the growth and succession of ancient cultures. In his own training at Harvard University,

There was no theory, nothing was said, so far as I can remember or find in my old lecture notes, of what anthropology was all about, of how it and other disciplines could, to their mutual advantage, link arms in attempting to understand the fellow human being with whom we must share this ever-shrinking planet. Nor did American archaeology, certainly at Harvard and I believe pretty generally elsewhere, have chronological depth, in spite of what was known, and was then being taught us by W. C. Farrabee, of the age-long development of Old World cultures. . . . There were several causes for such neglect of the time element. Many of the claims for vast antiquity of New World man had been obviously fantastic. W. H. Holmes had shown that various objects, held to represent Palaeolithic industries, were recent workshop rejects. Hrdlička often rightly, but always furiously, attacked every attempt to demonstrate a respectable age for any find. In those days it had become heresy to think back, even into the upper B. C.'s. Also, Boas' refutation of

77

over-simplistic theories of cultural evolution played a part in the almost dead-leveling of American prehistory. Furthermore, in the early 1900's, the few Americanists active in archaeology were busy tilling fields at once so rich and so nearly virgin that collection of data seemed most immediately essential. There was likewise a growing realization of the necessity for new standards of accuracy in typological observation and description.

Looking back upon his educational career, Kidder wanted students of Americanist archaeology, especially Mesoamericanists, to have the benefit of a well-ordered plan of analytical attack for archaeological problems. He believed that their first and most basic task was the establishment of a system of cultural chronologies, based upon what was found in the ground. This emphasis on chronology and stratigraphy may be traced to his reading of Edward Sapir's (1916) "Time Perspective in Aboriginal American Culture." Although Sapir did not discuss archaeological data, his paper intensified Kidder's interest in chronological ordering and in providing a foundation for judging the relationships among cultures (Kidder 1959a:2). During the period between 1906 and the involvement of the Carnegie Institution of Washington in 1914, the archaeology of Mesoamerica was in a preproblem stage. Data collected were few, geographically spotty, and generally imprecise; only the most spectacular received attention. Thus data regarding typology and "chronological relations necessary for the formulation of meaningful historical or cultural problems . . . were generally lacking" (Kidder 1959a:2).

ARCHAEOLOGY AT THE CARNEGIE INSTITUTION BEFORE A. V. KIDDER

The intellectual climate of Middle American archaeology prior to Kidder's work there in 1929 somewhat paralleled that of North America in general trends, but its emphasis was different from that of the archaeology practiced in the United States. Middle American archaeology had also been influenced by Europe, but more by individual Europeans than by "general intellectual or archaeological developments there, in contrast to North America" (Willey and Sabloff 1980:57). Other differences between the archaeology of Middle America and that of the United States were the richness and grandeur of the Middle American remains, coupled with indigenous writing systems. These systems became the focus of study for both European and North American scholars; their decipherment would one day allow Middle Americanists to date their sites more accurately, as well as to propose a means by which to correlate Mayan and Western chronologies.

The intellectual climate of this period was marked by exploration and description of ruins, and like the American Southwest, Middle American and Mayan archaeology was at its preproblem stage. The lack of questions to be tested in the field certainly can be traced to archaeological training at universities of that time; there was little emphasis upon constructing a well-ordered plan of attack, let alone more profound theoretical guidance.

The beginning of this period was marked by two explorations in Yucatan and Central America by John L. Stephens (a lawyer) and Frederick Catherwood (an architect and artist) and the publication of Stephens's (1841) *Incidents of Travel in Central America, Chiapas, and Yucatan* and (1843) *Incidents of Travel in Yucatan* and Catherwood's (1844) *Views of Ancient Monuments in Central America, Chiapas, and Yucatan.* Stephens had previously traveled in the Old World and had published three accounts of his explorations (1837, 1838, 1839). The accounts of Stephens and Catherwood opened the field of Mayan archaeology, which was to be developed by Sylvanus Morley and A. V. Kidder. Stephens had correctly noted that the Mayan materials lacked great antiquity, at a time when much speculation suggested a much older time frame.

The work of Stephens and Catherwood was followed by that of a diverse groups of investigators, including Desiré Charnay, a Frenchman, who was the first to photograph early Mayan ruins (Charnay, 1887). LePlongeon made some early excavations and was one of the most "fantastic characters in American Archaeology" (Willey and Sabloff, 1980:58).

In 1889 Alfred Maudslay, an Englishman, explored, mapped, and photographed many Mayan sites, among them Yaxchilán and Copán. Based upon his explorations he published *Biologia Centrali Americana,* which includes four volumes on archaeology (Maudslay 1889–1902). Later Teobart Maler, who worked for the Peabody Museum, photographed many Maya hieroglyphic inscriptions (Maler 1901, 1903, 1908); their work enabled Goodman (1897) and Forstemann (1906) to solve the mystery of the Maya long count. This accomplishment, in turn, led to the formulation of interesting and significant questions concerning Mayan astronomical and mathematical systems. Adolph Bastian wrote about the sculptures of Santa Lucia Cotzumalhuapa, in the Guatemalan highlands (Bastian 1876). Karl Sapper, a geographer and ethnographer, classified Mayan ruins into architectural types and related them to ethnographic and linguistic areas (Sapper 1895). At the turn of the century, Thomas Gann surveyed and excavated in Honduras, and E. H. Thompson, the American consul in Yucatan, dredged the Sacred Cenote at Chichén Itzá and excavated other sites (Gann 1900; E. Thompson, 1897, 1898, 1904). Exploration and description of ruins was the only type of archaeology in Mesoamerica during that period.

While the Maya area was the center of most of the archaeological activity of this period, work was also being done in central Mexico. Leopold Batres (1906) had done work at Teotihuacán, and Zelia Nuttal (1910) published studies on a wide variety of topics in Mexican archaeology. W. H. Holmes also made contributions to Middle American archaeology. In *Archaeological Studies of Ancient Cities of Mexico* (Holmes 1895–97), he classified ceramic vessels and various types of ceremonial architecture and attempted to make comparisons between the two.

The first large-scale excavation of a site in Middle America was undertaken by M. H. Saville, at Copán, Honduras, under the auspices of the Peabody Museum of Harvard University (Saville 1892). His report and others of that time were almost entirely descriptive in content. Alfred M. Tozzer and R. E. Merwin, in the Maya Lowlands, and Edgar Lee Hewett and Sylvanus G. Morley, at Quirigua, wrote descriptive treatments of their investigations in reports that "were virtually modern in the accuracy of recording and completeness of presentation" (Willey and Sabloff 1980: 62). They also attempted to derive a chronological system for their sites, based upon the excavations of buildings in relation to hieroglyphic inscriptions and Maya calendrical dates (Tozzer 1911, 1913; Hewett, 1912, 1916; Morley 1913; Merwin and Vaillant 1932). The interest in this field of study was dominated by Europeans like Abbé Brasseur de Bourbourg, Ernest W. Forstemann, and Edward Seler, but Americans such as Cyrus Thomas, D. G. Brinton, Joseph T. Goodman, and Charles P. Bowditch also made contributions.

The work of Forstemann on the Dresden Codex led him to decipher

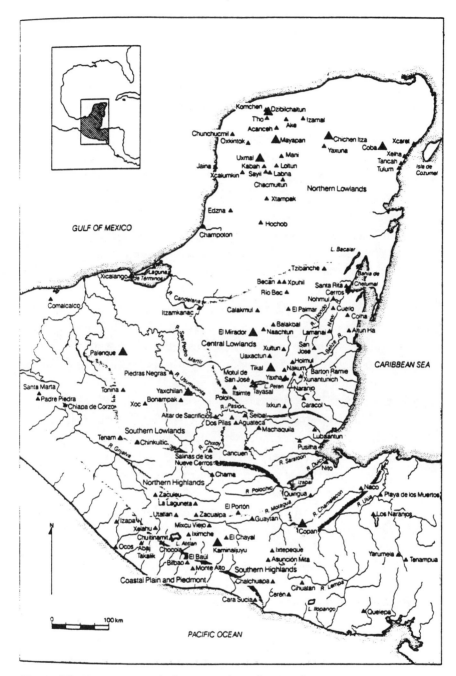

Map 3. The Maya area, principal sites. (Morley and Brainerd 1983)

81

much of the numerical and calendrical data in it. With his work it became possible for archaeologists to date inscribed monuments at their sites. Brasseur de Bourbourg worked on Landa's *Relación de las Cosas de Yucatán* and various Mayan documents from Yucatan and the Guatemalan highlands (Brinton 1882, 1885).

Contributing to the intellectual climate of this period was William H. Prescott's authoritative work on the conquest of Mexico by the Spanish (Prescott 1843), which gave investigators a glimpse into the more recent past in Mexico.

In 1914, at the end of this period in Mayan archaeology, Thomas A. Joyce, an English archaeologist, wrote a very general synthesis of what was known about Middle American archaeology, in *Mexican Archaeology* (Joyce 1914). He attempted to create a chronology for the area based upon dates on Mayan stelae in relation to native legends and traditions. One year earlier, Herbert J. Spinden, in *A Study of Maya Art,* had attempted to order Maya art "with the evolutionary development of stylistic traits as the framework for [his] chronological synthesis" (Willey and Sabloff 1980:66). By the close of 1914, a new era in Middle American archaeological method and theory was on the horizon.

Middle American archaeologists did not develop a stratigraphic method for obtaining cultural chronologies until Manuel Gamio, sometime after 1909, discovered a superposition of cultures at Atzapotzalco. It was with this discovery that the period of purposeful excavation in Middle America began. In 1911 Gamio returned to Mexico from Columbia University, to work with Franz Boas (Adams 1960:99). His efforts were encouraged by Boas and Alfred Tozzer, who were affiliated with the short-lived International School, in Mexico.

Boas had accumulated a vast surface collection of pottery from sites in the Valley of Mexico, which he had divided into three typological groups: Tipo del Cerro, Teotihuacán, and Aztec (Adams 1960:99). He wanted to confirm this sequence and recommended that Gamio undertake a stratigraphic excavation at Atzapotzalco to this end. Gamio dug there in 25 cm. levels; at the conclusion of his excavation he was able to confirm Boas's ceramic typology (Boas 1913:176–79).

Like the work of Nels C. Nelson (at San Cristobal Pueblo, Galisteo Basin) in the American Southwest, Gamio's observations at Atzapotzalco and his pioneering stratigraphic work at Teotihuacán opened a new chapter in the development of field methods in Middle American archaeology (Gamio 1913:150–57). To answer questions about cultural development in Middle America, it became necessary to perfect methods of stratigraphic excavation and to pay special attention to the deposition of artifacts. Gamio must have recognized the need to excavate a long-occupied site, where sequent remains would yield data about cultural development; he conceived such an investigation, at Teotihuacán, in 1917. He worked there with the distinguished Mexican archaeologists Marquina and Noguera and sponsored the stabilization and preservation of many architectural monuments by Regadas Vertiz.

Gamio's policy of site preservation was continued by Alfonso Caso, at Monte Albán; Acosta, at Tula; Morley and Erosa, at Chichén Itzá; Ruiz at Palenque; and by Gustav Strömsvik, at Copán. Kidder credits Gamio with putting "Mexican archaeology solidly on its feet" (1959a:3). The question remains, however, of whether Kidder was significantly influenced by Gamio. In terms of stratigraphic excavation, Nels Nelson was undoubtedly the most influential. In 1957, during an informal interview, Gordon Willey asked Kidder if he had been influenced by Gamio, to which Kidder replied:

> No, I don't think so. He was influenced by Boas. That broad scale attack that he worked {out} at Teotihuacán—I first heard of it when I was down there with him in twenty-two (1922) with {Clarence} Hay. I knew him first in 1922 {sic} and then his big book {on his Teotihuacán studies} came out. . . . I read it with a great deal of interest. Gamio was really a very remarkable fellow in a great many ways. He was about the worst archaeologist I have ever known, but, he had very broad and very intelligent interest in the people of Mexico.

Why Kidder should remark that Gamio was one of the worst archaeologists he had ever known is a mystery; there is nothing in his unpublished papers to explain the remark. In any case Kidder's first encounter with stratigraphy was with Nels C. Nelson's San Cristobal investigations, not with Manuel Gamio. And Gamio certainly did not travel to Pecos, New Mexico, to view Kidder's work there.

A. V. Kidder's association with the Division of Historical Research—

Carnegie Institution of Washington was an extension of his remarkable work at Pecos Pueblo. He brought to the division his expertise in administration and his precise methods for attacking problems in the field. Kidder had thought about changing his geographic interest from Pecos and the American Southwest to the Carnegie Institution and Middle America shortly before 1929. He had "very definite plans for Pecos of the same sort that [he] afterward [planned] for Central America, Guatemala and Mexico" (AVK II:43).

The Carnegie Institution was beginning to expand its archaeological researches when Kidder became one of its high-level administrators, in 1929. The institution had carried on archaeological work from its founding, in 1902, including a search by W. H. Holmes for ancient evidence of humans in America and excavations at Anau, in Turkestan, by Raphael Pumpelly (Woodbury 1973:52). From 1914 onward it had supported a program of Maya research by Sylvanus Morley, who held the status of "associate." His direction of the Carnegie's Chichén Itzá project, before Kidder's arrival, is notable for Morley's ability to establish a foothold in the Yucatan at the time of the Mexican Revolution.

After the 1907 surveying of the McElmo area, the friendly working relationship between Morley and Kidder was in abeyance for eighteen years. Morley's desire to work with the Maya was overpowering, and he directed his energies toward that end. Between 1907 and 1914 Morley worked for Edgar Lee Hewett, in Santa Fe, New Mexico. He saw no future in his job with Hewett, but rather harbored an ambitious plan to excavate Chichén Itzá, a site that had not been investigated with any level of intensity since the work of Alfred Tozzer, in 1903 (Phillips 1955:73). Morley knew that Hewett's School of American Archaeology and its modest budget could not afford such a grand plan, but in 1912 he heard from William Barclay Parsons (a member of the Carnegie's executive committee) that the institution was going to expand its activities in anthropology. Included in the expansion was a new Department of Central American Archaeology.[1]

Morley quickly wrote his friend F. W. Hodge, of the Smithsonian Institution, about qualifications and his specific plans to excavate Chichén Itzá. Hodge, by all accounts, was sympathetic, and Morley hoped that he would communicate his proposal to the Carnegie Institution as a project to be undertaken by the new department. Robert S. Woodward, then president of the Carnegie, however, reacted with silence to a new archaeology department. He did remark to his colleagues that archaeology existed to aid museums in the acquisition of collections; since the Carnegie had no museums, archaeology was therefore not part of its mission (Brunhouse 1971:67).

F. W. Hodge and W. H. Holmes were two of Morley's most ardent supporters for the new Carnegie position (Morley to Hewett, 15 February, no year, ELH). Letters and telegrams passed between them about Morley's prospects for directing the Carnegie's archaeological efforts in Middle America. But the progress of the Carnegie's executive committee in narrowing down their field of candidates was slow, and this increased Morley's frustration during the course of the selection process.

His sense of frustration turned to anger when he received a letter from Hodge, on 12 January 1914, indicating that Alfred Tozzer was being pushed for the same position by Charles Bowditch, F. W. Putnam, and Clark Wissler. But Hodge wrote that"[he] thinks it is a 100 to 1 shot that he will win. [Hodge] believes outcome may be that T [Tozzer] will get the direction with me as second in command. This arrangement would be more satisfactory than any other provided I cannot get the directorship myself" (Morley 1914a:12, Morley to Hewett, 1 November, no year, ELH). Morley also commented in his diary: "That gets me. I wired back that his activity in the ceñote work would certainly disqualify him if it were known. The thing is now in the lap of the gods. All I can do is wait."

Morley waited very impatiently for 15 January 1914, the day of the Carnegie's decision on who would head their new department of archaeology. As Morley wrote,

> This is the day, though I can hardly hear before tomorrow. I am good for nothing today. My anxiety is such, when I try to concentrate my heart jumps into my mouth. A thousand times I look at my watch. If it reads 12, I think it reads twelve in Washington. And so it has been all day. I have done my best and now the only thing to do is wait. (Morley 1914a:14–15)

The morning of 16 January 1914 brought him excellent news:
> They gave it to me. Early this morning the following telegram came from H {Hodge}. 'Decision of Committee in your favor. Will proba-

*bly be called east soon.' It has seemed all day as though my horizon
was not big enough to hold me. This means that my sole ambition
for me {these} last {few} years is about to be realized. Rarely, I
think are aims so clearly defined in life as mine have been. Ever since
visiting Chichén Itzá 7 years ago this year, it has been my fondest
wish to someday excavate that city. (Morley 1914a:16)*

On this same day Morley received a telegram from Edgar Lee Hewett,
saying, "You win in Committee" (Morley 1914a:16, cf. Holmes to Hewett, Telegram, 15 January 1914, ELH).

On 17 January 1914 Hewett contacted Morley and congratulated him
on his new position with the Carnegie Institution. He told Morley that
the blame for the foot-dragging should be placed on the "Tozzer/Boas
combination," while at the same time "omitting all reference to his own
contra-activities" (Morley 1914a:17). Hewett's objective was evidently to
"poison [Morley's] mind against Tozzer" (Morley 1914a:17).

During the years that Morley was dreaming of excavating Chichén
Itzá, he quietly but persistently pressed the project upon President Woodward. His activities were not quiet enough, though, as Edgar Hewett got
wind of his covert project and demanded to know who Morley was
working for, him or the Carnegie. As Morley wrote in his diary:

*Hewett threw me into an uneasy mood, by telling me he was going to
send a night letter to Holmes asking him if Thursday's action was
definite enough to warrant my resignation and Earl Morris' appointment. I pointed out to him that our news was unofficial and as
such I also judge confidential. (1914a:18)*

Morley succeeded in persuading Hewett to postpone his contact with
Holmes until the following day. Underlying this maneuvering was the
mistaken assumption, given by Hewett to the Carnegie's executive committee, that Morley was a tool of Franz Boas and therefore could not be
trusted (Morley 1914a:19). Morley was unaware, after this confronta-
tion, that Hewett was working in the background, urging the Carnegie
to reject Morley's plan. Hewett quite possibly felt upstaged, and this led
him to attack Morley's plan. At any rate Hewett's efforts did not deter
Morley's plans, and he continued to remain quiet (Brunhouse 1971:67).

On 28 July 1914 Morley tendered his resignation to Hewett and the school, "because [his new position] promises to very largely increase the sphere of my usefulness to American archaeology" (Morley to Hewett, 1 July 1914b, ELH).

In a letter to Kidder, J. Eric Thompson referred to Hewett's egotistical personality, through a limerick written by his friend Beatrice Blackwood:

> There was an old duffer named Hewett
> Who was head of the School, and we knew it.
> When anyone came
> Who knew naught of his fame,
> He took out his trumpet and blew it.
> (Thompson to Kidder, 29 April 1961, AVK).

Morley's application was eventually accepted by President Woodward, and he began his work with the Carnegie in 1914. The Carnegie's Chichén Itzá project gained quick approval by Mexican authorities, for one major reason: Since the Carnegie had no museums to house collections and Mexico had enacted a tough antiquities' law barring trafficking in stolen artifacts, the Mexican government trusted that no artifacts would be permanently removed from the Yucatán peninsula. Morley was an excellent choice to take direction of the program in Middle America. He had several years of fieldwork experience behind him and had been exposed, like Kidder, to the work of George Reisner while he was a student at Harvard (Kidder 1959b:778).

Kidder's interest in the Maya can be traced back to his educational career at Harvard University and to Professor Alfred M. Tozzer. His first visit to Mexico was in 1922, with a Harvard classmate, Clarence L. Hay. In 1925 Kidder became a formal advisor to the work of his long-time friend and associate Sylvanus Morley, who had by then been directing the excavations at Chichén Itzá for eleven years. In February 1925, as consultant and member of an advisory committee, Kidder met with the new president of the Carnegie Institution, J. C. Merriam (an eminent palaeontologist), and Clark Wissler, of the American Museum of Natural History. That meeting signaled the beginning of Kidder's twenty-five year association with the Carnegie. His first appointment was in 1926, when he became a research associate; from 1928 to 1929 he was an associate of the institution, in charge of archaeological investigations.

Evidently Kidder did not know of the intense competition for funding within the Carnegie Institution prior to his chairmanship of the Division of Historical Research. But the first published accounts of the institution's budget for anthropological fieldwork show that, in 1913, ethnology and archaeology were engaged in a heated struggle for available monies.

The archaeological program with which Kidder became associated was a long-term, significant one, with its beginning charted in a remarkable volume published by the institution in 1913, "Reports upon the Present Condition and Future Needs of the Science of Anthropology," by W. H. R. Rivers, A. E. Jenks, and S. G. Morley. Rivers's chapter, "Report on Anthropological Research Outside America," stressed the urgency of ethnographic research among fast-disappearing native peoples, and supported Oceania as the area that would best combine important theoretical problems with a significant relationship to the origins of American indigenous culture. Jenks's proposal, "Report on the science of Anthropology in the Western Hemisphere and the Pacific Islands," suggested a world clearinghouse for anthropology, in the form of a research laboratory devoted to studies in ethnic heredity, environment, and amalgamation. The final chapter, by Morley, "Archaeological Research at the Ruins of Chichén Itzá, Yucatán," was just as ambitious, but far more specific in its proposals. Following a documentary and archaeological review of the history of the Maya Indians and their civilization, he outlined the need for a twenty-five-year excavation program at a major site, presenting detailed information on Chichén Itzá to justify its selection for this purpose. He included details of labor resources, climatic problems, health, and restoration of architectural remains, together with many handsome illustrations, and a selected bibliography. All this was in marked contrast to the broad-brush approach of Rivers and Jenks (Woodbury 1973:53).

Morley's plan for fieldwork at Chichén Itzá was selected by the Carnegie Institution over the proposals of Rivers and Jenks, and Morley was appointed research associate in Middle American Archaeology, "one of about fifty scholars in various fields with such appointments by the Institution" (Woodbury 1973:54).

President J. C. Merriam provided some guidance to Morley about how the Carnegie should begin its investigations at Chichén Itzá. He told Morley that the institution would have to decide whether to approach the archaeology of the site in a big way or as a small project, to be "done in a specially fine way" (Morley 1923a:62). He also told him that he would have to approach the proper Mexican federal authorities in Mexico City and find out what they would do for the institute to further the project. Once the Mexican government had agreed in principle to the Carnegie's investigations, Merriam and Morley would present a definite proposal concerning "a large archaeological project covering a long term of years at the ruins of Chichén Itzá" (Morley 1923a:63).

THE SELECTION OF A. V. KIDDER TO ADMINISTER
THE DIVISION OF HISTORICAL RESEARCH

The intellectual climate of Middle American archaeology when Kidder became associated with the Carnegie Institution of Washington was no longer at the purely exploratory, descriptive stage. There had already been some chronological ordering of data in the Maya lowlands prior to 1914, made possible by the translation of Mayan inscriptions and the correlation of calendrical dates with those of the Western calendar (Willey and Sabloff 1980:113). The result was a "floating chronology" of almost six hundred years in length, dating back almost to the first millennium A.D. However, this was applicable only to the Maya lowlands, where usable inscriptions were to be found.

Herbert Spinden (1928) and George Vaillant had begun their own syntheses of Middle American archaeology just before Kidder moved to his new position. Vaillant had begun his detailed synthesis of the area in 1927, in an unpublished Ph.D. dissertation (Vaillant 1927).

Nevertheless there was no well-defined body of archaeological method or theory until Kidder arrived at the Carnegie. He proposed a well-coordinated, pan-scientific attack upon the life of the Maya.

The Carnegie's archaeological program in Mesoamerica continued to grow during the years from 1926 to 1929, until it was decided to form a larger administrative body to coordinate its efforts there. The institution's board of trustees designated the new administrative body the Division of Historical Research. A. V. Kidder's selection, in 1929, as chairman of the new division was the result of two separate circumstances. The first was Kidder's realization that the 1929 field season would be the final one at Pecos; much in the way of analysis and publishing still remained, but he knew the time was right for a change.

The second circumstance was the perception by the board of trustees that a new direction must be taken in its Maya program, one of better coordination of field efforts (AVK II:2). However Kidder says in his unpublished memoirs (AVK II:5) that he was hired also as the result of an unfortunate violation of the Mexican Antiquities Law, a case involving Thomas Gann and Sylvanus Morley.

Morley was a great admirer and a great friend of Gann. Morley had him appointed by Merriam as the physician without salary to the Carnegie Institution project at Chichén. I was then a member of an advisory committee {on archaeology, in 1925} which consisted of Wissler and myself. Merriam {then president of the institution} assured Gamio that anybody who violated the Mexican Antiquities Law ipso facto *was no longer a member of the Carnegie Institution. He got a letter one day from Gamio in which Manuelo said 'Your Dr. Gann has exported illegally from Mexico the famous Teotihuacán jade.' Merriam wired or telephoned to me to go to Washington. I had been to Yucatán with him as a member of the advisory board. We knew each other very well. I was at Andover at this time. When I got to Washington Merriam told me about this thing. I knew that Gann had that damn jade. I hoped that he would be able to get away with it. How Gamio found out about it I don't know. I knew he had it because he had shown it to me up in the Southwest. Morley brought him up there one time when he was still a member of the Carnegie Institution's staff. I think he did have a salary or honorarium or something. Merriam said, 'I can't have Morley running this organization anymore. He gets a man like Gann into our staff and, after what I got our Trustees to put into the record, I want you to take charge of our archaeological work.' (AVK II:6)*

In many of his yet unpublished records, Kidder mentions the importance of cultural resource management and programs to combat the theft of antiquities (AVK III:1–200). It is unlikely that Kidder personally condoned Gann's behavior, but rather was protecting his friendship with Morley when he let the matter drop. Kidder's unpublished diaries and papers, however, do not mention speaking with Morley on this subject.

Morley's diary entries for 29–30 August 1923 contain the following description of the affair:

> *After dinner and when we had come back to the hotel and were resting and chatting, Gann got up in a sort of self-conscious way— he had no coat on and said 'do you notice anything about my back?'*
>
> *At first I did not but a closer examination revealed a flattish pad on the small of his back.*
>
> *He said 'do you remember that jade plaque that Weston had?' I let him go no further. 'Gann you Devil, did you buy it?' 'Yes', he replied, 'even before we went to Yucatan.'*
>
> *He carefully undid it from a cotton swathing inside of a Turkish towel which looked for all the world like a bustle, and there it was.*
>
> *It was beyond doubt the most magnificent piece of Maya jade I have ever seen both in coloring and execution.*
>
> *He had bought it from Weston for $250.00 gold. It is the first piece of jade I have ever seen, and there is nothing in the Cenote jades to touch it. (Morley 1923b:443–44)*

Leopold Batres had excavated the jade from the Temple of the Sun, at San Juan Teotihuacán, many years before it came into the possession of Gann. Batres had given the jade to a Señor Limantour, minister of finance in the Porfirio Diaz cabinet. Limantour later left Mexico and sold it to Weston, who then sold it to Gann (Morley 1923b:445). In June 1923 Morley requested instructions from Merriam on presenting the jade to the Mexican government as a gift, a matter of face-saving for all concerned (Morley 1923b:144).

Kidder had known J. C. Merriam since 1925, when he became a member of the Carnegie's advisory committee on the excavations at Chichén Itzá. It is quite possible that his appointment was due to their shared enthusiasm for a multidisciplinary approach as a way of attacking Maya research at the site. In 1923 Merriam had wanted Morley to approach the work there through studies in geology and geography, climatology and meteorology, botany and zoology, physical anthropology and linguistics (Morley 1923a:64). It is also quite possible that Morley had recommended Kidder to Merriam as a consultant and advisory committee member, although Kidder did not mention any influence on the part of Morley. The two other members of the advisory committee were Clark Wissler, of the American Museum, and James H. Breasted, of the Oriental Institute.

When the Carnegie decided to expand its Maya program, Merriam realized that he needed a competent administrator to keep it in line. This led to his request, in 1928, that Kidder make a study of the program and visit all the localities where the institution was working. Although Kidder's unpublished papers do not mention giving his Pecos *vita* to Merriam, there can be little doubt that Merriam had known of his remarkable administrative qualities when he was asked to serve in an advisory capacity in 1925. At the conclusion of his study, Kidder reported to Merriam the organizational changes needed to keep the Chichén Itzá project on track. The immediate effect of Kidder's study and administrative abilities is seen in Merriam's report to the Carnegie's board of trustees in the closing days of 1928:

In early American History Dr. Alfred V. Kidder has made wide studies of the work of the Institution and related investigations in the past year, and has visited all of the localities at which researches of the Institution are under way. This re-examination of the program has made possible a better vision of our problem. With the plans now formulated, the investigations in each of the several projects, while conducted with increased emphasis upon detail, have a clearer relation to the larger scheme of studies in this field in America.

As compared with earlier years, the past season's activities in Middle American Archaeology have brought relatively large results in terms of scientific achievement. Improved organization of excavation work at Chichén Itzá in Yucatan has given all of the investigators a somewhat larger percentage time for the study of results already attained, as also for consideration of the scientific significances of investigations under way. (Merriam 1928:4)

Neither Merriam's published works nor Kidder's unpublished papers mention whether Morley had suggested Kidder's appointment to head the new division. Morley was so interested in hieroglyphs and his overall plan for Chichén Itzá, that it might be assumed he would devote little time to the institution's administrative needs there.

Before Kidder officially accepted the Carnegie offer, he secured permission to continue working on his Pecos reports during his tenure as chairman of the division of historical research. Then, in 1929, he assumed control of one of the most ambitious programs in Mesoamerican archaeology. His direction of the division's work in the Maya area was patterned after what he envisioned to be a "collection of all pertinent sciences," with their mutual input into the facilitation of archaeological analysis and interpretation. He believed the only way archaeologists could get to the basics of their work, in terms of cultural development and the "development of the human race," was by making use of all the sciences—social, natural, and environmental (AVK II:72–74). Kidder communicated this opinion to J. C. Merriam:

> *In connection with the program of continuing study on problems of Middle American civilization, it is our hope to carry forward a plan involving not merely architecture and art, but comprising as well a careful examination of the development of this civilization in relation to its environment. To this end it is important that studies be made ranging from the general geology, ethnobotany, and ethnozoology of the region up to and including the story of those specific difficulties which have beset the human group as expressed in what may be called its medical history. Through this consideration of the record of human development we may expect to relate the history of the Maya people to problems of the present day, in such manner that the historical evidence will contribute directly toward interpretation of questions of the present and future. (1928:753)*

Kidder (AVK I, AVK II) credited J. C. Merriam with many of the successes of the division. He noted that Merriam had an excellent grasp of the implications of anthropological science (AVK III).

The Carnegie Institution's support of the Maya program is well documented in archaeological literature. The success of their program consisted of two separate aspects: the organization and direction of the division's work by Kidder, and Kidder's numerous papers within the program, on archaeological methods and future goals. Examples of his publications on this point include "An Archaeological Research and Its Ramifications: A View Point of An Archaeologist" (1930b) and his report to the Carnegie Institution in 1946, "Memorandum Regarding Future Archaeological Activities" (1946b).

The final report of Sylvanus Morley as director of the Chichén Itzá project, before Kidder took over his new duties, can be viewed as an ambitious status report on Middle American archaeological research. His plan emphasized linguistic, architectural, ceramic, hieroglyphic, and historic studies, with archaeological excavation being the central focus of his work (Woodbury 1973:57). Kidder's program, in turn, was a broader attack upon the problems of Maya archaeology than Morley had originally conceived. In addition to the foundations that Morley laid, Kidder would add nutritional, medical, sociological, and aerial site-survey studies to the program.

Kidder's redirection of the division's efforts in Mesoamerica began in a broadening of the program to include all pertinent sciences in studying the cultural development of the Maya (cf. Kidder 1936:218–19). He had, however, already begun the task of formulating the needed changes in the division's archaeological work, in 1928. His thinking appeared in summary form in a short paper published in 1928 in the *Bulletin of the International Committee of Historical Sciences* (1928). In this paper Kidder proposed a research program involving four emphases. First, studies of the sequence of prehistoric cultural development in the Valley of Mexico, from the earliest appearance of horticulturalists to advances in cultural complexity early in the Christian era. Second, an archaeological survey of the Guatemalan highlands, in order to increase knowledge of the ancient Maya and their living descendants. Third, selection of an ancient Mayan site for thorough excavation, in order to trace its growth and to create new techniques for locating sites too remote for complete clearance. Fourth, a comprehensive study of the Yucatan Peninsula, in cooperation with workers from other disciplines (Kidder 1928:749–53). He also noted that the tasks of archaeology and allied sciences are three-fold: to supply historical perspective; to interpret results in terms of "basic laws of human evolution; to utilize methods developed and knowledge gained from laws for attack upon similar problems elsewhere" (Kidder 1928: 750).

It is interesting to note that Kidder gave thought to "basic laws of human evolution." He did not take a Darwinian approach to the definition of such laws in his 1928 paper (1928:749–53). In 1938 Kidder saw them in the context of human culture, which is "extra-organic and unrestrainted by the slow-working laws of biological evolution" (Kidder 1938: 494). "Man . . . is born intellectually naked. Nothing is transmitted to him from former generations beyond his physical makeup, a receptive but empty mind, and the urge to exercise such purely organic functions as feeding and reproducing himself" (Kidder 1938:494).

In Kidder's mind the laws governing the growth of culture depend on the control mechanisms that regulate its development through time. In order to ferret these laws and mechanisms, we must know of the history of cultural growth and the relationship between humans and their culture, by asking the following questions:

> Given proper opportunity, will all men take certain cultural steps? Are some {populations} more capable than others of building culture? Are others unable to cope with it? Is culture subject to laws of development comparable to those which we know control the material world? (Kidder 1940:532)
>
> • • •
>
> {D}oes culture, although not biologically transmitted, develop and function in response to tendencies—it is perhaps too connotative of inevitability to call them laws—that are comparable to those controlling biological evolution? (Kidder 1946b:54).

For Kidder there seemed to be some evidence of just such tendencies. In 1946 Kidder formulated his own definition of culture with respect to the "basic laws," as he understood them. His idea of culture is reminiscent of those of both E. B. Tylor and Ralph Linton:

> One of these super-questions, in many ways the most fundamental that faces all students of man, concerns the evolution of culture, that complex of knowledges and custom and beliefs which distinguishes man from all other mammals. Culture is not inborn, it is passed

*from generation to generation by the teaching-learning process; it has
no physical existence, because it is carried solely in men's minds, yet
it exercises the most potent of all influences in shaping the actions
and through them the destinies of every individual and of all peoples
(Kidder 1946b:56).*

THE PAN-SCIENTIFIC APPROACH

Kidder's plans for a pan-scientific approach to the resolution of archaeological problems were presented to Carnegie archaeologists in 1930, when he called them to gather at Chichén Itzá, Yucatan, in January of that year. The Conference at Chichén Itzá was called two months after his appointment to the new division. The purpose of the gathering was to provide a forum for new ideas about the problems of on-site fieldwork and the archaeological analysis of recovered remains.

*The purpose of the gathering was to discuss, without agenda and
in a purely preliminary way, the desirability of bringing to bear
upon the historical problems of the area the resources of various disciplines and to consider methods for the prosecution of cooperative research. (Kidder 1930c:391)*

The Carnegie archaeologists accepted Kidder's premise that historical evaluation of the archaeological knowledge derived from the excavations of Sylvanus Morley and his staff could be made more precise by an accurate knowledge of environmental conditions, supplied by specialists in biology, geology, meteorology, etc. Data on the social condition of the Maya, past and present, would be collected by workers in documentary history, medicine, comparative linguistics, and the several social sciences (Kidder 1930c:391).

Kidder pointed out during the conference that the knowledge gained from such a multidisciplinary approach would benefit not only the individual disciplines, but would also gain cumulative importance, because "geographical concentration would permit pooling of data, interchange of ideas, as well as formulation of combined attack upon problems of common interest" (Kidder 1930c:391).

Kidder felt that all scientists interested in the resolution of archaeological problems in addition to accumulating knowledge in their own fields should be in continuous communication with other investigators working on similar problems. The Chichén Itzá Conference concluded *that all studies should be independent, intensive and highly specialized, and that limited and definite goals within each science should be aimed for. A historical view-point, in the broadest sense, should, however, be adhered to; and close but informal touch should be maintained among all workers in order that they should keep cognizance of the methods, the general trends and the bearing upon their own fields of each other's activities (Kidder 1930c:391).*

The conference, like the initial Pecos Conference of 1927, sought to bring together investigators from diverse fields; nevertheless, Kidder later admitted that the scope of the work recommended by the conference was too great. The Carnegie Institution did not have the funding or the manpower to undertake all that needed to be done; Kidder's program would require many more resources than would ever be available to him. Even so the conference set the stage for new directions in Middle American archaeology, just as the Pecos Conference had for Southwest archaeology.

The first formal indication of Kidder's desire to combine history and archaeology in the Carnegie's program for Middle American research can be found in his first annual report on the division. The division was composed of three sections: Early American History (that is, the archaeology of Middle America and the Southwest), Modern American History (continuing the conventional research already being supported by the Carnegie Institution), and the History of Science (Kidder 1930a:391, Woodbury 1973:58). The role Kidder envisioned for the section of Early American History was the following:

In designating the group engaged in studies of the pre-Columbian career of the American Indians, the term history has been used as symbolic of a desire to do away with the somewhat rigid distinction which has generally been drawn between archaeology and history. The work of the Section is, of course, archaeological in that it deals with material remains rather than with written records. But archaeologists seek to gather from ruined buildings and potsherds the

*same sort of knowledge that historians derive from books and manu-
scripts, and while the subject matter and therefore, the primary
methods of the two disciplines are naturally unlike, their ultimate
aims are identical, for both archaeology and history strive to recover
and to interpret the story of man's past. Archaeology, however, has
all too generally been prosecuted as if the excavation of specimens
were an end in itself. Antiquities have, as a rule, been collected
more for their beauty than for what they might tell of the doings and
the thoughts of human beings who made them. Emphasis in archaeology is gradually shifting, however, from things to what things
mean; and archaeological finds are fortunately coming more and
more to be considered as historical documents (Kidder 1930a:391).*

Kidder noted that Mayan research could be likened to historical
research, if certain definite and logical methods were employed. In his
plan the first step was to make a record of the sequent events that
characterized the career of the people under investigation. The second
step of Kidder's plan was to seek causes and explain the interrelations of
those events. His plan called finally for studying the previous two classes
of information for use in formulating "those fundamental laws which
have governed the past and which therefore may reasonably be expected
to shape, in the future, the course of human affairs" (Kidder 1937:218).

The fundamental laws Kidder referred to are the human behavioral
patterns that make cultures successful and adaptable to a changing physical and social environment, often over many centuries. Kidder's use of the
word *law* suggests scientific statements used to classify or characterize a
range of behaviors, in order to create an organized system of general and
universal propositions to explain the course of Mayan cultural development.

Kidder wanted to provide a clear and well-documented account of the
Maya, broad in scope as well as analytically deep. His concern was with the
overall relation of human groups to their habitats, the spread and interac-
tion of cultures, the origin of higher civilization, the decay of social orders, the relationships between native and European peoples, "the adjust-
ments between conquerors and conquered, and the impact of twentieth-
century ideas upon aboriginal populations" (Kidder 1937: 220).

One of the more important contributions to the division's Maya project was Kidder's implementation of an "environmental factors" program, to take into account the constraints within which a prehistoric culture had developed. His program included the efforts of ecologists, medical professionals, and experts in the study of agricultural technology, analyzing the lives of contemporary and prehistoric Maya. This plan came well before such a focus was generally accepted in Americanist archaeology.

Although this pan-scientific approach never reached total fruition, Kidder did succeed in collecting a wide range of data about the Maya, regarding their habitat, agricultural base, technology, and living descendants.

But in spite of all uncertainties, one may feel confidence in the soundness of this type of approach. For the activities of the physical anthropologist {and other scientists} have not only helped the archaeologist but have already resulted in the formulation of a host of special problems of modern life, which are themselves insoluble save on the evidence of what has gone before. Thus the present and the past have been firmly interlinked; and the realization has been driven home that neither one can be understood save in the light of the other. (Kidder 1937:222)

Kidder, as well as his colleagues, recognized the value of this pioneering approach to archaeological field research. "It was Kidder's retrospective opinion, in the late 1950's, that this conception of an over-all approach to Maya culture history and the natural environmental settings of this history was his most significant contribution to anthropology" (Willey 1967:303).

During his tenure with the Carnegie, Kidder complained of the general failure to study and classify material properly and to publish the results. He traced this shortcoming to a difficulty in raising publication funds, to a lack of time available to the average archaeologist, and to the lackadaisical attitude of many institutions toward the "issuance of reports as an essential and immediate sequel to field work" (Wauchope 1965: 159). Kidder advocated shorter digging seasons, fewer workmen, and annual publications, or at least the preparation of completely up-to-date finished manuscripts before the start of a new field season (Wauchope 1965:159).

There is no doubt that Americanist archaeology greatly benefited from Kidder's broad theoretical vision and his field administrative abilities. Mayan archaeology was enriched and changed forever.

THE BEGINNINGS OF AERIAL ARCHAEOLOGY IN MIDDLE AMERICA

Kidder early saw the potential use of the airplane for locating Mayan sites in Yucatan, and explored various possibilities during several aerial surveys he made with Charles Lindbergh, beginning in 1929. Among Kidder's personal papers is his correspondence with Lindbergh during 1929 and 1930 (1929d; 1930d,e), in which are discussed various topics related to the use of the airplane in Middle American archaeology (see appendix 3 for reproductions of selected correspondence between Lindbergh and Kidder). Kidder concluded, however, that the airplane was not of great advantage for locating archaeological sites in the jungles of the Yucatan and Guatemala (AVK 1929a), although it was useful for ecological studies and for transportation.[2]

The relationship between Charles Lindbergh and A. V. Kidder was based on their mutual interest in archaeology. When their association began, Lindbergh had been associated with the Daniel Guggenheim Fund for the Promotion of Aeronautics, and was eager to promote the utility of the airplane; Kidder was interested in finding a more effective way to complete an archaeological survey of the Maya area. Lindbergh and Kidder first flew together over Yucatan and Guatemala, in October 1929. It was the first time Kidder had flown. He was so excited about the flight that he had Lindbergh radio a telegram to his wife, Madeleine: "Just wound up in five days flying eight years worth of mule back Stop Miami tonite Washington Saturday home Sunday Federal Stop Love this from air over Cozumel Channel Ted" (Kidder to Madeleine Kidder 10 October 1929, AVK). At Kidder's request Lindbergh also made a short aerial survey of Guatemala, with camera film provided by the Carnegie Institution (Lindbergh to Kidder 18 December 1929; Lindbergh to Kidder n.d., from the Hotel Pancoast, Miami, Florida).

Lindbergh's willingness to lend his aeronautical expertise in the furtherance of the Carnegie's work had greatly impressed Kidder. About the middle of 1930 Kidder received a letter from Lindbergh that a member of his wife's family, Dwight Morrow, Jr., wished to visit with Earl Morris in the American Southwest (Lindbergh to Kidder 1930, no day or month noted, AVK). Kidder immediately set up plans for the visit, taking care that the trip be as comfortable as possible. On 25 June 1930 Kidder wrote back to Lindbergh:

> Everything, I think is set for Mr. Morrow, Jr's trip. Mrs. Morris has arranged to have a Ford touring car purchased and broken in. I imagine that it will be in Gallup {New Mexico} to meet the party on July 6th, but if not, Morris will have transportation there anyhow. Recent word from Earl expresses his pleasure at the prospect of having . . . {Dwight Morrow, Jr.} with him and I am sure {he} could not be in the field under better auspices. Morris is one of the finest characters I know. (Kidder to Lindbergh 15 July 1930, AVK)

On 15 July 1930 Lindbergh wrote back to Kidder:

> Thank you very much for your letter of June 15th. I am sorry I have not been able to answer it sooner.
>
> Dwight Morris, Jr., left for the West in time to meet Dr. Morris at Gallup on July 6th. We cannot thank you enough for arranging for him to go on this expedition. (Lindbergh to Kidder 2 December 1930, AVK)

During 1929 and 1930 Lindbergh was a valuable member of Kidder's "unpaid staff." He served as Kidder's advisor on the use of the airplane in archaeology and consented to serve on a division committee regarding its use. During 1930 and 1931 there were more flights to locate archaeological sites over Yucatan and Guatemala. On 1 March 1932, however, an event occurred that shocked the people of the United States and put an end to Lindbergh's association with the Carnegie Institution: the kidnapping of the Lindberghs' infant child. On 21 February 1939 Kidder received a letter from Lindbergh, written in Paris, saying that he could no longer take an active part in the Carnegie's Mayan program:

*There is no need for me to outline to you the conditions which have
caused us to make our home in Europe recently. I can only say that I
hope that they will change in the future although present trends are
not at all encouraging (Lindbergh to Kidder 8 February 1939,
AVK).*

Lindbergh's first flight to photograph archaeological sites had come in
1929, when Lindbergh and his wife, Ann Morrow Lindbergh, flew over
parts of Canyon de Chelly, the Hopi country, Chaco Canyon, and the
Pajarito Plateau. Kidder considered these flights to be highly significant
in terms of data gathered on the area's water supply and arable land. It was
this effort that caused him to urge a similar series of flights over Yucatan
(Woodbury 1973:60).

After Kidder became chairman of the division, he met with Lindbergh once again to consider the value of the airplane in jungle archaeology. In September of 1929 Lindbergh was sent by Pan American Airways
to inaugurate the first regular flight from Miami to a South American
destination, Surinam (Dutch Guiana). The flight would coincide with a
full-scale aerial exploration of the Maya country. Pan American supplied a
twin-engine Sikorsky amphibious plane, and the Carnegie Institution
agreed to sponsor the aerial photography (Deuel 1969:194).

Pan American had a major maintenance installation at Belize, the
capital of British Honduras, which was also chosen as the Carnegie's
archaeological base of operations. From there all Maya centers within a
radius of some four hundred miles were surveyed by air. The Lindberghs
arrived on October 5, after establishing an air route to northern South
America. William I. Van Dusen, a Pan American representative, was
designated as the historian of the expedition. On behalf of the Carnegie
Institution, Kidder sent Oliver H. Ricketson, an expert on the Petén
area. Mrs. Lindbergh acted as official photographer. After an initial flight
over Uaxactún, which Ricketson had worked on some years earlier, he
was heard to say: "It is not good for an archaeologist to fly over this
region, especially if he is going back. The thought of all day on a mule in
contrast to six minutes in an arm chair is unsettling. Besides, the ticks
don't fly" (Deuel 1969:198).

Final arrangements for the inauguration of Middle American aerial archaeology were made in New York, between the Carnegie Institution and Pan American Airways. The parties to the New York meeting were Colonel Lindbergh, James Eaton (traffic manager of Pan American Airways), and a member of the Carnegie's archaeological staff (Kidder 1929a: 1200).

The first flights in the Yucatán made by Kidder and Lindbergh took place in October of 1929, over parts of British Honduras, Yucatan, and the Petén. While the flights did not yield information concerning the location of new Mayan sites, they did give "promise of ecological information hitherto unavailable, such as boundaries of forest types" (Woodbury 1973: 60). Kidder hoped to organize extensive air reconnaissance and air transport and supply for remote camps, and also envisioned the use of the Goodyear blimp as a means of extending time in the air for aerial survey of archaeological sites. The latter idea was impractical, however, due to the expensive logistical preparations needed for the blimp in the Yucatan jungles (Lindbergh to Kidder 2 December 1930). Kidder therefore decided to rely on Lindbergh's willingness to continue his flights in the airplane on loan from Pan-Am.

Kidder quickly recognized the utility of the airplane for making geographical surveys (Kidder 1929a: 1204–1205, 1929b:xii–xiv). Areas could be surveyed in minutes or hours by airplane, rather than in days by mule on jungle trails.

Even more important than the finding of ruins was the demonstration of the extraordinary ease and rapidity with which geographical knowledge of the Maya country can be gathered from the air. The details of topography, the exact relation, for example, between mountain and plain, between forest, swamp, and watercourse, are absolutely vital for true understanding of the distribution and manner of life of an ancient people. But in regions of dense vegetation such phenomena are, from the ground, exceedingly difficult to observe and to record, while from a thousand feet up entire areas lie spread before the eye with the clarity and definiteness of a relief map. There can be made out the distribution of forest types, which, of course, reflects the nature of the underlying soil; there can be seen the gradual change in tree growth which takes place with increased altitudes and increased rainfall. These and many other studies, all necessary for

*adequate comprehension of the environment under which the Maya
lived, can be carried out by plane with a speed and accuracy
positively bewildering to one who has day after day labored on
muleback through the hot, green tunnels of the jungle trails. (Kidder 1929a:1204–1205)*

It would take many decades and some astonishing technological developments before the modern arsenal of remote-sensing techniques could be brought to bear on actual site analysis.

From the beginning of Kidder's tenure with the Carnegie Institution and for twenty years into the future, his administrative abilities at directing long-term archaeological investigations would be severely tested. Problems of funding and personnel would repeatedly take Kidder away from writing his Pecos synthesis. Nevertheless during this time Kidder did produce and publish three monographs on his Pecos work.

Although he made periodic trips to the Southwest during the summers of 1931 and 1932, Kidder continuously maintained his administrative direction of the Carnegie's efforts in Yucatán, Guatemala, and Mexico, a dozen or more simultaneous projects (Woodbury 1973:60). This heavy administrative load, plus the pressures to get out the Pecos publications, made Kidder realize that the day of one-man research had come to an end. Seizing the opportunity in this overwhelming situation, Kidder created a style of teamwork in which he gave other Carnegie archaeologists a free hand in the conduct of everyday fieldwork decisions.

*Dr. A.V. Kidder . . . has made many helpful suggestions, and
more than once has coaxed me off a dangerous limb. From his initiation of staff meetings to discussions of general strategy and specific
problems I, together with every participant, have derived great benefit. One could hardly ask more than a free hand to follow one's own
investigations when it is coupled with the advantages and profitable
obligations of teamwork. (Thompson 1960:ix)*

Such statements indicate how effective Kidder's redirection of the Carnegie's Maya project must have been. No longer were archaeologists left in isolation, but were encouraged to work together to solve mutual field problems. Kidder's initiation of staff meetings allowed investigators to thrash out problems and to receive suggestions from the team as a whole. Staff meetings were useful in providing a general plan of action so that effort was not expended on interesting but unrelated inquiry by individual researchers.

KIDDER'S FIRST DECADE AS CHAIRMAN
OF THE DIVISION OF HISTORICAL RESEARCH

Kidder initiated a greatly expanded, pan-scientific approach, to supplement more conventional archaeological work in Middle America. Initially he wanted to investigate the highland cultures of Yucatan, British Honduras, and Mexico, along with the Pre-Classic Maya of Guatemala.

{this} was my particular interest, and it was a mistake that I ever took it up, from the point of view of the Carnegie, I should have stuck in the Yucatán. It was too big. There weren't funds to do both areas in the way that I wanted to have them done. All sorts of difficulties cropped up. (AVK II:7)

Although Kidder admitted that this grand scheme could not be fully implemented, he pointed the way to the beginning of a synthesis of Maya culture. Prior to Kidder's chairmanship, Sylvanus G. Morley, Oliver Ricketson, Karl Ruppert, and Harry Pollock had already been hard at work in various archaeological sites in Middle America. Pollock, however, was not a formal member of the Carnegie staff, which added an air of uncertainty to his relationship with the division (AVK II:8). Evidently official links with the Carnegie were always in doubt:

That was always a difficult thing to know what was what in the Carnegie Institution. They had no titles nor any tenure. The Chairmen of the various divisions brought that up again and again in meetings that we used to have in Washington. We tried to get some statement out of the Administration about status and salary. (AVK II:8–9)

Soon after Kidder was selected as chairman of the division of historical research, in 1929, he "decided to put Vay [Morley] in complete charge [of the Chichén Itzá Project because] any other administrative arrangement [was] impossible" (Kidder 1930f:25). His diary for that period does not contain any other information about these administrative problems. However, Morley was more interested in deciphering glyphs than in administering the Carnegie's efforts there, and when Kidder assigned him to administer the work at Chichén Itzá, Morley became somewhat discouraged; he wanted to work on glyphs, not be Kidder's representative for a more global attack upon that site. Morley wanted to glorify the Maya in every possible way. He even thought of having his birthdate, in the form of a Mayan glyph (13 Pax) tatooed on his body "real artistically"; "[i]t wasn't the pain [that he dreaded], that would be nothing, it's the idea of a blemish on the skin one would have to live with for life" (Morley 1919). Morley's discouragement was heightened by Kidder's instructions that the work at Chichén Itzá was

> growing into a most complex and interwoven job with the biologists, medical people, sociologists, archaeologists, and, in the future, geologists, climatologists, etc. {Our} idea {is to} pitchfork as many lots of workers as possible into the Peninsula, get them to thrash . . . out their own problems and see what the result will be. (Kidder 1930f:32).

Of Morley's Chichén Itzá assignment, Kidder also wrote, in 1957, that

> Chichén Itzá was a most unhappy place. This is of course off the record. It was a very unhappy job because Morley—his two great interests were A— the Hieroglyphics and B— the glorification of the Maya and at Chichén there weren't any glyphs and there was every opportunity to glorify the Maya by putting their buildings on the map. His lectures and his articles in the Geographic—he did an enormous amount of that—but Chichén was the wrong place for him for there he played up the less worthy of his two interests. . . . The way Morley was running Chichén, it was costing a tremendous lot of money. I almost persuaded Merriam, a couple of times, to pull out of Chichén and, do some of the things that just stuck out to be done in Yucatán. (AVK II:9—10)

Kidder finally realized, after his retirement, that Morley had neither gift nor drive to be an administrator.

One of Kidder's major contributions to the study of the Maya was his selection of Robert Redfield to study a variety of folk cultures within the Maya sphere of influence. Redfield's 1930 book on Tepoztlán, a village near Mexico City, is a classic contribution to ethnography. He and several colleagues undertook studies of modern Yucatec Mayan communities, from the city of Mérida and the town of Chan Kom to the simpler villages of Quintana Roo. Redfield's research was an integral part of the Kidder's multidisciplinary approach to the study of the Maya. The final product of the work at Chan Kom was an ethnography by Redfield and Alfonso Villa Rojas (Redfield and Villa Rojas 1934).

Alfonso Villa Rojas was born and raised in Mérida, where he became a teacher; in 1927 he took charge of the Chan Kom school. When the University of Chicago gave Redfield a leave of absence to undertake the investigation of Chan Kom for the Carnegie Institution, Redfield asked Villa to join the study because of his knowledge of the local Mayan language (Redfield and Rojas 1934:X). In the winter of 1930 Redfield met Villa during a short visit to Chan Kom. He then spent the first few months of 1931 in Yucatán, with half of his time devoted to the study of Chan Kom. During this period and for several months thereafter, Villa also devoted much time to the study of the community, remaining in Chan Kom until December 1931.

The writing of the {Tepoztlán report} was done by {Redfield} . . . {and} Villa . . . made many small changes. . . . The support and sympathy and sound advice Dr. A. V. Kidder, Chairman of the Division of Historical Research of the Carnegie Institution, has carried the authors along through their work (Redfield and Villa Rojas 1934:ix–x).

Kidder's second annual report to the Carnegie Institution, in 1931, reflects other new directions. Besides continuing the program of archaeological and ethnological work, Kidder sought to expand Maya research by taking into account medical survey studies and biological investigations. He asked George C. Shattuck, from the Department of Tropical Medicine of the Harvard School of Public Health, to conduct medical surveys of the Yucatán; Morris Steggerda, of the Carnegie's Department of Genetics, to undertake physical anthropological studies, and Manuel J. Andrade, of the University of Chicago, to do linguistic research among the modern Maya. Subsequently F. W. Gaige, of the University of Michigan, conducted biological studies of the Maya area, and Ralph L. Roys undertook a translation of the Maya books of Chilam Balam (Kidder 1931b:31–65).

In the years after 1931 the Carnegie's Maya research program continued to expand, with the participation of other scholars and institutions. J. H. Kempton and G. W. Collins, of the Bureau of Plant Industry of the U.S. Department of Agriculture, studied the past and present agricultural methods of the Maya and also the problem of the origin of maize, of great importance since maize appeared to be a common thread between the civilizations of Mesoamerica and the Andean area. H. A. Emerson (of Cornell University), Wilson Popenoe (of the United Fruit Company), and Raymond Stadelman also participated in these agricultural studies. The fresh-water fauna of Yucatan was studied by A. S. Pearse, of Duke University (Woodbury 1973:62–63).

Climatological and geological studies were carried out by interested researchers from Harvard University's Blue Hill Observatory and by the U.S. Geological Survey. Ethnological work continued among the Maya, with Sol Tax's study of Indians in the Guatemalan highlands; the resulting monograph, *Penny Capitalism, A Guatemalan Indian Economy* (1953), was dedicated to Kidder, "with affection, respect, and gratitude" (Tax 1953:iv).

During the 1930s Kidder brought to the staff of the Carnegie two individuals who were to be key figures in the development of Maya research: Gustav Strömsvik and Anna O. Shepard, both frequently mentioned in the 1957 unpublished memoirs and the diaries of 1935–36 (AVK II:62). He was interested in Strömsvik's talents at repairing ancient buildings and so sent him to restore Copán, Honduras. Anna O. Shepard was brought in to study Mayan ceramics. Her addition to the Carnegie's staff can be seen as an extension of Kidder's own interest in ceramics, which he carried with him from Pecos.

The funding of the division's work grew from a total budget in 1929 of $80,000 (4.3 percent of the total budget) to a peak of $162,000 (12 percent of the Carnegie's total), in 1936, then gradually slipping below

$100,000 (8 percent), in 1953 (Woodbury 1973:64). This funding was very important to American archaeology in the 1930s; there was no Wenner-Gren Foundation or National Science Foundation to support such research, so that Mayan archaeology relied heavily on private contributions.

The first decade of Kidder's administration can be summed up as a period of increased activity within the scope of the program and of the acquisition of multidisciplinary data to enable better understanding of Maya cultural development. The new research initiatives made by the Carnegie's staff under Kidder's direction would show the value of his interdisciplinary approach, although it would later be argued by Clyde Kluckhohn and Walter W. Taylor that Kidder's program was too broad, with insufficient direction (Kluckhohn 1940, Taylor 1967).

In April 1931 Kidder called upon academics to work together toward the mutual resolution of research problems, in "The Future of Man in the Light of His Past: The View Point of an Archaeologist" (1931c). Originally read before the American Society of Naturalists, in Cleveland, Ohio, the paper suggested two important actions by scientists: teamwork and stocktaking (using a period of reflection to determine the most effective course for research). In the case of the Carnegie's Maya program, Kidder (1931b:239) suggested that this stocktaking should involve writing a culture history of the Maya, "based upon a correlation of all branches of investigation." Ordinarily archaeologists find so much of interest in excavations that they only grudgingly climb out, to be "dazzled and confused by the glare and hurry of the present" (Kidder 1931c:289). Looking forward to a continuing supply of ruins to excavate, they are "supremely indifferent" to advances in field technique or to what they have learned thus far (Kidder 1931c:289):

> *That, of course, is just the trouble with archaeology. When forced to justify his existence the archaeologist solemnly states that one can not understand the present without a comprehension of the past. Granted. But he is peevishly resentful if it be suggested that he can not interpret the past save in the light of the present.*
>
> *. . . And so it is very good for a digger to be brought out of the ground, to be forced to face the meaning of his finds; to take stock and to determine what, if any, bearing his labors may have upon the present and the future of mankind.*

As far as the Maya project was concerned, "We might well expect intelligent collection of data, clearer classification and sounder interpretation. But of even greater importance would be, I believe, the breaking down of the barriers which modern specialization has erected" (Kidder 1931c:292–93). The implementation of this ambitious research plan set a new standard for other Americanist archaeologists to emulate in creating their own field methodology.

From 1932 through 1941 Kidder was busy with the mundane affairs of the division and with his continuing work on various reports on the Pecos excavations (see Kidder, Jennings, and Shook 1946; Kidder and Shook 1952). In addition, however, from 1935 through 1936, Kidder became personally involved with the excavations at the large ceremonial center of Kaminaljuyú, in the suburbs of Guatemala City. This site had been investigated in the 1920s by Manuel Gamio and Samuel Lothrop, from whose findings Kidder and Oliver Ricketson formulated a three-year program of limited scope. Kidder's participation in the excavations continued intermittently until 1952. The work with Ricketson and later with Robert Wauchope, Jesse D. Jennings, and Edwin M. Shook, resulted in his first major book in Mayan archaeology: "Excavations at Kaminaljuyú, Guatemala" (Kidder, Jennings, and Shook 1946a). In the brief introduction to the report, Kidder first used the term *Mesoamerica,* a geographical designation coined by Paul Kirchoff, in 1943.

Kidder chose Kaminaljuyú for excavation because of Manuel Gamio's stratigraphic work there, in 1925. Gamio had made stratigraphic tests at Finca Miraflores, which was one of the several private properties that constituted the site. His work revealed deep cultural deposits and had the important result of bringing to light potsherds and clay figurines recognized by him as analogous to those of the Formative, or Pre-Classic Period of the Valley of Mexico, then called Archaic. Kaminaljuyú was thus shown to have been settled at an early date. At the same time Lothrop (1926) published a study of its numerous stone sculptures, which demonstrated that occupancy had extended into the period during which the Classic, or "Old Empire," civilization of the lowland Maya was at its height (Kidder 1961:561). The finds of Gamio and Lothrop gave Kidder the hope that further investigation at the site would yield data on cultural developments in the then little-known Guatemala highland cultures.

Kidder drew up a program for an orderly two- or three-season excavation of Kaminaljuyú; investigations would actually be carried out intermittently, over an eight-year period. Whether Kidder had decided to extend his pan-scientific approach to Kaminaljuyú is not known for two reasons. First, his program quickly turned into one of the first examples of salvage archaeology in Mesoamerica, because of a building boom in Guatemala City, with increased need for bricks, roofing tiles, and adobe. Building material to fuel the boom "ready mixed and puddled by the ancients was most easily and cheaply to be obtained from the mounds" (Kidder 1961:561). Woodbury (1973:66) also pointed out that a local football club near the site wished to lengthen their field to the regulation one hundred meters and that this would require cutting into the Kaminaljuyú mounds. Rushed salvage archaeology was obviously not the best way to conduct the work at the site, but it would never have been possible at all, without the aid of the Guatemalan Department of Public Works, which provided the labor to clear and excavate the vast amount of dirt. Second, interruptions of fieldwork, caused partly by the Second World War and the necessity to write descriptions of the unexpectedly large and rich collections, drew labor away from any orderly program of excavation there (Kidder 1961:561).

The years between 1929 and 1941 allowed Kidder to work on the administrative organization of the Carnegie's Maya research program, as well as to fulfill his obligations to the Phillips Academy with regard to the Pecos excavations. Kidder had maintained office space with both organizations. The diaries of this period indicate that he spent much of his time traveling between Cambridge, Andover, and Washington, D.C.; no doubt the trips became a burden. The Kidders initially spent their summers making short trips to the Southwest, with the rest of the time spent in Andover working on Pecos reports. This continued until pressures from the Carnegie became sufficiently great to prevent further fieldtrips to the Southwest.

From the mid-1930s on Kidder and Madeleine spent their winters in Yucatan and Guatemala, surveying the progress made by Morley, at Chichén Itzá, and by the Ricketsons, at Kaminaljuyú. These winter sojourns took place with regularity until 1954, when A. V. Kidder's health worsened. In these later years he also spent some time with his daughter, Barbara, in Guatemala.

In 1938 the Carnegie Institution moved the headquarters of the

Division of Historical Research to Cambridge, Massachusetts, and the Kidders then moved to a house nearby, at 41 Holden Street, where they lived for much of the remainder of his career. This move allowed him a more sedentary lifestyle, and a new role: counselor to anthropology graduate students from nearby Harvard University. Kidder's unpublished papers do not mention the names of the students who dropped by his home to discuss various archaeological topics, but only that he always welcomed them and was interested in their progress (AVK III:passim).

Under Kidder's leadership the Division of Historical Research inaugurated a new publication series, in 1940, entitled "Notes on Middle American Archaeology and Ethnology." The editorship of the series was placed in the hands of J. Eric S. Thompson. It consisted of short notes on specific specimens or topics, and totaled 131 short papers by the time the Carnegie closed out its operations in Mesoamerica, in 1957 (Woodbury 1973:69).

Thompson, Kidder recalls, was a valuable addition to the Carnegie staff in Mesoamerica.

{When} Eric first came out {to Mesoamerica} from the British Museum, he worked under Tom Joyce. During an interim between two appointments from the British Museum he worked for the Field Museum {Chicago}. I remember in '28 the British Museum did him wrong. Morley sent him a telegram saying 'Perfidious Albion better join the C.I.' Then he went to the Field Museum but he was unhappy there. It was a miserable place to work under that German, Lofter {Laufer}. I couldn't come to the Museum and see Eric or any other member of the staff without reporting first to Lofter {Laufer}. (AVK II:12)

Thompson contributed greatly to the understanding of hieroglyphics; it is likely that Morley was eager to have him on the Carnegie staff because of their mutual interest.

The diaries from 1935 onward suggest that time was becoming a major problem in the conduct of the Carnegie's investigations in Guatemala and the Yucatán. The practical pressure of trying to promote field research with no time limitations probably led to the realization that the Carnegie Maya program was too ambitious.

The first hint of this, outside of Kidder's diaries and personal papers, can be found in his 1935 report to the Carnegie Institution (1935a:115). Kidder had by this time come to realize that time schedules for completion of a project were essential to building a synthesis of what had been learned. Yet the closest thing to a synthesis by a Carnegie archaeologist was a single work by Morley, *The Ancient Maya,* not published until 1946. Although the book is focused on the artistic and calendric achievements of the Maya, it also deals with topics such as Maya farming (as inferred from modern practices) and the life of the common people (Morley 1946, Woodbury 1973:70).

In 1939 Kidder suggested that the Carnegie should attempt a synthesis of the division's work. This would lead, he reasoned, to better planning for future fieldwork. Kidder did not intend that it be ready in less than a decade. Between 1939 and 1953 Kidder added to his knowledge of the Maya so that the synthesis of what was known of Mayan archaeology could be put together. By 1953 he realized that the time element must also be taken into account because the materials of Maya archaeology are practically inexhaustible. Since there were gaps in the knowledge of the Maya that had to be filled, Kidder reasoned that much more data would have to be accumulated before a complete cultural synthesis would become worthwhile. Nevertheless Kidder decided that it was necessary to set an arbitrary time limit, establishing a data when all investigations would come to a close, all findings be recorded, definite conclusions be stated, and problems delineated for future research. Kidder believed a ten-year period to be sufficient for this purpose. New projects should be only undertaken if they could be completed within that time frame (Kidder and Shook 1952:115).

No matter how over-ambitious Kidder's plans may later have proved to be, his introduction of the interdisciplinary approach as part of routine field methodology allowed for a fuller explanation of ancient human habitation in Mesoamerica. What he initiated changed the face of archaeology there forever.

KIDDER'S SECOND DECADE AT THE CARNEGIE

The second decade of Kidder's administration at the Carnegie saw the specter arise of reduced funding, through reallocation to the hard sciences as the result of the impending conflict of World War II. The dissolution of the division's work in Mesoamerica was a slow but steady progress; Kidder found that he was spending much of his time arguing for funds to continue the investigations. Accompanying this shift was a change of leadership at the institution, where the physicist Vannevar Bush replaced J. C. Merriam as president. Bush was no friend of the humanities and thought that resources would be better put to use in the hard sciences. Just before Bush began his plan to shut down the Carnegie's operation in Middle America, Kidder proposed to him that the institution underwrite the use of radiocarbon dating for archaeology. Although this would definitely have involved some sophisticated physics, Bush would not hear of any more funds being spent on archaeological research.

Woodbury suggests another reason why Kidder ran into funding problems during the second decade of the Maya program:

> *The failure of Kidder's archaeological program to win a more permanent place in the Carnegie Institution may also derive in part from a view of archaeology that was widely held in the 1930s and even later. Archaeology was seen as chiefly the pursuit of adventurous young men of good family and private income. It was respectable and required energy and talent, but was hardly a profession with the same serious demands as engineering or the physical sciences. Although Kidder himself did much to dispel the notion that archaeology's aim was to fill the shelves of museums, the 'lost cities of the jungle' overtones of some of the Carnegie's archaeological work and the personal background of many of the individuals involved could hardly dispel the impression that it was still something of a gentlemanly adventure. (Woodbury 1973:71)*

Although Kidder's archaeological research program clearly was very ambitious, the appointment of Vannevar Bush to succeed J. C. Merriam ended any hope of putting together a synthesis of Mesoamerican archaeology. If Bush had not cut his budget, Kidder might have had the opportunity to make the needed strategy changes to fit a reduced time frame; as it was, Bush's action left Kidder out on a limb.

In 1947 Kidder and Morley had communicated about the possibility of the Carnegie Institution withdrawing funding from the division. Bush had already directed that funds for research within the division be stopped for areas other than archaeology. Both Kidder and Morley had a sense of foreboding about the future (AVK III:1–83; Morley 1947:16 March). Morley's diary entry of 16 March is revealing:

> {A} . . . *far more serious threat faces the Institution, no less than the extinction of the Division, its liquidation after Ted's retirement. Bush, apparently, is not interested in Historical Research as a field of investigation for the C.I. and so would close us out.*

Morley received a communication from Kidder saying that he would recommend to Bush and the trustees that the name of the division be changed to the Department of Archaeology, to reflect the research that would continue into the near future (Morley 1947b:1 April). In the same communication, Kidder outlined four possibilities available to Bush:

1. *The division would be completely liquidated and all the rest of the staff except Earl Morris, who would retire in 1954, would be dismissed.*

2. *There would be no new division scientists taken on, but the present staff would be kept until the last staff member retired, around 1975.*

3. *The original plan of archaeological research would continue, either at a division or department level.*

4. *There was an outside chance that Morley and Kidder could convince Bush and the trustees to undertake a large project at Tikal, which be financed mainly outside the institution; the entire staff of the division or department could be concentrated at that site (Morley 1947b:8–9).*

Kidder thought that Bush would choose the first option, while Morley thought the second much more likely.

In 1946 Kidder had proposed a new program of research that would turn attention from the Maya to relations between the two major centers of civilization in the New World, Mesoamerica and the Andes. In a memorandum to the institute's Committee on the Division of Historical Research, Kidder outlined future goals for Middle American archaeological research (1946b:51–59). Kidder's plan was not accepted by the Carnegie Institution, but it was partially carried out, about fifteen years later, through the Institute for Andean Research, an organization that Kidder almost single-handedly created. Mrs. Truxton Beale, who was an ardent amateur archaeologist (see Beale 1930, 1932), had met with the Peruvian archaeologist Julio Tello, in Lima, in 1931. Tello showed her some of the mummy bundles from the Paracas graves. Much impressed by their beauty and fired by the enthusiasm of Tello, who explained that funds were needed for expert assistance in reproducing their complex polychrome designs, Mrs. Beale told him that he could count on her for what would be necessary.

The first that Kidder knew of Beale's interest in archaeology was a wire from Alfred Kroeber, in Berkeley, that said he had seen Tello and learned of Mrs. Beale's offer, and that Tello had advised her to make her donation available through the School of American Research, at Santa Fe. Kroeber told her that he did not consider this "the most desirable agency" (AVK I:140). He suggested that Kidder see Mrs. Beale and find out if some other arrangement could be made. Kidder fully agreed with Kroeber's assessment, because there was then no Peruvian scholar on the school's staff. Kidder went at once to Washington and called on Mrs. Beale. He told her he was convinced that her money would be better put to service by some other agency. Mrs. Beale replied that she did not want to be seen as a funding source for any institution whose work she cared little about (AVK I:140). Her comment put Kidder into a quandary, until suddenly an idea struck him:

'Why not the Institute for Andean Research?' 'What is that?' said she, 'I never heard of it.' 'Well, its quite a new outfit.' I replied, not feeling it necessary to add that its age was less than one minute. 'It's a group of representatives of the organizations in the United States that are most actively concerned with Peruvian antiquities.' I then named several men I was sure she knew all about and I was equally certain would, so to speak, play ball. Mrs. Beale said that would suit her exactly.

Feeling very guilty about misleading a lady whom I greatly liked and admired, even for the few minutes necessary to reach the nearest Western Union office, I pleaded an urgent appointment and hastened to wire Alfred Kroeber, Sam Lothrop, Alfred Tozzer, Wendell Bennett, George Vaillant and Duncan Strong: 'You were today elected to the Institute for Andean Research letter follows.' Back at the Cosmos Club, I wrote each one what I'd done and why. All accepted. The Andean Institute held its first meeting not long after.

As I said, above, I consider the founding of that body a real contribution to New World archaeology. It was a great success from the first. (AVK I:140–41)

The institute has served Peruvian archaeology well, although it now survives in a different form.

RETIREMENT

From 1906 until his retirement, in 1950, Kidder introduced many new techniques in archaeological analysis. His Middle America research program and his later interest in the cultures of South America provide ample evidence of the scope of his archaeological influence. In 1950 Kidder published his own stocktaking of the impact he had on Middle American and Mayan archaeology, by discussing the role of the Carnegie's Maya research program.

I hope to write a paper shortly on this program, bringing out the many errors and failures which resulted and some of the successes. The successes, I think, were that we gave a great many men in other disciplines an interest in archaeological and cultural-historical problems and an opportunity to do a great deal of publication which they might otherwise not have done. One of the great errors was that we bit off a great deal more than we could chew. We can see now that we should have confined ourselves to the Old Empire region, the Petén and north Yucatan, instead of going wandering off into the Guatemalan highlands. . . .

Another difficulty was the fact that the program attempted to follow the history of the inhabitants of the area from the earliest time to the present; in other words, it was a vertical program. Our great trouble all through was that the workers, myself included, tended to go off horizontally. The people interested in the Pre-Classic cultures did not want to work up into the early Classic, they wanted to go off and see what was happening in Pre-Classic times in Mexico, South America, and elsewhere. . . . The same was true of the students of colonial history, who became interested in the encomienda and refused to work up into the later periods, such as the pre-revolutionary time and independence, because they wanted to study the encomienda all over Latin America. Naturally, that was a great mistake.

The depression came, the war came, the administration changed to one which was not interested in these problems, and the work has been very much cut down. (Kidder 1953:257–58).

Kidder's primary contribution to Mayan research was certainly the introduction of the pan-scientific approach; the idea that various scientific disciplines could complement each other in the resolution of archaeological problems was a new and even radical approach to archaeology in the 1930s and 1940s.

After Kidder's retirement he was awarded the Viking Fund Medal in archaeology, an award given by the Wenner-Gren Foundation for Anthropological Research. He also received the University of Arizona's Medal of Merit, presented by Kidder's old friend, Emil W. Haury.

Retirement allowed him to accept an invitation from the Department of Anthropology, University of California at Berkeley, to teach a seminar in archaeology: "[it was] my first venture into the teaching field since I was a section-hand under Farrabee in Anthropology I at Harvard during the late Pleistocene" (AVK II:33–34). The seminar was a success and Kidder enjoyed the experience very much.

Kidder saw field archaeology and the analysis of archaeological remains as a team effort; in the process of promoting this view he was instrumental in promoting the careers of various archaeologists whose names have become household words in the field today. It is important to realize that Kidder's tenure with the Carnegie Institution was an important milestone on the road to Americanist archaeology as it is known today.

NOTES

1. The new department had actually been proposed in early 1909, by Parsons, but the rest of the executive committee ignored the proposal; Parsons had chosen the wrong specialist, Hiram Bingham, to draw up specific plans. Bingham was involved from 1909 through 1913 in investigations of Machu Picchu, in Peru (Brunhouse 1971:64). He was primarily a historian, not an archaeologist, and the executive committee may have viewed his sensationalistic accounts of his Machu Picchu discoveries as a major drawback to his consideration.

2. Lindbergh also consented to aid A. L. Kroeber to locate archaeological sites in Peru.

3. See Robert Brunhouse's *Sylvanus G. Morley and the World of the Ancient Maya* (1971) for further reading on the life and work of Morley.

KIDDER'S IMPACT ON
AMERICANIST ARCHAEOLOGY

There are great similarities between Kidder's work at Pecos and that with the Carnegie Institution. Emphasis on field excavations to trace antiquity and cultural development was of paramount importance in both areas. In the Southwest he preached the importance of stratigraphy as first practiced by Nels C. Nelson at San Cristobal, and he also stressed Manuel Gamio's pioneering stratigraphic method at Teotihuacán. "[It was not] until the 20's, when the Carnegie Institution undertook excavations at Chichen Itza, Uaxactun, and Tayasal, did "dirt" archaeology begin to play a significant role and [stratigraphy and] the humble potsherd come into its own" (Kidder 1946a:26).

An analysis of Kidder's tenure with the Carnegie Institution reveals several important contributions to Americanist archaeology.

DIRT ARCHAEOLOGY AND CERAMIC EVIDENCE

The year 1929 began a new era in the development of Middle American archaeology, when Kidder was selected to chair the Division of Historical Research of the Carnegie Institution. From that date until his retirement, in 1950, Kidder continually enlarged the Carnegie's efforts in Middle American archaeology.

He also noted that archaeologists must study the sequent culture development of a particular site, and that only stratigraphy could provide such developmental information. To answer questions about culture development workers first had to perfect methods of stratigraphic excavation and to pay attention to all types of artifacts. Long-occupied sites were the most immediately valuable, since sequent remains there would "yield data as to the course and the mechanics of cultural developments" (Kidder

1959a:3). Kidder also spoke to the value of carefully controlled excavation, because it yields sequential data for any given site. The surface archaeology practiced by Morley and did result in an analysis of visible remains, but dirt archaeology provided the researcher with the necessary continuum of cultural development at any given site.

> *On "dirt" archaeology, product of the shovel, we must rely for fullest and more revealing evidence of man's past. Digging bares not only the temples and tombs of the mighty but also the homes and the graves and the belongings of the masses who, Atlas-like, supported the governmental and religious super-structures of all societies. Digging, too, reveals the time-relations of what is uncovered, on the simple but irrefutable principle that if one thing lies upon another it must have reached that position after the lower was deposited. On superpositions established by stratigraphic observation have been based all major chronological conclusions of geology, palaeontology, and archaeology. . . . When man has passed away, the archaeologist from Mars will learn more of American life from the dumping grounds of Flatbush than from the ruins of Rockefeller Center. (Kidder 1946a:25–26).*

Kidder continued to point out the value of ceramics and their analysis in the delineation of cultural development. When discovered in superposition, such "stratisherd" relationships not only define cultural type but also duration of habitation at each site.

> *The value of the potsherd cannot be more happily expressed than in the words of the historian Myers: 'When with the soft clay which has, so to say, no natural shape or utility at all, the human hand guided by imagination, but otherwise unaided, creates a form, gourd-like, or flask-like, or stone-bowl-like, but not itself either gourd, or skin, or stone, then invention has begun, and an art is born which demands on each occasion of its exercise a fresh effort of imagination to devise, and of intellect to give effect to, a literally new thing. It is a fortunate accident that the material in question, once fixed in the given form by exposure to fire, is by that very process made so brittle that its prospect of utility is short; consequently the demand for replacement is persistent. The only group of industries*

*which can compare with potmaking in intellectual importance is
that of the textile fabrics: basketry and weaving. But whereas
basket-work and all forms of matting and cloth are perishable and
will burn, broken pottery is almost indestructible, just because, once
broken, it is so useless. It follows that evidence so permanent, so copi-
ous, and so plastic, that is to say so infinitely sensitive a register of
the changes of artist's mood, as the potsherds on an ancient site, is
among the most valuable that we can ever have, for tracing of culture.' (Kidder 1946a:26; original source not given)*

Kidder believed that ceramic analysis was of the utmost importance
in establishing antiquity and for working out the geographic range of
given cultures and subcultures at various periods. "Traded pottery indicates commercial and chronological relations between cultures" (Kidder
1946a:26). The morphology and design of vessels gave evidence of the
daily life of ancient peoples, "ceremonial pieces as to religious cults, the
finer wares often bear pictorial decorations illustrating costumes, orna-
ments, weapons" (Kidder 1946a:26–27). But Kidder also realized that
preoccupation with ceramic study can have a negative effect upon other
aspects of archaeological analysis:

*It may well seem that its ceramic tail has been wagging the Di-
vision's archaeological dog. There is, indeed, danger of over-
preoccupation with this or any other single line of evidence which can
become so interesting as to blind the investigator to broader problems.
But pottery, as we have shown, is of the greatest service, in the preliminary stages of research in every archaeological field in which it
occurs, for determining the all-important time-relations of cultural
phases and for linking them chronologically with phases of other cultures, to say nothing of the knowledge it affords of the daily life of
its makers. The Division has realized these values and several of its
members are ceramic specialists, but sight has never been lost of the
fact that study of pottery is merely one of several means toward the
end of reconstructing Maya prehistory. (Kidder 1946a:29)*

Kidder also incorporated the earlier ideas and techniques used by
Alfonso Caso at Monte Albán. The position in Mesoamerican archaeology

that Mexico had attained under Gamio, and which had been sustained by Marquina and others of Gamio's group, was greatly enhanced by Caso.

MULTIDISCIPLINARY RESEARCH

In January 1930 Kidder's program for a pan-scientific attack on archaeological problems was formulated, during the Chichén Itzá Conference. One result was the application of his methods to Yucatecan archaeological studies. In such an investigation the archaeologist would supply the prehistoric background; the historian would detail the documentary record of the conquest, the colonial, and the Mexican periods; and the sociologist would consider the structure of modern life (Kidder 1928a:753). At the same time studies would be made of the botany, zoology, and climate of the region under investigation, in addition to the agriculture, economic system, and health conditions of contemporary urban and rural populations (Kidder 1928a:753).

Although Kidder's unpublished diaries and personal papers understandably do not argue the value of multidisciplinary research as do his published works, they reveal his clear awareness that once the shovel or trowel has altered a site, its context is destroyed forever. Field notes record the site context for the archaeologist, but the site context of zoological, botanical, climatological, and human osteological remains must also be recorded, by multidisciplinary researchers working alongside the archaeologist.

Although the participants at the 1930 Chichén Itzá Conference embraced the new plan for Mayan archaeology, Kidder continued to preach its worth to newer members of the Middle American archaeological community, through many of his Carnegie publications from 1935 through 1946. He stressed the complexity of human culture and continually asked for the help of other researchers to carry out comprehensive and detailed investigations.

While man's progress has been ever upward, no single people has been able to maintain preeminence for more than a relatively brief period. All civilizations have collapsed, as did that of the Maya. Various reasons have been advanced for the fall of this or that people, but the fundamental cause seems, in each case, to have been the over-rapid growth of the material side of culture resulting in situa-

tions too complex for human intelligence to cope with. We appear to
be approaching such a condition at the present time. Our command of
the physical world, through progress in the exact sciences, has
brought about social, economic, and international political diffi-
culties which we are as yet unable to solve. Success can only come
through better understanding of the laws governing human action.
We must bring our knowledge of man to something like par with our
knowledge of material things. But this is exceedingly difficult, be-
cause man is so complex a creature and his career has been, and con-
tinues to be, affected by so many diverse factors that cooperative effort
of workers in all the social sciences is necessary for reaching sound
conclusions. Methods for such a cooperation are for the first time
being worked out in the Division's studies upon the Maya, a re-
search which began as a purely archaeological undertaking, but has
grown through participation of historians, ethnologists, medical
men, and investigators in many other lines, into a pan-scientific sur-
vey of the Maya from the earliest days to the present (Kidder
1946b:91).

The effect of Kidder's approach upon Middle American archaeology
and, indeed, upon Americanist archaeology in general, was the expansion
of archaeological interpretation. His contributions were twofold: He was
a pioneer in the generation of newer analytical and field-excavation techniques; and he recognized that archaeologists must have the aid of outside
specialists in order to resolve archaeological problems more effectively
and to enhance data interpretation.

In 1946 Kidder also expressed his evaluation of the usefulness of the
"culture area" concept for widening archaeological interpretations of the
Maya, a concept he had gotten from his long-time friend Alfred Kroeber.
Kidder, however, modified Kroeber's concept to create his own principle
of "core attack." This method advocated examining a large archaeological
region and its subareas, all of which would require intensive study. Such
an approach would necessarily be protracted and costly, but the information gained would give invaluable clues to cultural identification and
chronology. "Spheres of influence" could readily be determined by surface
survey and minor excavation, both of which would be rapid and economi-

cal to carry out (Kidder 1946a:14). Such work would then allow the specification of elements making up a culture trait, of particular value in studying a culture's material and artistic growth, "intellectual status, and . . . estimating the influence it has received from or radiated to other cultures" (Kidder 1946a:14).

The value of the core attack approach should have been evident, but this principle was seldom followed consistently. Kidder characterized most archaeological undertakings even during his time with the Carnegie as "more or less hit-or-miss affairs whose primary objective has been the recovery of specimens for museum display rather than of data to throw light on historical problems" (Kidder 1946a:14). Since the Carnegie possessed no museum, its energies were perforce channeled to more scientific ends; in fact, his researchers were practicing the principle of core attack even before he had fully expressed the idea.

Kidder justified the preoccupation with the Maya by the principle of "core attack, but the purpose of core attack is to make possible the eventual widening of an investigation and the achievement of an over-all picture" (Kidder 1946a:49).

DIRECT HISTORICAL APPROACH

Throughout his archaeological career, Kidder emphasized the importance of ethnographic work in interpreting archaeological remains; he strived to link a prehistoric site or culture with its living descendants. He pursued this course with the Maya by having Robert Redfield and Alfonso Villa Rojas undertake ethnographic studies of specific Mayan villages.

He called for the use of the direct historical approach to the study of the Maya, by noting that the "gap between the present and the prehistoric past can be bridged by study of the documentary history of the four centuries that have elapsed since the conquest" (Kidder 1946a:21). He even called for a form of glottochronology, to compare sixteenth-century Mayan idioms with those of the language spoken in Yucatan during modern times. Such a study would be based upon archival resources in Seville and in other repositories around Europe (Kidder 1946a:21).

The use of ethnographic analogies in archaeology was seen by Kidder as another necessary tool for linking the past with the present. Proceeding from the known present to the unknown past could provide a fuller account of that past (Kidder 1930a:145). His work remains impressive, in spite of the current debate over the usefulness of ethnographic analogies in archaeological research (see Ascher 1961; L. Binford 1968a, 1968b, 1978; S. Binford 1968; Gould and Watson 1982; Wylie 1982; Watson, LeBlanc, and Redman 1984:259–263; Glock 1985; and Yellen 1977).

INTENSIVE INVESTIGATION

Toward the end of the Carnegie Institution's involvement in Middle American archaeology, Kidder realized that in order to understand how the Maya developed over time, a rich ceremonial site such as Kaminaljuyú must be selected for thorough investigation. It was his hope that the mechanisms of development at one thoroughly investigated site might provide a model for others. This idea never reached fruition because of Vannevar Bush's impact on Carnegie resources after the retirement of J. C. Merriam.

LOCATIONAL ANALYSIS

Kidder contributed to Middle American as well as to the entirety of Americanist archaeology by devising methods for locating Mayan archaeological sites. With the help of the Lindberghs, he inaugurated aerial archaeology in Mesoamerica, as well as the early stages of a coherent site-distribution analysis program. Kidder and Oliver Ricketson began speculation about the possible linkage of highland and lowland sites, either by roads or deliberate choice of a population. Flights over the Mayan enclaves of Guatemala and Yucatan provided hints of trade avenues, as well as possible lines of communication between one location and another. In all of this activity, Kidder was trying to work out the Mayan logic for selecting certain locations for their cities. Flights of this nature also enabled archaeological teams to move rapidly in and out of remote locations.

ARCHAEOLOGY AND HISTORY

Kidder saw no difficulty in aligning archaeology with history and often suggested that such a combination is in fact necessary for archaeological analysis. Kidder believed that the archaeological end product would be the history of a culture from its beginnings to its present condition.

ADMINISTRATION

Next to Kidder's multidisciplinary approach to the study of the Maya, his greatest contribution to Middle American archaeology was through his outstanding administrative talents. From 1929 to 1950 Kidder directed one of the largest and most complex research organizations in the United States. Although his responsibilities involved directing the entirety of the Carnegie's Division of Historical Research, his major administrative contribution to Americanist archaeology came from his research organization of the Section of Early American History. His task was to coordinate efforts by Carnegie staff and related Middle American governmental interests in order to resolve relevant archaeological problems. Kidder excelled in the organization of large-scale archaeological research projects. In addition he was successful in soliciting additional Carnegie funding support during the early years of the division's work in Middle America and was persistent in procuring the funding that allowed his program to continue until 1958, long after such support was normally available.

A. V. Kidder set methodological precedent both through his own innovations in archaeological method and theory and through his multidisciplinary approaches to archaeological problems. Not only was he an expert field archaeologist, but he was also a forward-thinking scholar who was continuously interested in assessing the human condition from a humanistic viewpoint.

Let the final word be Kidder's:

Everyone knows out of what you can't make a silk purse. I couldn't ever have been a Kroeber; nor could I have had Loren Eisely's precious combination of brain and pen. But one cannot help trying a little to excuse one's deficiencies. How about the intellectual climate of the age in which I grew up? Would I have done any better if I'd been raised during the first decade of the 20th Century instead of the last years of the 19th? And what of my education at Harvard? That certainly wasn't what's now known as 'general' (AVK I:20).

Taking a retrospective look at myself as an archaeologist, I can think of many sins of omission, fewer of commission because I've always stuck pretty closely to factual reporting, mostly regarding one aspect or another of material culture. In this, if one is careful and a close observer, its hard to go wrong, except in failure to distinguish the significant from the trivial. However, in spite of the present general dimming of interest among United States anthropologists in such reporting, its fundamental importance eventually will become realized. But in two other quite distinct ways I think I have been of real service to American archaeology. One was the holding of what I believe was the first field get-together of anthropologists to report on current activities and discuss matters of common interest. . . . (AVK I:18)

EARLY TRAVELS

This appendix contains transcriptions from A. V. Kidder's diary of 1907 and his unpublished memoirs of 1957. Here the reader will find additional information about Kidder's earliest travels and surveying activities in 1907, under the direction of Edgar L. Hewett, as well as personal reflections concerning his lifelong friend, Sylvanus G. Morley.

SUNDAY, 30 JUNE 1907
(DURANGO TO CORTEZ; 1907:34)

Pitilessly clear all day. Left Durango on the seven o'clock train. We crawled along, twisting up around a great mesa-like shoulder, the hills became more the shape of mesas as we went along, until at 10:30 we came out into a sort of valley where lies the little town of Mancos. Across the plain rose the sharp profile of the Mesa Verde and behind us was a high snow capped mountain with large névés. Was driven to the hotel, a small wooden building with the inevitable 'porch'. Was directed to the house of one Mills, an elderly wood-chuck-looking man who gave me some information as to Hewett. Decided to go right on to Bluff via Cortez, where I spent the night, catching a mail buggy in the morning. Accordingly, after lunch another buggy came for me and we set out on the 20-mile drive to Cortez. The driver, a stoutish old-timer with a tobacco-stained moustache, took great pride in the beauties of the mountains and was delighted when I under-estimated distances in the clear air. We circled the end of the Mesa Verde and followed a broad valley around it until we came to the town, which was scattered about, a score or two of rough plank houses on a little rise. The country is dry, parched, the earth cracked and seamed by the fierce sun. Arrived at Cortez in 2½ hours. I made my arrangements to start at five tomorrow and then came out on the board walk in front of the hotel to look about. A couple of saloons opposite with the usual false facades and patient ponies waiting outside. A Ute and a couple of Navajos riding in from their reservations. Talked with the druggist, a fiery little man, an ex-doctor with a craze for archaeology, his businesslike phraseology when discussing these erudite problems was most amusing—'Now as to this Pueblo proposition,' he would say, 'facts line up all right, but—.' Before supper I got into conversation with a couple of young fellows come into 'town' for Sunday. They were on the government survey near here—a Wisconsin University and an Ann Arbor man. Supper, most of the guests in spurred boots and shirt-sleeves and all keeping the sealed silence of Western meals. After a pipe in the cool evening air, the mountains and mesas sharp and blue, in the crystal atmosphere, went up to my room where I packed up my things in most compact form and got out of my campaign clothes.

ON THE WAY TO BLUFF CITY
(1957:17)

I felt when we pulled out, as the sky to the east was just beginning to pale, that I was really on my way. It was a fine clear morning, cool with the desert's wonderful early morning freshness; as the day wore on it grew blisteringly hot. 'Wore on' is wrong, there wasn't a moment's boredom; no bend of the pair of ruts that was the road, when it didn't rattle the buggy over a stretch of bare sandstone, failed to open new marvels of erosion, new trees, new birds. That day I saw my first dashing black and white Magpies, heard for the first time songs which through the years came to mean so much: The Canyon Wren's clear notes, running down the scale; the tinkle of the Western Meadow Lark, so much more musical than that of his eastern cousin; and that evening from the cottonwoods at Bluff the pensive, rather than mournful, sound of Mourning Doves. A good part of the way to Bluff was down the valley, which further below became the canyon, of the McElmo. In its upper reaches were ranches with fields of alfalfa and orchards that bore, as I learned later, peaches and apricots such as are grown only on dry land that can be irrigated, or maybe they taste extra luscious because they're so welcome in that kind of country. Cultivation along the McElmo lessened as the red sandstone walls heightened and in places pinched in. Toward noon we passed, close to the road, a low, sun-baked adobe house and a parched-looking field. 'No mail for here today', said Hunt, 'It's the last ranch this side of Bluff. Belongs to Jim Holley'. I little knew how many vivid, long-lasting memories I'd have of that place and its owners. A mile or so below, an equally big and deep, equally barren canyon came in on the right, a high, cliffy mesa towering like a giant ship's prow between it and the McElmo. Hunt pointed past it, 'Yellow Jacket, that is. When it's up you can't get a rig across.' It didn't look to me as if, far from being 'up', it could ever have had a drop of water in it. But I'd yet to learn the rushing, tearing force of desert floods, or know the treacherously hidden top-dried beds of quick-sand they sometimes leave behind them where two drainages meet or some sharp bend or rocky jut causes an eddy.

SYLVANUS G. MORLEY
(1957:53-54)

[I must now] pay tribute to Sylvanus Morley, the sparkplug of our three-man team. Sylvanus had really studied Anthropology intensively during his two years as an undergraduate at Harvard. He'd entered as a Junior, coming from the Pennsylvania Military College, where he'd learned some surveying and had become a good horseman. From boyhood much interested in antiquities, especially hieroglyphic systems of writing, he'd made the transfer in order to study Egyptology under G. A. Reisner. However, when he arrived in Cambridge he consulted Professor Putnam, then head of the Department of Anthropology, who, always anxious to stimulate research in the New World, and finding that hieroglyphs were Morley's principal concern told him that the Egyptian systems were well understood and that great progress had been made on cuneiform, but that the meaning of the Maya glyphs of Mexico and Central America was almost entirely unknown. Then and there was recruited the most ardent of all students of the Maya. He elected Tozzer's inspiring Anthropology 9, a half course, ending at midyear, and his keenness was so evident that Tozzer advised him to spend the remaining winter months of 1907 in Yucatan. He did, and it drove from his head all thought of becoming anything but a Mayanist. His graduate career in anthropology at Harvard required a certain amount of work in other fields; hence his presence in the Southwest that summer. Of the three of us, Vay was the only one who knew what an archaeological survey was all about. It should, he said, be a stock-taking of all the remains in an area and their description in the form of notes, plans, and photographs in as full detail as was possible without excavation.

WEDNESDAY, 3 JULY 1907
(THE HOLLEY RANCH; 1907:38)

We got up at four, shook the sand out of our hair and clothes . . . saddled up and got away just as daylight began to strengthen. After going a little further along the mesa we found a gully down which we led our horses and got again to the river road. About ten miles under the red cliffs and along the flood plain brought us to the store, where we had stopped on our way to Bluff.

We set out again about eight-thirty, followed the river for a while and then turned up upon the mesa tableland. It was a long climb and we walked our horses. As we got higher and higher the view out across the great desert plateau beyond the San Juan opened up, mesa after mesa square-shouldered and bare. As we came out atop we passed through a flock of many hundreds of sheep, drifting, with their mounted Navajo tenders across the sage brush plain. We now had good springy road, a cool breeze and a filmy sky to cut the sun, so for ten miles or so we made good time . . . [and] . . . we went into the ranch house, a low stone and adobe building where he introduced me to the family: Mrs. Holley, one-armed, work-worn by hospitable, Mr. Holley, a tall bronze man with a limp, and seven children, ranging from one to ten or twelve years of age, all barefoot, all ragged, and all supremely healthy.

[Later], Mr. Hewett rode up to Hill's ranch, a few miles along the valley, to meet the other two lads [Fletcher and Morley].

9 JULY 1907
(FIELD ADVENTURE; 1907:46)

Our first adventure came as we were riding along the narrow trail beside the dry arroyo of lower Ruin Canyon—our horses suddenly shied far over to the left side of the road, even the little shambly-legged colt that was following Morley's mare pricked up its ears and cowered against its mother's side. A dry incessant whirr was coming from somewhere on our right, a distant, impersonal buzzing. 'Rattler'! we exclaimed simultaneously, and in a minute we made him out behind a sage-brush beside the trail, his body tightly coiled, head drawn back and resting on the coil and tail held stiffly in the air—a first for us both. We left him severely alone and continued up the narrow rock-walled canyon. We dismounted twice to examine small ruined buildings, watch towers apparently, placed on huge, almost inaccessible rocks at curves of the canyon. We were beginning to wonder how the place deserved its name when we came around a jutting rock and on a spur far ahead of us saw the tall red-brown walls of a large ruin. As we came nearer we made out another and then another, perched here and there in commanding positions. We tied our horses to a little cedar tree and made our way to a prow-like point on rock that seemed to split the canyon in two. We worked our way, back and knees, up a cleft and stepped out on the flat top with the sage-plain stretching far away on every side. From here we could make out our position and the 'lay of the buildings'. We were at the very end of the canyon where it split into two final little branches. All about the forks stood buildings, scarcely ruins, one can call them, so straight and high do the walls stand, yet at the base and within each were piles of the fallen blocks which had carried the structures even farther in the air.

MORE DISCOVERIES
(AVK II:43)

These buildings consisted of two large house-towers, if such they be, the walls standing some fifteen feet high and the interiors cut up into many chambers connecting with each other by low narrow doors in many of which the wooden lintels, gray and split with age, are still in place. From within we could make out the butts of wooden joists still imbedded in the masonry, and in two cases extending clear across the rooms, where the storeys of the old dwelling had been. These two ruins extended around the head of the gorge in a sort of horseshoe, below them was a cliff of twenty or forty feet. They were set exactly upon the edge, the masonry often almost overstepping and, under, where the otherwise sheer cliff overhung, were nestled many smaller houses or cubby-holes, built into the recesses of the rock. The most impressive of the upper set of ruins was a square-tower, placed on a corner of a ledge near the bottom of the canyon. Its walls rose straight up, course after course of trim, well-cut stones, to a height of over thirty feet. It was so small in cross-section, so slim and delicate looking that one wondered how it could have withstood the wear and tear of the centuries which must have elapsed since those hunted, peaceable masons were driven for refuge to such places as this.

Morley and I worked here all the morning, mapping the locality, exploring and measuring the ruins and admiring the skill of the stone-layers who dared build upon such narrow edges with such perfect abandon. As we left at twelve, we started down an opening in the cliffs which led to the opening of a rising V of talus and debris some ten feet below. I was ahead and groping for a hold with my foot, I felt a firm incut step; I tried lower with my other foot, struck another, and so on down by the old stairway of the vanished people. It was a finishing touch.

THURSDAY, 11 JULY 1907
(1907:46–47)

Our start was delayed this morning by my having to go down to the 'haystack', a pasturage half a mile away, and drive up the horses. My white mare was in good fettle and we had a splendid gallop in the cool of the early hours as far as Ruin Canyon. We were looking for Holley Canyon, a north branch of Ruin, but as many gulches run off the main line our only key to the right one was a watch tower guarding the entrance of a small canyon a couple of miles from the mouth. As we rode up this on a faint old trail it opened out, and lengthened up surprisingly. We must have ridden over a mile and a half without seeing any sign of habitation when we arrived at a fork guarded, as before, by a tumbledown tower. The right prong ran north for a distance and then began to broaden out and rise to the mesa top. Morley went up one side and I the other and in a minute I heard him call out that he had seen ruins on the plain ahead of him. I kept on until I had got clean out of the canyon and upon a little rise of the mesa top. Instead of the ordinary level, the country fell away from me, terrace on terrace, to another large system laid out below like a map. Leaving this . . . for another trip I rode around the head of Holley through the stunted cedars and over the flat shaley ledges to where Morley and

Fletcher were already tying their horses to examine the ruins. These were not on the plain as had at first appeared, but set about the head of a little rocky canyon that leads into the main branch a bit lower. The arrangement is much the same as at the top of the Ruin: tower-houses a series of ruined cell-rooms only to be made out in ground plan, and guard-towers straddled upon jutting rocks. The walls here, though, standing in many cases over twenty feet high are in a very precarious condition, some leaning out, some in and making a very ticklish business of sketching and measuring. In one place a large building had been placed upon a great rock at the edge of the plain, and this rock has since slowly slid down the slope and canted over to an angle of nearly forty-five degrees. On the upper edge some five feet of the wall are still in place though at perilous inclination; below is a monstrous tumbled heap of shaped stones, and broken roof-beams from the lost building.

Desolation, these ruined settlements of a lost people are its typification. Flat tops of the mesas with their dusty sage brush and dried-up, tortured cedars; the rock upper stretches of the canyons; and between stand the broken brown walls. Rabbits dodge above the towers, lizards whisk in and out of the gaping windows; the only sound is the far-off coo of a wild dove, and upon all the sun beats down out of the cloudless sky.

SUNDAY, 21 JULY 1907
(UTAH RUIN; AVK II:52–53)

Started out with blankets, tea pot and some provisions to work up the Utah ruin. We let our horses take it slowly, finally got away from the McElmo and struck along the trail across the highland, where at a turn in the road we found a Navajo sound asleep in the flaring sun beside his tethered horse. Our passing waked him up, he soon came galloping after us; but when we turned aside to hunt a spring we had heard of he passed on ahead and off out of sight around the mesa. An hour or so later we rounded a point and saw against the sky the sharp brown outline of the walls. We led our horses up on top of the mesa and without unsaddling mine I tied him to a bush and ran down to the cave to see if the water still held. Under the overhanging ledge I stopped: the faint drip, drip of falling drops came softly from the dark recess! I crawled in, wriggled until my face was over the little pool and drank deep, then I lit a pipe and lay on the cool rock until the others came scrambling down among the fallen walls.

Our horses cared for we started to work with tape and note-book. The first ruin was a largish pueblo in such fine preservation that every wall stood from six to fifteen or twenty feet high. No ceilings, of course, were in place but we could see the dried cedar beam butts still embedded in the masonry. The doors, some with wooden and some with stone lintels were as usual very small, and being often nearly choked with debris made it difficult for one of generous proportions to scramble from room to room. A feature of this building which we have not noticed in any other was a sort of vestibule on the cliff side. Through this was the only way into the rooms, the outer walls being blank except for the little 'loophole-windows' never over six inches square. Apparently, guarding this entrance was a tower, now half tumbled away, which was perched or rather straddled on two large rocks over the talus below. We finished up the ruins on this side of the little gully, and while Morley drew a working plan of the pueblo opposite, Fletcher and I looked to the horses. Water we brought up from the spring in a bucket which had to be filled with my canteen cup, so low was the roof of the cave and so shallow the pool; oats we poured out on saddle blankets and set on the ground before them. When we got back to the cave we found Morley laying out the food, eggs, bacon and crackers, and keeping an eye on the tea pot which he had set to boil on what he told us was a Maya three-slab hearth. Fletcher finished first and climbed up upon the mesa-top; a minute later we heard him calling excitedly. It was a scene which in its way outrivalled the grandest sunsets of the high Alps. The great darkening plain; the terraces of the distant San Juan marching one above another, bare and canyon-riven, off to the high southwestern mesa-desert with its lonely square-shouldered buttes blue in the distance; and to cap all the sun setting to the left of a towering thundercloud, and making a golden curtain of the sweeping sheets of distant rain. When the last glow had faded from the high-banked clouds in the east, we went back to the cave again to sit around the little sage-brush fire and tell stories. Then the full moon came into its own, powdering the ruins above us with silvery light and casting the broken doorways into coal black shadows.

About eight o'clock we climbed up on the edge of the plain, scraped little holes in the sand and with our saddles for pillows settled ourselves for the night. The thunderstorm had passed off to the south but now, to our disgust it began to creep back again in our direction. A sighing in the brush, a little cold whisking wind blowing the dust in our faces and then the flash and rattle of an electrical bombardment. I thought uncomfortably of our steel saddle horns, the only metal probably in fifteen miles, and made mental calculations of the time between lightning and thunder. Then with a rush the rain was on us. Morley and Fletcher made a break for the cave. I struggled for a moment to keep my flapping poncho over me, partly lost hold of it, and grabbing up my bedding scrambled in my stocking feet down the debris. The moon was hidden and I could just make out the black opening of a little cliff-house under a shelving rock. I dove in there, cowering down by the old wall. By this time the storm had become a regular cloudburst, the spray from the dashing rain was driven clear into my retreat, and over the ledge there began to flow an ever strengthening cataract. I drew my blanket about me but thoughts of rattlesnakes and of the great rock so close over my head kept sleep away for some time. I must have dozed off though, for my next recollection is of the moon shining on the rocks outside and the voices of Morley and Fletcher further up the canyon. The rain had stopped and they were going back up to the saddles. I joined them and we found the sand only damp, as it was a bit slanting, and we again settled ourselves for the night and I slept soundly. When I woke the sun was just getting over the horizon and Morley was sitting up in his blankets rubbing his eyes.

FIELDWORK AT PECOS

KIDDER'S ABSENCE, 1917–18
(1957:41–42)

While I was away, during the war, Carl Guthe did a field job. He excavated a site near Pecos, one just below Pecos at the town of Rowe. He took this remarkable old Ford of ours and made an exploration of the San Luis Valley in Colorado, to work out the northern extension of Pueblo culture, which he did very satisfactorily. It has never been written up but, he got a lot of very good dope. I spent the summer of '19, after I got back from France, in Andover, getting caught up with various notes and things. Then, I went out in 1920 with a full-dress field season. Guthe was with me again that summer and I also had Earnest Hooton which was great fun. I had been kicking about my skeletons. He said they had an awful lot of fresh breaks on the bones. In the Southwest, a bone will often crack and not come apart. When you take it out, it comes in two pieces and, it looks like a fresh break but, it isn't a fresh break. I tried to explain that to Earnest, but that didn't do any good, so I said, 'You come out and dig some skeletons yourself'. So he did. Then I discovered that Earnest had done practically no excavation at all. He had worked a little in a long barrow and then he had been to the Canaries and worked in a cave but as far as digging skeletons, in bad conditions, he knew very little about it. He would clean out a long bone and put his knife under it and pry and the damn thing would break. It was very interesting having him there, because he gave us a lot of information about the age of children, the dentition, and he made out a whole lot of tables for us, of one sort or another. Of course, he was always fun to be with and excellent company. That same summer, Guthe and I went over to Zuni to visit Alfred

141

Kroeber, who was with Leslie Spier. He lived on a house-top in Zuni and, cruised all around, picking up potsherds and looking at ruins, and having a good time.

1920 FIELD SEASON
(1957:24–26)

The excavation of the field season of 1920 was principally devoted to a long cross-cut trench from the head of one of our three salient trenches, that had come out from the bottom or edge of a rubbish heap up through the deep rubbish heap and just to the edge of the mesa. From there, we carried it clear across through the ruin. We also began on the west edge of the mesa working in to meet. We ran the trench in through one of the gateways of the pueblo. We went in through that entry-way going down to bedrock, into the plaza. We immediately got into trouble. First, with Black and White ruins, very badly down, then, into a kiva, which had been built and rebuilt. There were a tremendous amount of changes that had been made in this kiva in the course of its occupancy. It had been sunk in Black and White times and, was used right up to the end of the occupation of Pecos. It had some seven fire-pits. It was very, very complicated going down through the different floors. Then we came into a large kiva. This had been both built and abandoned during Black and White. That was the only good, Black and White kiva we found at Pecos. There was a Black and White burial made through the floor, and it was full of other burials and a ceremonial cache practically on the surface. That trench kept on to the end of the ruin proper. This second, big kiva was right up against the pueblo itself the ruins of the late pueblo. In the meantime, our trench from the west had run into all sorts of troubles. You couldn't put a shovel into the ground at Pecos without getting into a mess. We first went through a series of ruins, beginning with Glaze I and running up into Glaze III, which had been torn down and stone-robbed and beam-robbed and burials made in all them. It was very profitable archaeologically but it was very difficult digging. That trench, which was a couple of hundred feet long, yielded a great deal of information. We got a sequence of pottery types and the methods of burial, etc. The skeletons were in rather better condition than they were in the rubbish-heap. We came into the ruin from both sides and, then, we were in trouble. The pueblo, itself, was in most frightful condition. The late wall was standing eight and nine feet high but, with ten or twelve feet of old ruins underneath them so, when you got down to the floor of the late ruins, which you could find all right, because they were hard, flat adobe floors, you weren't anywhere near the bottom, to see what was there, to find out what the architecture of these earlier ruins was, because the ones we had struck on the west terrace had been so pulled down and stone-robbed that the walls were only a few inches high. But the walls were standing pretty well under the main ruin. It was a dangerous job because of getting down underneath the floor. The late walls were very likely to come down. We pulled some of them down, others we were able to brace up with timbers. We were able to get down to bedrock all the way across so our cross-cut trench was completed. We found a lot of very interesting conditions down in these holes underneath the later ruins. We got the information there from when the main pueblo was built, which was during Glaze III. From Glaze II which was apparently in the middle of the 15th Century on to the end of the occupancy of Pecos there was no change in the Pueblo. They used those rooms—they had to patch some of them up—as long as there was a roof over them—water didn't get down and freeze in the wintertime they were all right. So we were able to date the building of the main Pueblo and, later on were also able to date the two annexes that were built against it and an independent ruin which we called the South House that ran from the Quadrangle down to where the Church is. That was, in many ways, the most profitable season we had . . .

1922 AND THE LATER YEARS
(1957:45–47)

We worked again in '22. In '21 we didn't go into the field. In '21 Guthe made his study of pottery making at San Ildefonso. That same summer Elsie Parsons made her study of the Jemez. Jemez being the Pueblo to which the remnant of the Pecos went in 1838. Some Jemez came over and invited the Pecos. They had heard about what a bad way they were in. They were reduced to about 15 to 16 people. A good many people had oozed out. I talked with a woman from Cochatee [Cochiti] who said that her folks had come from Pecos. Leslie White found some Pecos descendants at Santo Domingo. By the early part of the 19th Century the Mexicans had settled the town of Pecos about three miles above the ruin. They kept the Comanche out. The Comanche raided them once or twice but it wasn't worth the Comanche trouble to do anything about Pecos. That was why I was so anxious to have Elsie Parsons to do a job at Jemez. It was one of the Pueblos she hadn't studied. As a matter of fact, she got very little about Pecos from the Jemez. All the originals had died though there was the son of one of them who had heard a good deal from his father. And there were two societies at Jemez which had been brought from Pecos. She got some information as to them. But by and large the Pecos people at Jemez worked right into the group but they didn't get on well ceremonially. One of the Pecos told her that these Jemez don't know how to run ceremonies.

Some real funny things happened there. The Pecos descendants, during the last couple of years, have all become evangelistas, and have split away from the Jemez people. Father Chavez, a wonderful fine man, did the splendid history of Comingos. He is now acting as the clergyman at Pecos, I mean in Jemez. He is very much annoyed at the Pecos people. There is a split even though there has been inter-marriage.

The whole summer of 1921 I was here working in the Andover museum. That was when I got interested in the Andover rubbish heap. I was, of course, very keen on refuse and stratigraphy. I didn't do near as much on the Andover rubbish-heap as [it has often been said] I did. That story has grown. [We have no further information on this summer.] One thing that I did find in that rubbish-heap which was amusing was a lot of little flat pieces of rusted iron, some twelve or fourteen inches long. I couldn't imagine what they were. I took one of them and Madeleine didn't know what they were and, I showed them to my mother who was visiting us at that time. She said, "Oh, those are corset bones. When your corset wore out we used to roll it up and tie it with strings and throw it in the rubbish." They were made of metal. The whalebone ones had gotten to be so terribly expensive that no one used them anymore. When I was at Zuni with Kroeber and Spier I tried to put a hole in the rubbish-heap there but they wouldn't let me. The reason for that, I have since learned, is the rubbish-heap is full of ashes and they belong to a creature known as ash-boy who is the guardian of the rubbish-heap and who takes care of children at night if they go out. If they have to go out for a call of nature their mother smears a little ash on them and they go out to the rubbish heap and do their business and ash-boy looks after them. And the kiva ash has a lot of ceremonial potency. I got a lot of information about that. I found that the ash in the kivas at Pecos was entirely different from the ash in the rubbish-heaps. In fact, the kiva ash didn't get into the rubbish-heaps. This ash-boy that Florence Ellis tells me about—any old ash will do for him apparently. The ash in the kiva fireplaces were pure white and there was an ash-pit or repository in the kiva. It had no charcoal in it. Old Gregg, the Santa Fe trader visited the Pecos when it was still occupied and was taken into some of the kivas and, he said that the kiva fire was fed with light, quick-burning material which didn't char, warmed the kiva up and particularly lighted it, quite different from the stuff they burned in the fireplaces in their houses. I wondered about the kiva ash, so perfectly pure white and occasionally with little pieces of white flecks and white flint arrowheads. Elsie Parsons was told that if you held a white arrowhead in your hand you could see what was going on at home. Very often you would find that your wife was carrying on with some fellow and you would go home and do something about it. I got Madeleine to start a test-pit in the plaza away from the kivas. The first thing that she ran into was a hollow that had been dug in the packed living surface, full of kiva ash and a little further along we found another one. One of them had a very nice pipe in it. I was walking down with Freddy Wilson one day in the Pecos Arroyo and I found a whole lot of these ash-pits being washed out. It is very interesting, the whole ash business.

Although the Pecos River is full of trout, and the Spaniard Casteñanda talks about what fine trout there are in the Pecos River, I found a single trout bone in the rubbish. Fish bones don't last well anyway but the rubbish I found underneath the rooms in the pueblo is very much better preserved and you find baskets, mats and sandals and things like that and in that I found no fishbones. I asked Elsie (Parsons) about that if any pueblo had a taboo against eating fish like that of the Navajo. No pueblo had as far as Elsie knew, but she discovered from the Pima though they had no fish taboo, they get a lot of fish out of the Gila, but they save the bones and throw them all back into the water to make new fish. Elsie wonders in her Jemez book if that was done in Pecos. Clyde [Kluckhohn] doesn't know of any taboo against fish among the pueblos. Of course, it is very strong among the Navajo. Mrs. Wetherill told me that the reason for that was that the Navajo say that when they came into the Southwest they chased the Anasazi into the San Juan River and that they turned into fish and if you ate any fish you got them right where they could do their worst to you. I never asked Clyde about that.

I lasted a long time at Pecos. First, it was a grand place to be with the kids. I could always find an excuse for digging some more. We worked there in '20 and '22 and '24 and '25 and in the summer of '25 I put a trench into the campsite where we had built our house and were living just across the crick from Pecos. You couldn't see any sight of ruin there but way back in the eighties Bandelier had seen sherds in the face of the arroyo cut and I had made a collection of sherds there. At that time, unfortunately I didn't have sense enough to realize that there was a recognizable sequence of Black and White types. Charlie Anderson was the fellow who found that. He and Anna Shepard worked it out. I didn't pay any attention to this campsite ruin because I knew there were Black and White sherds at Pecos and I thought it was a small unimportant ruin. When we built our camp, digging refuse holes and other things we found other sherds but I didn't think it was much of a ruin. In '26 I put a trench into that darn place and I found it was an enormous ruin and I worked there in '26, '27, and '29 and I never did get to the end of it. It was a very strange ruin to us because we had been working at Pecos. We might have known what the situation was but we didn't. In the earlier sites if a room became unsuitable they just gave it up and filled it with rubbish and robbed it of stone if they wanted them but mostly of beams, because they were hard to cut. On this campsite I found at the least five different pueblos. One built up against another. I have kicked myself ever since for not doing a lot more there than I did. I don't know to this day and no one else, how the kiva developed. It got very strange above ground. Stanley Stubbs and Sid Stallings got the same kind of queer surface kivas at a ruin they dug near Santa Fe. They hadn't published when I was digging and I hadn't published when they were digging. Unfortunately, neither of us were cognizant of the other fellow's problems. I was awfully dumb when I was working in Pecos.

1929 was the last season. That was the season that Lindbergh was there with us.

CONVERSATIONS WITH GORDON WILLEY
ON PECOS AND THE SOUTHWEST (AVK III: 10–16)

AVK: My original idea was that the Pecos Valley would give material, dating back to the very first working up of agriculture out of Mexico, was not so. I couldn't find anything in the valley or in the Parjarito Plateau which was really early. The earliest stuff that I could find was definitely

Pueblo III. That interested me in the whole question of where in the dickens they did come from and, what was going on in other parts of the Southwest, which I didn't know anything about. I had worked up in the San Juan with Hewett for just one year. And also I had worked for a couple of seasons at the Pajarito Plateau north of Santa Fe. I put in the season of 1923 in cruising all over the Southwest. I covered pretty nearly the whole country. I particularly wanted to see what was in the country lying between Albuquerque-Gallup Railroad and the San Juan. I went through that country—spent the whole summer with Monroe Anderson [Amsden?] cruising about. At that time Sam Guernsey with whom I had worked on the Basketmakers had started in a season up in the north up in the Saline country. He had got a bad case of dust poisoning so he had to quit and pull out. I learned about this and took over Sam's outfit and went with Bill Claflin and the man I had been with before, Monroe Anderson, up to the Saline country which I hadn't seen in a good many years. Toward the end of the field season of 1923 I had a pretty good idea of almost everything in the Southwest with the exception of the Hohokam. I didn't know that at all. I set about that Autumn writing a description of the work at Pecos up to that time. That led me into trying to work out what had gone on in general in the Southwest. The work was definitely finished in Pecos in '29; even if it hadn't been for the Carnegie job which I took over in that year, I would have pulled out pretty soon. The problems of the San Juan had been worked out very thoroughly while I had been at Pecos by Earl Morris, who was then preparing his big book on the archaeology of the La Plata.

Willey: Which didn't come out for a good many years.

AVK: Yes, he got switched off like me in Middle America. That was the period when he was working in — he began in 1924 in Chichén and, worked there pretty much through the rest of the twenties.

Willey: In the *Introduction to Southwestern Archaeology* you didn't use Pecos classification, did you?

AVK: That was formulated in '27.

Willey: What sort of scheme did you use?

AVK: I used the old terms that Sam Guernsey and I had worked out. Sam Guernsey and I were the fellows who worked on the growth of the

Anasazi culture. The Basket-makers were known but nobody knew just where they came in. Nothing whatever was known of what we took to calling the Slabhouse Culture. It is now known as Pueblo I and, then, still later, Sam found and recognized immediately, what afterwards became to be known as Basket-maker III. Sam and I together really worked out the sequence of cultures of the Anasazi. And I used those terms— Basket-maker and Post Basket-maker, which is Basket-maker III. Slabhouse, which is Pueblo I, and Cliff House. Those were the terms I used and, I also recognized what I called a Proto-Mesa Verde which is really an early Pueblo III. It was worked out more thoroughly, mostly by Paul Martin. J. O. Brew didn't get down that late with his work on Alkali Ridge. But I knew that that region west of Cortez and north of Cortez was a very important area, and I suggested to Scott and Jo that Jo should work up there. They had a terrible blizzard the first year that he worked up there and, the Navajo got into bad trouble and, they had to drop food to them by airplanes and, poor Jo {Brew} was snowed in up on Alkali Ridge. Scott asked me about it and I said, "It doesn't amount to anything. The snow doesn't lie up there and it will be gone in a few days." Jo's never got over that.

Willey: What was the reaction to the *Introduction,* at that time?

AVK: It was very interesting. Everybody said it was a swell job, except in the region that they knew about. They found lots of errors and misconceptions in that. In general, it was pretty good. And the book sold like hot cakes. It was very well reviewed in the *New York Times.* It was their leading review in that weekly. The first printing sold out immediately and they made a larger one.

I had very definite plans for Pecos of the same sort that I afterward tried to carry on in Central America, Guatemala, and Mexico. Namely, to attack the problems of the upper Rio Grande. That was the country that I was particularly interested in. Pecos was the largest site in it in prehistoric times. I wanted to attack that from many angles. I did get Elsie Parsons to work at Jemez and, I wanted to get a historian, Franz {Blom?}, whom I afterwards did get in Central America, among various other people. I knew very shortly after 1929 that I wasn't going to be able to carry on at Pecos. But I still feel that the only way we are eventually going to get the real meat from archaeological work in terms of cultural development and a development of the human race is by using the abilities of all pertinent sciences, social and environmental. That is why I have felt so very sadly, aside from the effect it had had on the men themselves, of the dropping of that program by the Carnegie Institution.

A great deal of exploration was done by Guthe during the war years. Guthe wasn't in the army. He explored a great deal in the Pecos Valley below Pecos. Then he pursued the Pueblo culture to its dying out in the north—not in the northwest but directly north.

My interest in the Southwest never entirely lapsed. I was connected with Gladwin and Gila Pueblo right from the start of the Gila Pueblo Program.

Willey: Did you encourage him to go into the south, into the Hohokam?

AVK: Yes I did. I also, suggested Awatovi to Jo. I had been in '25, I think it was, to Awatovi. No, no it was in 1917. When I went to the Hopi country before I went into the service. It was a place where archaeology carried on into historic times. And, it was also, obviously, a very important site ceramically. What caught my eye was the pottery and, just going over the mounds at Awatovi you could see that everything was there, just as there was at Pecos, and a lot of things, of course, came over to Pecos, such as the Black on Yellow and the Sigiatki, both found at Pecos.

Willey: As of 1929, what did you think of as the major problems in the Southwest?

AVK: It's awfully hard to remember back. There are so many problems while I was writing this paper that I never thought of while I was at Pecos. I think I was just a plain fact gatherer and, what was very much wanted at that time. I have always been a fact-gatherer rather than a thinker.

Willey: I don't think that's quite fair. What about the *Introduction?* That's more than facts.

AVK: I am under no illusions as to my intellect but, if I have been useful in Anthropology it has been as a gatherer and a presenter, making available . . . general significant facts.

Willey: I am inclined to think that that has always been Anthropology's greatest role, and perhaps today. That is why archaeology has moved to the forefront as a great many facts have been gathered in ethnology are no longer available. The great wealth now is archaeology.

AVK: I really can't remember what I felt were the particular problems of Southwestern archaeology. But, I did realize very keenly how much more data we needed and still do in that field. I wasn't then and isn't yet the sucked orange that Hewett told Morgan and Meade it was.

Willey: You went into Pecos with the conception that in the Rio Grande Valley you had an avenue from Middle America into the Southwest and, that you might very well find where the beginnings or introduction of agriculture was in the Southwest. After you had worked the area this you found was obviously not true. The picture was infinitely more complicated.

AVK: Yes, much more complicated and, I now remember what I did have particularly in mind when I quit Pecos and, that was to follow down into northern Mexico—I had been interested in Chihuahua—and I wanted to go in 1922—I got to see the Chachauitas sites with Gamio and Hay. Hay and I were going up to Zapay which we couldn't do because Hay was taken sick. That was what I had in mind for the Southwest was to work on down into Mexico.

Willey: And also, into southern Arizona.

AVK: Yes, I had no conception of the importance of the Hohokam at that time. I realized perfectly well that the Hohokam pottery was not in the Anasazi tradition. But, I had no conception of the extreme unlikeness to all the rest of the Southwest that the Hohokam was. Kroeber was the first person who really grasped that. It still isn't by any means worked out. I think Gladwin balled things up badly. He had and still has crazy ideas about the thing. Mainly that the origin of Hohokam culture was in Guerara [Guerrero] and that they sent up a group of scouts to find some place that would suit them. Of course, there was nothing to that. But, there are still a great many problems regarding relationship between the Hohokam and the cultures of Mexico. Because it doesn't hook up a hoot with Northwestern Mexico. It does much better in the highlands and down into Chachahuitas. That whole problem was balled up by Gladwin.

I can't believe for a moment his lion and lamb lying down together in the Gila. I never could get him to excavate at Big House, Casa Grande. There is a great house at Snaketown and, I was very anxious to get them to work that. No great house has ever been properly done. Emil got as much as he could out of the old Cushing notes. Odd Halseth has been right along side of Pueblo Grande right along but has never got anything out of it. He has never done much with it except to collect specimens. There is no question but that Salado pottery was coming in. There were Salado people who died down there and were buried but I don't believe for a minute that two cultures so utterly distinct, in every way, could live side by side for any length of time. They were living in the same environment and practicing the same arts. It's a very interesting problem. I haven't read Gladwin's new book thoroughly. I have just skimmed it. He did a great deal of valuable work both himself and the men he backed and he brought out that very valuable series of Medallions. There are three great conglomerations of sherds: the one at Gila Pueblo, the Laboratory at Santa Fe, and the Museum of Northern Arizona. It is a very cheap and effective way, sherd collecting, of getting things lined out, but it has got to be backed by intensive excavation.

Willey: What do you see today as our future needs for research in the Southwest?

AVK: Of course, these ties to Mexico which are just beginning to come a little clear—there is Charley Kelly's work—should be followed up. I still feel that the most important thing to do is to tie the Southwest into northern Mexico and, then so on down. As Erik [Thompson] and I pointed out a long time ago, it's the best hope we have of solving the correlation problem. There is no question of the accuracy of tree-ring dates if they are done by competent people. A good many were done by McGregor which turned out not to be good. All the ones done by Gladwin, Douglass and Emil, himself, and by Sid Stallings, have turned out very well indeed. There is no question about them. They are accurate to the year. The Carbon 14 is not competent to pass on the correlation questions because they have got this plus or minus. I still believe in the Martinez-Thompson correlation, in spite of the fact that the Carbon hits Joe Spinden's right on the nose. But I am awfully bearish on Carbon 14 these days. They need a great many more readings and I doubt if you can get dependable readings in a wet tropical climate.

THE INDIAN—SOUTH OF US

This unpublished paper probably was written in 1930, as implied by Kidder's mention of the conference "held during the past winter at Chichén Itzá"; the gathering was held in January 1930.

In the early history of the United States the Indian was of course an element of much importance, and until almost the close of the last century he continued to be more or less a factor in influencing the direction and nature of the westward extension of our frontiers. For this reason knowledge of the Indian, and appreciation of the very great differences which existed between the various tribes, are necessary for comprehension of many events and trends in our national growth. But now he is gone, like breath from a mirror; the Indian question of today is merely a matter of rendering tardy justice to the dwindling remnants of a sadly maltreated race; and in our future he will play no active role.

In Mexico, however, and in many parts of Central and South America the situation is quite otherwise. Not only in days of Pizarro and Cortez, and during the whole Colonial Period, was the Indian the single most potent force in shaping the course of conquest and settlement; but also at the present time he is, to a large extent, responsible for the contours of social and economic life and the nature of government. Throughout vast territories aboriginal blood still predominates, and the destiny of several great countries depends in considerable measure upon proper development of their Indian citizens. The problem of Latin America, as has often been pointed out, is therefore largely the problem of the Indian.

So the United States is after all still vitally concerned with the Indian, for we are drawing ever closer to the nations south of us. If our relations, economic, political, and intellectual are to be well and solidly founded, it behooves us to understand the race which bulks so large in the make-up of our neighbors. Practical considerations alone should dictate research. The subject has also, as will be shown, the most fundamental scientific implications. Finally, we of the United States are singularly well placed for at least its inauguration. We are near, but not too near, we can view the entire field in a way hardly yet practicable for any group within it; we can consider dispassionately many phenomena which are locally too beclouded with prejudice to permit impartial judgement.

Comprehensive study of the Indian obviously demands teamwork. It is a task far too great for any one group of scholars. The conditions of today lie in the province of the sociologist, the economist, the ethnologist. The past, without a knowledge of which it is impossible to evaluate the present, must be attacked by the archaeologist and the historian.

Taking stock of what is now known of Indian history, we find that it presents three phases of outstanding interest: the populating of the New World, the building of native civilization, and the contact with Europeans.

In naming the race which he came upon in 1492, Columbus was at least correct within the limits of a continent, for the Indians did, without much doubt, originate in Asia. They are physically allied to certain Asiatic peoples; they entered the New World from the northwest. But when they came, why they came, and the manner of their coming, are still largely matters of guesswork and inference. These questions are inextricably intertwined with the primary diffusion of mankind—one has only to read Dixon's "Racial History of Man" and the reviews thereof to realize both the importance and the complexity of the subject. It is still highly controversial, and its solution depends upon studies of physical anthropology in both hemispheres, upon the collection and weighing of multitudinous data in geology and palaeontology, in linguistics and in comparative ethnology. But among the many problems involved there is one of preponderating interest and importance. What did the Indians bring with them? Did they enter these continents as palaeolithic savages, and were all their subsequent achievements due to native genius? Were they, until the sixteenth century, unaffected by cultural stimuli from the Old World? Or did they owe, as Elliot Smith and Perry and their school would have us believe, all progress to transoceanic, ultimately Egyptian sources? This again is a controversial matter, but it serves sharply to define questions of the ability of mankind to reproduce basic inventions; and of the inherent mental capacity of different races; issues which lie at the very root of all historic and anthropologic judgement.

The second great epoch of New World history was ushered in by the discovery of maize agriculture. The exact place of origin, and the botanical relationships of course are still uncertain, but a subtropical plateau region seems indicated. Maize, at all events, made possible, just as did wheat in the eastern Mediterranean, the rise of civilization. Cultures founded upon maize—such as the Maya, the Toltec, the Aztec, the pre-Inca, and the Inca—developed various and elaborate social and religious systems, architectures, horticultures, methods of metal working, of loom weaving, of animal husbandry, of mathematics, and of writing, which, although they were in most cases chronologically of later appearance and so attained less maturity than corresponding phenomena in Europe and Asia, were of the same intellectual order and held the same potentialities for further progress. The trends of pre-Columbian history; the growth, efflorescence, and decay of independent political units; the coagulation of empires; the break-up of agricultural states under pressure by nomadic invaders; all these provide most striking parallels to what took place on similar evolutionary horizons in the Old World.

Although the rise of aboriginal American civilization is largely undocumented, the archaeological record is remarkably complete and singularly straightforward. Furthermore, as it was laid down in comparatively recent centuries, it has not suffered the long erosion of time, which has dealt so cruelly with the remains of many vital periods in Europe and Asia. Nor, for some as yet uncomprehended reason, was it nearly so complicated by the sweep and countersweep of migrant races that passed across those continents. The Americas, therefore, offer rare opportunity for comparative studies of the growth of civilization; and they should also enable us to develop methods for collecting and evaluating data from regions and from periods whose materials are more fragmentary or more complex.

Here there enters again the matter of origins. What elements, if any, of higher culture did the Indians derive from the Old World? How much of their achievement is their own? This is a question of transcendent importance, for upon its solution depend many of our ultimate conclusions, not only as to the physical possibilities of cultural diffusion, but as to the very nature of civilization, and as to the psychological unity of the human race. America offers the great test case. This invests research upon the Indian with a meaning not as yet fully grasped even by many of its students; and it calls for our best efforts in intensive and most critical consideration of the details of New World history and culture. The superficial generalities hitherto mostly indulged in will get us nowhere.

The coming of Europeans opened the third major phase of New World history. Viewing the continents by and large we find that one of two things usually happened, either the Indians were exterminated or they were not. Where, as in most parts of [the United States] and of eastern South America, the aborigines were few and [had a] rude culture, they quickly disappeared. In Middle America and western South America, however, the native populations were dense and relatively civilized. What might have happened had the Conquest been delayed but a few centuries, and the Aztec and Inca states been given time to expand, to stiffen, and to weld themselves together, forms fascinating food for speculation. The whole course of world events would doubtless have been changed. But the Spanish came, the flimsy political structures of Mexico and Peru felt apart, the nations were intellectually decapitated by the destruction of the theocratic upper classes, in whom resided all power and all learning, and there were left the teeming millions which from the sixteenth century on have formed the body of the population. They have influenced the Caucasian immigrants quite as much as the latter have affected them. The social system and the government of a large part of Latin America are, as I have said, the outcome of the blending of the two groups. Analysis of the interplay of racial and cultural forces, past and present, is essential to understanding conditions in those countries; and knowledge of what [. . .] occurred will supply invaluable material for the scientific study of often more complex, but fundamentally not dissimilar, conditions produced by military adventure and colonization in other parts of the world.

I believe this matter of race and culture contacts to be perhaps the most portentous which faces us today. We have abolished space, and we are busily engaged in veneering western material civilization and ideas over the entire face of the globe. The resultant clash is responsible, at bottom, for much of what is now happening in China, in India, in Egypt, in South America, even in Russia. I think it, indeed, not unlikely that the historian of the future will see in these phenomena vastly greater significance for the formation of his world, than he can observe in the politics of nineteenth century Europe. Yet to the details of that period a hundred scholars now devote their lives, for every one who considers those fundamental ethnic relationships of which the Indian-White contact forms so perfect, because relatively so simple, an example.

The three outstanding phases of Indian history, which I have sketched so summarily, all lie, it is true, in the domain of the Americanist, and their immediate problems are essentially American. But each one has world-wide implications, and each is of vital importance to the entire range of the sciences of man. They are of appalling intricacy because they deal with human beings, and they are, therefore, beset with the multitudinous psychological bafflements, biological obscurities, and gaps in the historic record which render the study of mankind so much more complex than any other research can possibly be.

Such inherent difficulties are, of course largely responsible for the slow development of human as compared to biological knowledge; and for its snail-like progress when contrasted with the rapid advance of the physical sciences. But we students of man have also, I believe, been highly culpable in failing to face the issue. The awesome bulk of human history, or human evolution, or the nature of man, or whatever one chooses to call it, we have feared to regard, as the mind shrinks from the contemplation of eternity. Daunted by the grievous magnitude and the seemingly endless ramifications of our task we have buried our heads, ostrich-like, in the comfortable sand-heaps of specialization.

Specialization, of course, is necessary, for it is the splitting up of something too large for immediate comprehension in its entirety to permit intensive consideration of its parts. The process, however, implies eventual reassembly of those parts, and ultimate visualization of the whole. But each of the many sections, the so-called disciplines, into which the study of man has perforce been subdivided pursues its own ends with almost deliberate disregard of the objectives of every other. And within the disciplines each worker or group of workers does practically the same. We have, of course, realized the dangers of intellectual isolation and we have attempted to counteract them by broadening the scope of graduate instruction, by holding mixed conventions, by establishing academies, and research councils. Although such moves are certainly in the right direction, they are at best mechanistic set-ups rather than natural cooperations, and in our individual researches, our field, or laboratory, or archive investigations, in those activities which are nearest our hearts and to which our best efforts inevitably are given; we have made few and but half-hearted attempts toward real association or mutual understanding.

It may not yet be the moment for too close contact. It would indeed, probably be unsafe for the young and raging lion of sociology to lie down with the gentle historical lamb. They should, at all events, not be thrust arbitrarily into the same cage. Forced cooperation may lead to trouble. At best it is pretty sure to be artificial and therefore unproductive. But some form of cooperation becomes essential as the disciplines broaden their outlook and deepen their researches, and there begin to be encountered phenomena too great for comprehension by any single group, yet involving principles of fundamental importance to all groups: race, for example, or environment *versus* heredity, or the inherent ability of mankind to increase its capacity for understanding. These things must be attacked and their underlying problems must be formulated if the science of man is to go forward.

But how? Every scholar is fully occupied with his own researches, every 'ology has its own preoccupations. In the few cases, however, where forces have been joined and the efforts of workers in several disciplines have in one way or another been brought to bear upon a single body of significant data, or upon any important general problem, it has always resulted that not only was the gathering and digestion of specialized information in no way retarded, but that there has come about an interchange of ideas, and intellectual cross-fertilization immensely valuable for all participants. Such investigations have, however, been the exception rather than the rule, and for some reason, possibly from mere inertia, possibly because certain enterprises have been over-organized or their programs too rigidly defined, they have not yet become by any means standard practice in the social sciences. Further experiment is necessary.

A survey of Yucatan by the Division of Historical Research of [the] Carnegie Institution of Washington and associated agencies has been inaugurated with the above considerations in mind. It is based on the theory that we should concentrate, whenever we can, upon fields where specialized researches can go forward in entire independence of each other, but where results will be cumulative and findings comparable; and where mutual interest, if nothing else, will foster intellectual and practical cooperation.

The general problem toward the solution of which the investigation is directed may be formulated as follows: "What are the results of the meeting of two races of diverse physical make-up and differing culture?" This is obviously a matter of very great moment. No research in history, anthropology, sociology, government, religion, genetics, esthetics can be pushed very extensively or very profoundly without encountering one aspect or another of race or culture crossing. It is a problem transcending adequate comprehension by any one group, therefore it is an ideal one for joint attack. Even so approached, however, it is still too great. One cannot hope effectively to begin a study of ethnic contacts with the whole world as a field and throughout the millennia of history. We must pick a simple exemplification of the problem both in space and in time. It has already been shown that the New World offers a splendid laboratory for the study of culture growth and that the post-Columbian period in Latin America illustrates particularly well all the phenomena incident to the meeting of diverse peoples. But Latin America, again, is too big. We should still further reduce our preliminary objective and so we come to Yucatan.

The area of Yucatan is small; its environment is uniform. Natural barriers isolate it from continental Mexico. For upwards of a thousand years the peninsula was the seat of a high aboriginal culture. The Spanish conquest resulted in obliteration of the externals of native civilization, in the catholicizing of the Maya, and the reduction of the dense native population to serfdom. There took place the inevitable hybridizations, racial, religious, social, and economic; there were the same strifes, uprisings, readjustments, with far-reaching effects upon both elements, which have occurred wherever the Spanish found themselves overlords of crowded Indian nations. Yucatan presents an epitome of historical events and present-day conditions in large parts of Latin America; and, to a less precise but still significant degree, it illustrates what has happened at all periods and in all parts of the world when, after military conquest, the will of a potent minority is enforced upon a race of lower culture. And finally, the very helpful attitude of the Mexican governments, both Federal and State, and the fine climate of the country make conditions most favorable for research.

The survey has tentatively been divided as follows: The prehistory of the Maya will continue, as in the past, to be studied by the archaeological staff of the Institution, in close touch with the Direccion de Antropologia of the Republic of Mexico and such other agencies as are engaged in Middle American archaeology. The documentary history of the Conquest and the Colonial Period will be handled by the Division's section of Modern American History. Present day social and economic conditions have been the subject, during the past winter, of preliminary field reconnaissance by Dr. Robert Redfield of University of Chicago, who has submitted plans for future work. A program for study of recent history, which in Yucatan presents many aspects of intense interest, will be worked out by the documentary historians and the sociologists, as the nature and limits of their own investigations become clearer. Medical research is already in its second year under Dr. George C. Shattuck of the Department of Tropical Medicine of the Harvard School of Public Health. Physical Anthropology will be taken over by the Department of Genetics of [the] Carnegie Institution. A linguistic survey of the Maya is being carried on by Dr. Andrade for the Department of Anthropology of [the] University of Chicago. In [the] all-important field of environmental conditions, we have prospect of cooperation by [the] University of Michigan, which has already made a first examination of the region with a view to conducting intensive research in zoology and botany. Much is still unprovided for: meteorology, for example, and geology, and agronomy. It is manifestly impossible for the Carnegie Institution alone to staff or to support all the necessary investigations. But the project is designed to continue for many years, and it is hoped that other agencies will come to believe that it represents exceptional opportunities to pursue their own scientific interests, at the same time adding effectively to a sum of generally useful coordinated knowledge.

It has seemed wise to formulate only the following principles: Each unit of research should be intensive, employing the technical methods and striving for the special aims of its proper discipline; but there should constantly be kept in mind its ultimate bearing upon the basic question of race-contacts; and there should also be fostered a historical point of view, in other words, a consciousness of the time-relation of all phenomena. And, finally, by field conferences, such as the one held during the past winter at Chichén Itzá, by meetings between all concerned. This is thought to be perhaps the single most important aspect of the project.

INDEX TO THE PERSONAL PAPERS OF ALFRED VINCENT KIDDER

This book draws heavily on the unpublished papers and diaries of Alfred Vincent Kidder, some of them opened in the course of this research for the first time since his death. There is usually one bound diary per year, but occasionally two to three volumes were used. Where that is the case Roman numerals, put on the bindings by Kidder, have been used.

I. Personal diaries

1896 - 2 February–15 June
1900 - 1 January–31 December
1901 (I) - 1 January–31 December
1901 (II) - 12 September–15 September (Contents found in book I, which was accidently left on a train by Kidder but was returned to him).
1902 (I) - 1 January–31 December
1902 (II) - 10 September–17 September (Contents found in book I.)
1903 - 1 January–31 December
1904 - 1 January–31 December
1905 (I) - 1 January–13 June
1905 (II) - 1 July–25 August
1905 (III) - 13 September–20 October
1906 - 5 January–4 December
1907 (I) - 14 January–4 June

1907 (II) - 5 June–29 July
1907 - typewritten account of 1907 (II) with one carbon copy.
1910 - 31 July–4 August
1914 (I) - 5 June–30 June typewritten diary, pp. 1–11.
1914 (II) - 5 June–30 June, Handwritten in "Red Line Pocket Note Book", same material found in book I for 1914.
1917 - No days or months noted.
1923 - (Probably), work at Walpi, 2 pages.
1930 - 1 January–31 December
1931 - 1 January–31 December
1932 - 1 January–31 December
1933 - 1 January–31 December
1934 - 1 January–31 December
1935 (I) - 14 January–22 March

1935 (II) - 23 March–10 May

1935 (III) - 1 January–31 December
(Books I and II are incorporated in Book III. Books I and II were added into Book III by Kidder because of its larger size.)

1936 - 1 January–31 December

1937 (I) - 4 January–11 August

1937 (II) - 12 August–31 December

1938 (I) - 1 January–27 June

1938 (II) - 28 June–31 December

1939 (I) - 1 January–17 July

1939 (II) - 18 July–30 November

1939–1940 - 1 December–30 April

1940 - 1 May–30 November

1940–1941 - 1 December–30 April

1941 - 1 May–30 November

1941–1942 - 1 December–31 May

1942 - 1 June–31 December

1943 (I) - 1 January–19 August

1943 (II) - 20 August–31 December

1944 (I) - 1 January–30 June

1944 (II) - 1 July–31 December

1945 (I) - 1 January–24 April

1945 (II) - 24 April–25 November

1945 (III) - 26 November–31 December

1946 (I) - 1 January–12 May

1946 (II) - 13 May–23 November

1946–1947 - 23 November–17 May

1947 - 18 May–6 December

1947–1948 - 7 December–25 May

1948 - 26 May–31 December

1949 (I) - 1 January–5 June

1949 (II) - 6 June–31 December

1950 (I) - 1 January–26 April

1950 (II) - 27 April–11 September

1950 (III) - 12 September–31 December

1951 (I) - 1 January–15 April

1951 (II) - 16 April–29 July

1951 (III) - 30 July–17 October

1951–1952 (I) - 18 October–10 January

1952 (II) - 11 January–17 March

1952 (III) - 18 March–4 June

1952 (IV) - 5 June–24 August

1952 (V) - 25 August–15 November

1952–1953 (I) 16 November–7 February

1953 (II) - 8 February–3 May

1953 (III) - 4 May–12 July

1953 (IV) - 13 July–10 August

1953 (V) - 11 August–22 December

1953–1954 -22 December–26 February

1954 (I) - 27 February–7 May

1954 (II) - 8 May–17 July

1954 (III) - 18 July–2 October

1954 (IV) - 22 August–23 November

1954–1955 - 24 November–12 April

1955 (I) - 14 April–15 July

1955 (II) - 16 July–21 October

1955–1956 - 22 October–19 January

1956 (I) - 19 January–30 April

1956 (II) - 1 May–5 August

1956 (III) - 6 August–10 December

1956–1957 - 11 December–31 March

1957 (I) - 1 April–29 July

1957 (II) - 30 July–22 October

1957 Iceland trip, spiral bound notebook, handwritten, also contains
loose handwritten notes and ad-
dresses of people Kidder met
there.
1957 (III) - 23 October–31 December
1958 (I) - 1 January–6 April
1958 (II) - 7 April–24 July
1958 (III) - 25 July–5 November
1958–1959 - 6 November–18 February
1959 (I) - 19 February–20 May
1959 (II) - 21 May–31 July

1959 (III) - 1 August–30 September
1959 (IV) - 1 October–31 December
1960 (I) - 1 January–27 April
1960 (II) - 28 April–29 July
1960 (III) - 30 July–28 October
1960–1961 - 8 November–28 February
1961 (I) - 1 March–16 July
1961 (II) - 17 July–31 December
1962 (I) - 1 January–31 May
1962 (II) - 1 June–29 October
1962–1963 - 29 October–14 April
1963 - 15 April–10 June

II. Field Notes

1908 (I) - 11 May–6 June, Mesa Verde, also contains bibliographic references to
Egyptian archaeology.
1908–1910 (II) - 12 June–January, Montezuma Creek, Utah, Chaco Canyon,
and notes on pottery sherds during trip to Chaco Canyon.
1908–? (V) - Descriptions of sherd collections from Montezuma Creek, Peabody
Museum, and Denver Museum.
n.d. [1910–?] (III) - Excavations about Cave Springs, Alkali Canyon, San Juan
County, Utah.
1935 (0–1) - Finca Moreflores and San Agustin Acasaguastlan.
n.d. [1935–36?] (102) - Wares and descriptions of E-III tomb at Kaminaljuyu.
1936 (I) - Ayampuc, Mound I, Kaminaljuyu.
1936 (II) - Ayampuc, Mound I, Kaminaljuyu.
1937 (XI) - Descriptions, drawings of work at Kaminaljuyu.
n.d. [1938–39?] - Peten Polychrome, Grave at Roosevelt Hospital, Petrillo
pieces, Salvador notes.
n.d. [1938–39?] - Kaminaljuyu sherd lots.
1945 (32) - Descriptions and drawings from work at Kaminaljuyu and other
associated sites.
1946 (27) - Maya pottery notes.
1947 (31) - Zaculeu pottery descriptions.
1948 (24) - Nebaj, Tomb III mirrors, Kaminaljuyu sherd lots.
1949 (19) - Nebaj and E-III descriptions.

1950 - E-II tomb and Utila descriptions.

1952 (45) - Kaminaljuyu and original Santa Clara site descriptions.

1953 (74) - Kaminaljuyu descriptions, written in Cambridge, Massachusetts. Blank field note book.

III. Drafts of Memoirs

n.d. [1954?] "Rambling Reminiscences," typewritten manuscript, three-ring bound notebook, pp. 1–83. Contains a magazine photograph of William F. Libby, inventor of the Radiocarbon dating technique.

1954 "Rambling Reminiscences," typewritten manuscript, three-ring bound notebook, pp. 1–154.

1957 "Reminiscences," manuscript typed (perhaps by Mrs. Katherine Willey) from a tape-recorded question and answer session between Kidder, Gordon R. Willey, J. O. Brew, and Fay-Cooper Cole. The three-ring bound notebook, pp. 1–115, also contains a typewritten manuscript of a brief discussion by Kidder of what constitutes civilization and the development of material culture, pp. 1–6.

IV. Unpublished Manuscripts

n.d. "The Indian—South of Us," Typewritten, pp. 1–35.

1914 "Southwestern Ceramics: Their Value in Reconstructing the History of the Ancient Cliff Dwelling and Pueblo Tribes: An Exposition from the Point of View of Type Distinctions." Doctoral dissertation, Harvard University, Cambridge, bound with clamps, card stock cover, 2 volumes, 303 total pages.

V. Unpublished Materials by Other Scholars

Guernsey, Samuel J. Diary, 1914, 7 June–26 July, "Arizona Exploration—1914," pp. 1–54.

Ware, G. Diary, 1912, 15 May–15 August, with photographs, pp. 1–67.

VI. Correspondence Relating to Military Career

Bottoms, A. F. (Examining Officer, Presidio). Letter to Mr. Alfred Vincent Kidder, 10 August 1917, 1 page.

Brees, H. J. (Chief of Staff). Special Orders (#91) to 1st Lieutenant Alfred Vincent Kidder, 1 April 1918, 1 page.

———. Special Orders (#39) to 1st Lieut. Alfred V. Kidder, 29 August 1919, Coburn, H. D. (Adjutant), Special Order (161) to Alfred V. Kidder, 27 November 1917, 1 page.

French Legion d'Honneur (chevalier), by Presidential Decree of 4 June 1919, citation to Kidder, Alfred V., Captain, Infantry, Headquarters 91st Division, 1 page.

Honorable Discharge Form—Alfred Vincent Kidder, Form No. 525.3, A.G.O., 19 April 1919, 2 pages (front and back).

Johnston, William H. (Major General). Letter to Captain A. B. [V.] Kidder, 5 May 1919, 2 pages.

———. Letter to Captain Kidder, 8 December 1919, 1 page.

———. Letter to Captain Kidder, 30 December 1920, 1 page.

Pillsbury, Dennis C. (Adjutant). Special Orders (# 188) to 1st Lieutenant A. V. Kidder, 12 July 1918, 1 page.

Proctor, John R. (Colonel, General Staff). Special Orders (#114) to 1st Lieutenant A. V. Kidder, Inf., 10 July 1918, 1 page.

Jewett, Henry C. (Chief of Staff). Special Orders (#115) to Captain Alfred Vincent Kidder, 26 November 1918, permission to visit Nice, France, 1 page.

McAndrew, James W. (Chief of Staff). Special Orders (#300) to Alfred V. Kidder, 27 October 1918, 2 pages, promotion to Captain in the Infantry.

Plark, O. W. [Writer's name illegible] (United States Veterans Bureau). Letter to Alfred Vincent Kidder, 1 January 1925.

VII. Published Manuscripts by Other Scholars

Harrington, Margaret A. L. n.d. "Bibliography of Alfred Vincent Kidder." Pp. 1–19, typewritten, published in Willey's 1967 obituary "A.V. Kidder."

Mason, T. Alden. n.d. "Alfred Vincent Kidder 1885–1963." Pp. 1–6, typewritten, pp. A–B of Mason's obituary written by Tatiana Proskouriakoff.

Smith, Watson. n.d. *Review* of "Pecos, New Mexico Archaeological Notes," by Alfred Vincent Kidder, *Papers of the Robert S. Peabody Foundation for Archaeology,* Volume 5, Phillips Academy, Andover, Massachusetts 1958, carbon copy, 5 pages.

VIII. Guggenheim Fellowship Correspondence

n.d. Handwritten note, two lines, notebook paper.

Kidder, A. V. Letter to Dr. Henry Allen Moe, 5 August 1957.

———. Letter to Dr. Henry Allen Moe, 4 November 1957, with attachment of a request for a grant from the John Simon Guggenheim Memorial Foundation for preparation of an autobiographical sketch.

Moe, Henry Allen. Letter to Dr. A. V. Kidder, 14 October 1957.
————. Letter to Dr. Alfred Vincent Kidder, 21 December 1957.
————. Letter to Dr. A. V. Kidder, 17 February 1958.
————. Letter to Dr. A. V. Kidder, 10 June 1958.

IX. *Kidder Memoir Proposal*

Willey, Gordon R. n.d. "Kidder Project Proposal." [for tape-recorded interview] Recipient of proposal not designated, typewritten, carbon copy, 2 pages.

X. *Correspondence Between A. V. Kidder and Colonel Charles A. Lindbergh*

Kidder, A. V. Letter to Colonel Charles A. Lindbergh, 25 June 1930, carbon copy, 1 page.
————. Letter to Colonel Charles A. Lindbergh, 15 July 1930, carbon copy, 1 page.
Lindbergh, Charles A. Letter to Dr. A. V. Kidder, n.d., 1 page.
————. Letter to Dr. A. V. Kidder, n.d., 1 page.
————. Letter to Dr. A. V. Kidder, 18 December 1929, 1 page.
————. Letter to Dr. Kidder, 15 July 1930, 1 page.
————. Letter to Dr. A. V. Kidder, 2 December 1930, 1 page.
————. Letter to Dr. A. V. Kidder, 15 September 1935, 1 page.
————. Letter to Dr. A. V. Kidder, 8 February 1939, 1 page.

XI. *Correspondence from A. V. Kidder to M. A. Kidder Regarding Lindbergh Flight*

Kidder, A. V. Telegram to M. A. Kidder, 10 October 1929, 1 page.

XII. *Correspondence Between A. V. Kidder and Henry Cabot Lodge, Regarding Legislative Threats to the Pueblos of New Mexico*

Kidder, A. V. Letter to Senator Henry Cabot Lodge, 5 April 1943.
Lodge, Henry Cabot. Letter to Mr. A. V. Kidder, 30 March 1943.

XII. *Correspondence of the Division of Historical Research— Carnegie Institute of Washington*

Pollock, H. E. D. Memorandum to Division Staff, 20 April 1949, 1 page.

XIII. Correspondence to Kidder from J. Eric Thompson, Raymond H. Thompson, Donald Watson, Leslie White, and Gordon R. Willey

Thompson, J. Eric. 27 June 1959, 2 pages.
———. 5 November 1959, 2 pages.
———. 10 February 1960, 2 pages.
———. 31 May 1960, 2 pages.
———. 4 November, 2 pages.
———. 29 April 1961, 2 pages.
———. 17 May 1962, 2 pages.
Thompson, Raymond H. 8 January 1961, 1 page.
———. 7 March 1961, 1 page.
———. 24 May 1961, 1 page.
———. 8 June 1961, 1 page.
Watson, Donald. 12 September 1955, 1 page.
———. 12 October 1955, 1 page.
———. 9 October 1956, 2 pages.
White, Leslie A. 11 May 1959, 1 page.
———. 3 March 1963, 1 page.
Willey, Gordon R. 13 October 1952, 1 page.
———. 27 February 1959, 2 pages.
———. 21 February 1960, 1 page.
———. 19 March 1962, 1 page.
———. 19 October 1962, 2 pages, with answer by Kidder 31 October 1962, 1 page, carbon copy.
———. 9 February 1963, 1 page.

XIV. Correspondence to A. V. Kidder from Robert Wauchope and Richard B. Woodbury

Wauchope, Robert. 8 August 1952, 2 pages.
———. 5 February 1959, 1 page.
———. 20 February 1959, 1 page.
———. 9 April 1959, 1 page.
———. 22 December 1959, 1 page.
———. 6 June 1960, 1 page.
Woodbury, Richard B. 11 February 1959, 1 page.
———. 21 July 1959, 1 page.
———. 16 November 1959, 1 page.

————. 19 September 1960, 1 page.

————. 12 February 1961, 1 page.

————. 7 March 1961, 1 page.

————. 23 May 1961, 1 page.

————. 24 May 1961, postcard.

XV. *Miscellaneous Professional Correspondence*

?, Betty. Letter to Ted, 15 July, no year, 1 page.

?, Ed. Letter to Dr. Kidder, 8 February 1953, 3 pages (written on Carnegie Institution of Washington, Hieroglyphic Research, letterhead).

Appel, Ludwig. Letter to Mr. Alfred Victor [Vincent] Kidder, 26 February 1960, 1 page.

Anderson, Arthur. Letter to Ted, 29 January 1959, 2 pages.

————. Letter to Ted, 26 February 1959, 2 pages.

Arriola, Jorge Luis. Letter to Doctor Alfred Vincent Kidder, 10 May 1960, 1 page, with statement of charges due for 20 bibliographies of the Museum fur Völkerkunde, Hamburg, 1 page.

Beal [?], Marie. Letter to Ted, 15 June 1955, 2 pages.

Bliss, Mildred R. Letter to Alfred V. Kidder, 19 May 1937, 1 page.

Fuentes, Miguel Ydigoras [president of Guatemala]. Letter to Alfred V. Kidder, 2 August 1961.

Howe, M. A. DeWolfe. Letter to Ted, 31 May 1943, 2 pages.

Kidder, A. V. Letter to E. Wyllys Andrews, 3 January 1963, 1 page, carbon copy.

————. Letter to Prof. Dr. Franz Termer, 9 January 1963, 1 page, carbon copy, in answer to Termer's letter of 15 December 1962.

————. Letter to Dr. William S. Webb, 23 February 1959, 2 pages, carbon copy, in answer to Webb's letter of 13 February 1959.

Saltonstall, Leverett (governor Massachusetts). Letter to A. V. Kidder, 7 July 1944, 1 page.

Tax, Sol. Letter to Dr. A. V. Kidder, 19 February 1960, 1 page.

Tax, Susan. Letter to Kidders, 4 August 1960, 2 pages.

————. Letter to Kidders, 29 March 1962, 1 page.

Tebes [?], Harold (U.S. secretary of the interior). Letter to Dr. Kidder, 7 August 1942, 1 page.

Termer, Franz. Letter to Dr. Kidder, 3 April 1953, 1 page.

————. Letter to Alfred, 21 December 1955, 2 pages.

————. Letter to Alfred, 20 December 1958, 2 pages.

————. Letter to Alfred, 18 July 1959, 1 page.

———. Letter to Alfred, 9 August 1959, 2 pages.
———. Letter to Alfred, 20 December 1959, 1 page.
———. Letter to Alfred, 19 May 1960, 2 pages.
———. Letter to Alfred, 7 June 1960, 1 page.
———. Letter to Alfred, 20 July 1960, 2 pages.
———. Letter to Alfred, 11 September 1960, 1 page.
———. Letter to Alfred, 16 October 1960, 2 pages.
———. Letter to Alfred, 7 November 1960, 1 page.
———. Letter to Alfred, 20 November 1960, 1 page.
———. Letter to Alfred, 19 January 1961, 1 page.
———. Letter to Alfred, 15 December 1962, 2 pages.
Treganza, Adan E. Letter to Dr. A. V. Kidder, 4 August 1959, 1 page.
Warren, Bruce E. Letter to Dr. Alfred V. Kidder, 28 December 1959, 2 pages.
Webb, William S. Letter to Dr. A. V. Kidder, 13 February 1959, 6 pages.
Wendorf [?], Fred. Letter to Doctor, 31 August 1957, 2 pages.
Weyer, Edward M. Letter to Dr. Alfred V. Kidder, 29 June 1960, 1 page.
———. Letter to Dr. Alfred V. Kidder, 11 January 1961, 1 page.
White, Alexander M. Letter to Mr. A. V. Kidder, 26 December 1956, 1 page.
Williams, Howell. Letter to Dr. Kidder, 6 July 1952, 4 pages.

XVI. *Correspondance from Kidder to Madeleine A. Kidder*

Kidder, A. V. Letter to "Bestest," 30 May 1929, 11 pages.

XVII. *Correspondence from Kidder to His Father, Alfred Kidder*

Kidder, A. V. Letter to Papa, 12 (no month) 1922, 8 pages.

XVIII. *Miscellaneous Correspondence with Colleagues*

Britten, Marion Hale. Memorandum to the Members of the Committee on Survey of South American Indians, Division of Anthropology and Psychology, National Research Council, 7 July 1937, 1 page, carbon copy, with attachment, "Distributional survey of South American Culture: Outline of Project," written by Dr. John W. Copper, Chairman, Committee on Survey of South American Indians, 1 page, carbon copy.
———. Memorandum to the Members of the Committee on Survey of South American Indians, Division of Anthropology and Psychology, National Research Council, 26 July 1937, 1 page.
Bumpus, H. C. Circular letter to the Members of the Advisory Board, 19 November 1937, 1 page.

————. Letter to Dr. Kidder, 3 December 1937, 1 page.

Chapman, Kenneth. Letter to Ted, 2 June 1961, 2 pages.

DiPeso, Charles C. Letter to Dr. Kidder, 6 June 1961, 2 pages.

Fejos, Paul. Letter to Dr. Alfred V. Kidder, 1 page.

Flour [?], Fred. Letter to Mr. Kidder, 27 October 1945, 1 page.

Garrido, Luis. Letter to Sr. Alfred V. Kidder, 28 August 1951, 1 page.

Greenwood, Eleanor. 17 July 1945, 1 page.

Guthe, Carl. 19 March 1959, 1 page.

Haury, Emil W. Letter to Dr. A. V. Kidder, 11 December 1959, 1 page.

Hunter, W. S. Letter to Dr. A. V. Kidder, 18 November 1937, 1 page.

Cammerer, Arno B. Letter to Dr. Alfred V. Kidder, 1 June 1937, 1 page, with attachment of paper, "The Relationship of National Parks to Human Welfare," 10 pages.

Coleman, S. V. Letter to Professor Alfred V. Kidder, 7 June 1937, 1 page, with attachment, "Dictionary of American History," 1 page.

Caso, Alfonso. Letter to Sr. Dr. Alfred V. Kidder, 6 August 1941, 1 page.

Duane, William North. Letter to Ted, June, no day or year, 2 pages.

Kidder, A. V. Letter to Mrs. Truxton Beale, 1 August 1941, 1 page, carbon copy.

————. Letter to Dr. H. C. Bumpus, 1 December 1937, 1 page, carbon copy, answers Circular Letter from Bumpus of 19 November 1937, 1 page, carbon copy.

————. Letter to Dr. H. C. Bumpus, 6 December 1937, 1 page, carbon copy, answers Bumpus letter of 3 December 1937.

————. Letter to Mr. Arno B. Cammerer, 12 May 1937, 1 page, carbon copy.

————. Letter to Dr. Alfonso Caso, 21 August 1941, 1 page, carbon copy, answers Caso letter of 6 August 1941.

————. Letter to M. le Docteur André Cheynier, 16 July 1937, carbon copy.

————. Letter to R. V. Coleman, 9 June 1937, carbon copy, answers Coleman's letter of 7 June 1937.

————. Letter to William Duane, 29 June 1937, 1 page, carbon copy, answers Duane's letter of June, no day or year.

————. Letter to Mr. D. L. Hebard, 27 December 1937, 1 page, carbon copy.

————. Letter to Dr. Walter S. Hunter, 2 August 1937, 1 page, carbon copy.

————. Letter to Dr. Walter S. Hunter, 22 December 1937, 1 page, carbon copy, answers Hunter's letter of 18 November 1937.

————. Letter to Dr. James King, 2 June 1945, 1 page, carbon copy.

————. Letter to Mr. A. D. Krieger, 25 July 1945, 1 page, carbon copy.

————. Letter to Dr. Alfred L. Kroeber, 1 May 1945, 1 page, carbon copy.

————. Letter to Dr. Waldo C. Leland, 1 November 1937, 1 page, carbon copy, answers Leland letter of 3 November 1937.

————. Letter to Mr. Augustus P. Loring, Jr., 22 November 1937, 1 page, carbon copy.

————. Letter to Theodore Lyman, Esq., 7 December 1945, 1 page, carbon copy, answers Lyman letter of 30 November 1945.

————. Letter to Sr. Eduardo Noguera, 22 September 1941, 1 page, carbon copy, answers Noguera letter of 10 September 1941.

————. Letter to Dr. Frank Thone, 19 October 1937, 1 page, carbon copy, answers Thone letter of 16 October 1937.

————. Note to Dr. (Alfred) Tozzer, 5 October 1937, 1 page, with handwritten reply by Tozzer, 7 October 1937.

————. Letter to Hon. Grover Whalen, 20 May 1937, 1 page, carbon copy, answers Whalen letter of 17 May 1937.

————. Letter to Miss Eleanor Wilson, 18 December 1945, 1 page, carbon copy, answers Wilson letter of 14 December 1945.

Leland, Waldo G. Letter to Ted, 3 November 1937, 1 page.

Linglebach, William E. Letter to Ted, 16 November 1959, 2 pages.

————. Letter to Ted, 20 May 1961, 1 page.

Lyman, Theodore. Letter to Kidder, 28 November 1937, 1 page.

Meighan, C. Letter to Dr. Kidder, 18 May 1959, 1 page.

Millikan, Robert A. Memorandum to the Members of the Committee on Policies, National Research Council, 8 May 1937, 2 pages.

Morison, S. E. Letter to Ted, 11 October 1938, 1 page.

O'Neal, Vivan. Letter to Dr. Kidder, 17 September 1959, 2 pages.

Noguera, Eduardo. Letter to Sr. Doctor Alfred V. Kidder, 10 September 1941, 1 page.

Parker, W. Letter to Mr. Alfred V. Kidder, 17 December 1945, 1 page.

Thone, Frank. Letter to Dr. Kidder, 16 October 1937, 1 page.

Smith, Watson. Letter to Dr. A. V. Kidder, 22 June 1959, 1 page.

Thomas, Tully H. Letter to Dr. A. V. Kidder, 27 October 1951, 2 pages.

Whalen, Grover. Letter to Dr. Kidder, 17 May 1937, 1 page.

Wilson, Eleanor. Letter to Mr. Alfred Kidder, 14 December 1946, 1 page.

XIX. Miscellaneous Correspondence Not Addressed to Kidder

Ickes, Harold L. (Secretary of the Interior) Letter to Dr. Herman C. Bumpus, 15 November 1937, 2 pages, carbon copy.

————. Letter to The Director, The National Park Service, 15 November 1937, 1 page, carbon copy, with attachment "Statement by the Advisory Board of the National Park Service Respecting Its Functions and Duties and the Manner of Performing Them," signed by H. C. Bumpus, no date, 3 pages, carbon copy.

XX. *Condolences to Madeleine A. Kidder on the Death of A. V. Kidder*

Adele. 19 June 1963, 4 pages.

Alice. 12 June 1963, 2 pages.

Anne. n.d., 2 pages.

B. H. 24 July 1963, 1 page.

Babs. n.d. written Wednesday, 1 page.

Barr, Walwin. 3 July 1963, 1 page.

Barretto, Mrs. Larry. n.d. (written Thursday), 2 pages.

Bartlett, Joan H. 27 June 1963, 1 page.

Berlin, Heinrich. 2 July 1963, 2 pages.

Bill. 13 June 1963, 1 page.

Benton, Louise S. 25 June 1963, 2 pages.

Blum, Carole. 17 June 1963, 2 pages.

Boggs, Stanley H. 20 June 1963, 1 page.

Bosie. n.d., 2 pages.

Bowditch, H. 11 July 1963, 1 page.

Boyce, Eda. n.d., 2 pages.

Brambelles, Julia. 15 June 1963, 2 pages.

Bryan, Mary. n.d. (written Sunday—the sixteenth), 2 pages.

Bunoy, K. n.d., 2 pages.

Burnston, Clement M. 15 June 1963, 1 page.

Butler, Joseph (Mr. and Mrs.) and Mrs. Henry Butler. n.d., card.

Butler, Joseph G. 12 June 1963, 1 page.

Cabot, Gertrudo. 16 June 1963, 2 pages.

Chap. 11 June 1963, 1 page, with photocopy of original.

Charlotte, n.d., 3 pages.

Chimese. 7 July 1963, 2 pages.

Clarence. 13 June 1963, 2 pages.

Coffin [?], Aleie N. 14 June 1963, 1 page.

Colton, Harold S. 24 June 1963, 1 page.

Cook, Ruth. n.d. (written Saturday), 1 page.

Conklin, Ruth. 21 June 1963, 3 pages.

Coon, Carl. 29 June 1963, 1 page.

Cosgrove, Harriet S. n.d., 3 pages.

————. 12 June 1963, 3 pages.

Cur. n.d., 1 page.

Currier, Margaret. 16 June 1963, 2 pages.

Custer, Helen. n.d. (written Friday), 2 pages.

Danson, Edward B. 14 June 1963, 1 page.

Hall, Mrs. Bartow Harwood. n.d., card.
Marian. 19 June 1963, 2 pages.
Marjorie. n.d., 2 pages.
Martin, Paul S. n.d., 2 pages.
Mason, J. Alden. 16 June 1963, 1 page.
Mickey, n.d. (written Thursday), 2 pages.
Mixter, Dorothy T. n.d. (written Thursday), 2 pages.
Morss, Betty. 14 June 1963, 2 pages.
Morrow, Dwight, Jr. 13 June 1963, 2 pages.
Nan. 19 June 1963, 1 page.
Neil. n.d., 1 page.
Nick. n.d., 1 page.
Parker, Hoolie. 13 June 1963, 1 page.
Peabody, Mrs. Amelia. 27 June 1963, 2 pages.
Pollock, Mrs. Harry E.D. 17 June 1963, 2 pages.
Reed, Ellie, Cliff and Mary, and C.B. n.d., card.
Richardson, Francis B. 16 June 1963, 2 pages.
Risley, Mrs. Arthur Le Roy. 16 June 1963.
Riqua, Joan. n.d. (written Monday), 1 page.
Romero, Katie. 26 June 1963, 2 pages.
Rouse, Ben. 14 June 1963, 1 page.
Ruz, Alberto. 2 July 1963, 1 page.
Sanchez, G. 1 July 1963, 2 pages.
Satterthwaite, Mrs. Linton. 23 June 1963, 1 page.
Sayles, E.B. 13 June 1963, 1 page.
Schoelfort, Rudolf E. 17 June 1963, 2 pages.
Shapiro, Harry. 17 June 1963, 1 page.
Shepard, Anna. 14 May [June] 1963, 1 page.
Shields, M. Lawrence. 20 June 1963, 1 page.
"Sister." 19 June 1963, 2 pages.
Smith, Robert E. 13 June 1963, 1 page.
Smith, Mrs. Robert Eliot Smith. 20 June 1963, 2 pages.
Scholes, Marianne. 13 June 1963, 1 page.
Spring, John. 13 June 1963, 1 page.
Staff of the University Museum, n.d., card.
Stirling, Marion. 13 July 1963, 1 page.
Suzie. 22 July 1963, 1 page.
Sve. n.d., 2 pages.
Tax, Sol. 26 June 1963, 2 pages.
Tax, Susana. 6 July 1963, 1 page.

XXI. Condolences to Children of A. V. Kidder

XXII. Letter Fragments with No Identification of Originator

2 letter fragments

XXIII. Newspapers and Periodicals

Smart, James

　　1958 (9 November), "Museum's Jungle Team Uncovers the Glory That Was Tikal," *Philadelphia Sunday Bulletin,* 1 page.

Van Dusan, William I.

　　1930 (11 January), "Exploring the Maya with Lindbergh," *Saturday Evening Post,* pp. 40, 43, 44, 154, 155, 156, 157, 158.

————.

　　1930 (1 February), "Exploring the Maya with Lindbergh," *Saturday Evening Post,* pp. 6, 91, 92, 97, 98.

There are also thirty-nine newspaper articles without author or source, concerned with the flights over the Maya country by the Lindberghs and O. G. Ricketson, a colleague of Kidder's. There is also one article by Edward Weyer, with title of article and name of periodical missing.

XXIV. Reprints of Published Works by A. V. Kidder

1946a (16 December) "Memorandum Regarding Future Archaeological Activities," offset, 59 pages.

1946b "Memorandum for the Advisory Committee on the Division of Historical Research, Carnegie Institution of Washington," typewritten, carbon copy, 106 pages.

1950a *Review* of "Frederick Catherwood, Arch," by Victor Wolfgang von Hagen, 1950b, Oxford University Press, New York, in *American Historical Review,* no vol., 1 page.

1950b *Review* of "Incidents of Travel in Central America Chiapas, and Yucatan," by John L. Stephens, edited with an Introduction and Notes by Richard L. Predmore, 2 vols., Rutgers University Press, New Brunswick, 1949, in *American Historical Review,* no vol., 1 page.

1950c *Review* of "Scientist on the Trail: Travel Letters of A. F. Bandelier, 1880–1881," by George P. Hammond and Edgar F. Goad, Quivira Society Publications, Volume X, Berkeley, in *American Historical Review,* no vol., 1 page.

1951a *Review* of "La Ceramica de Monte Alban III," by A. Ignacio Bernal, Doctoral Dissertation, Universidad Nacional Autonoma de Mexico, 1949, mimeographed, 162 pages, in *American Antiquity,* XVII(1):67–69.

1951b *Review* of *Popol Vuh, the Sacred Book of the Ancient Quiche Maya,* English version by Delia Goetz and Sylvanus G. Morley from the Spanish translation by Adrian Recinos, University of Oklahoma Press, 1950, 267 pages, in *American Historical Review,* no. vol., pp. 105–106.

1951c "Story of the Pueblo of Pecos," *Papers of the School of American Research* 44:3–10, reprinted also in *El Palacio* 58(3), 2000 copies.

1953 *Review* of "Indian Tribes of Aboriginal America, Selected Papers of the XXIXth International Congress of Americanists," edited by Sol Tax, University of Chicago Press, Chicago, in *Hispanic American Historical Review,* no vol., pp. 260–61.

1954 *Review* of "Mogollon Cultural Continuity and Change, the Stratigraphic Analysis of Tularosa and Cardova Caves, by Paul S. Martin, John B. Rinaldo, Elaine Bluhm, Hugh C. Cutler, Roger Grange Jr., *Fieldiana: Anthropology,* Volume 40, Chicago Natural History Museum, 1952, 528 pages, in *American Antiquity,* 19(1):298–300.

1957a "European Knife Handles at Pecos—A Correction," *American Antiquity* 22(3):297–98.

1957b "Earl Halstead Morris—1889–1956," *American Antiquity* 22(4):390–97.

1959c "Diary of Sylvanus G. Morley," *Proceedings of the American Philosophical Society* 103(6):778–82.

1959d "Middle American Archaeology Since 1906," in *Middle American Anthropology,* assembled by G. R. Willey and others, pp. 1–10, Pan American Union, Social Science Monographs, Volume 5, two copies.

1959e (with E. M. Shook), "A Unique Ancient Maya Sweathouse, Guatemala," *Mitteilungen aus dem Museum für Völkerkunde in Hamburg,* 25:70–74.

1960 "Wanted: More and Better Archaeologists," *Expedition* 2(2):1–8. [This paper contains minor changes from its initial publication in 1940, "Looking Backward," in *Symposium on Characteristics of American Culture and Its Place in General Culture,* pp. 527–37, Proceedings of the American Philosophical Society, vol. 28.]

1961 "Archaeological Investigations at Kaminaljuyú, Guatemala," *Proceedings of the American Philosophical Society,* 105(6):559–70.

Also contained in the Kidder papers is a manuscript that was published by the Carnegie Institution of Washington as part of the periodical *Year Book* series.

XXV. Obituary of A. V. Kidder

Mason, J. Alden
1963 "Alfred Vincent Kidder—1885–1963," *Year Book of the American Philosophical Society,* pp. 167–72.

XXVI. Miscellaneous Materials

Byers, Douglas S.,
1956 "Annual Report of Robert F. Peabody Foundation for Archaeology," Phillips Academy, Andover, typewritten, pp. 2–3.

Davis, Emily
1937 "100 Babies Turned Loose on Desert Island Would Answer Hu-

man Riddle: 'Is Civilization an Accident?' Says Anthropologist; But It Might Take Million Years for Answers," *Science Service,* 18 November issue, offset copy, 1 page.

XXVII. *Maps of the American Southwest*

[Sent to author by Tristram Kidder, A. V. Kidder's grandson.] All maps are cut into sections and pasted on linen cloth so they could be folded and pocketed. Some have perspiration stains at the corners, and some have linen ties.

Contour map of Arizona—Verdi, dated 1910, with elevations.

Contour map of Navajo County, n.d., with elevations.

Contour map of Tusayan—St. John's Country, dated 1906, with elevations.

United States Geological Survey quadrangle maps, mounted on linen.

> Maps: Tusayan; (NE Utah—east Tavaputs); (NE Utah—Vernal-Roosevelt); (NE Utah—upper Minnie Maude—Argyle); Kaibab sheet; Diamond Cree; Mount Trumbull; San Francisco Mountains (2); Holdbrook; Chino; Canyon de Chelly; Marsh Pass; St. John's; Verde; (NE Utah, Duchesne-Myton), dated 1906.

> NE Utah, United States Geological Survey quadrangles mounted together showing route of Chaflin-Emerson 1931 expedition.

Original figures 2, 7, 8, 9, 10, 11, 12, 13, 17, from the E. T. Hall Awatovi Tree-Ring report, 1942.

E. T. Hall, tree-ring manuscript and maps for same.

XXVIII. *Dated Photographs*

Below is a listing of photographs by date and by the name of each person noted on the back of each by A. V. Kidder. Descriptions of photographs are Kidder's notes on the back of each.

1907 - Hovenweep Country, square masonry tower.

1908 - Alkali Ridge, Utah.

> Camp on Alkali Ridge, Bryon Cummings at head of table.

> Cliff Palace from Southeast rimrock, sundown, Mesa Verde.

> Jesse Nusbaum and A. V. Kidder, Mesa Verde. [photograph made into a postcard]

> Neil M. Judd, Alkali Ridge, Utah.

1911 - Pajarito Plateau, A. V. Kidder at mouth of a cave.

1912 - Mesa Verde, A. V. Kidder alongside tent "Tepee," 2 copies.

> Sprucetree House, Mesa Verde, picture of A. V. Kidder.

1914 - Clayton Wetherill and Uncle Jett, Kayenta.

> A. V. Kidder and "Boneyard Bill" Bryan, Kayenta.

A. V. Kidder and Bill Bryan, Marsh Pass, A. V. Kidder giving Bryan a haircut.

Hauling load of specimens to Kayenta from the Monuments.

On the road to Kayenta from Farmington, camp beyond Chinlee.

A. V. Kidder photograph.

Samuel J. Guernsey, Marsh Pass.

Samuel J. Guernsey, Marsh Pass excavations.

Samuel J. Guernsey, picture taken in Northern Arizona, location unknown.

Samuel J. Guernsey, different picture, location unknown.

Samuel J. Guernsey, end of season, note beard.

1915 - Visit to Pecos by Board of School of American Research, Identifications by K. M. Chapman, L–R: Mrs. Perch Jackson, J. L. Nusbaum, ?, E. L. Hewett, ?, A. V. Kidder, Percy Jackson, N. R. Fiarclough, C. F. Lummis, ?, Judge J. R. McFie, ?.

A. V. Kidder with his wife Madeleine Appleton Kidder.

Packing, Rachel and Sam Lothrop, A. V. Kidder.

Kate Murry (Romero), J. L. Nusbaum, Pecos.

J. L. Nusbaum, Pecos.

Pecos, A. V. Kidder drinking from canteen.

Burials under floor of Mission. The bodies in the coffin were those of priests.

Looking West at main mound showing three salient trenches, Pecos.

Central salient trench B, Pecos.

A. V. Kidder working on skeletons [?].

1916 - L–R: C. E. Guthe, A. V. Kidder, Cristino Varela, Martin Varela, and Mariano Quintana.

L–R: C. E. Guthe, Alfred Kidder II, A. V. Kidder, R. A. Kidder, Nicolas Encinias.

Charles Peabody, test IX [pit], Pecos.

1918- Camp Lewis, Washington. Hq. 182 Inf. Brigade, L–R: Gordon Voorhies, Adjutant, A. V. Kidder, George Hjelte, aides to General Foltz, Spring.

1920- Archaeological notes on way down Mimbres River. L–R: Wesley Bradfield, Hattie [Cosgrove?], Lansing B. Bloom, Kenneth M. Chapman.

Party in Chaco Country. L–R: seated ?, Mrs. Hewett, S. G. Morley, E. H. Morris; standing, N. M. Judd, Wesley Bradfield, ?, E. L. Hewett, A. V. Kidder, Jack Martin.

Camp of F. W. Hodge, Hawikuh. L–R: seated—F. W. Hodge, A. V. Kidder. L–R: standing—S. G. Morley, E. Coffin, S. J. Nusbaum,

Aileen Nusbaum, Eleanor Johnson, Deric Nusbaum, N. M. Judd, E. H. Morris, 3 copies.

Noon camp, Kimmenioli Valley, August 15.

National Geographic Society trip which selected Pueblo Bonito for work by Neil M. Judd, August, upper figure, S. G. Morley, Neil M. Judd at tail of wagon; driver—A. V. Kidder, E. H. Morris.

"Corn Mountain," Zuni. In photograph: Leslie Spier (side view) and A. L. Kroeber (back view).

1922 - Hattie and Dr. Kidder at mouth of Greenwood Canyon on the road out to the Gila River, "two Huskies, What?"

1923 - Preparing to start for Mesa Verde from Gallup, September. L–R: ?, Earl Morris, Ann Morris, S. G. Morley, ?, Fred Harvey lunch boxes from El Navajo.

?, E. H. Morris, Ann Morris, S. G. Morley, ?, September; provisioned before starting for Chaco.

1924 - Mrs. Morris, Mr. Morris, Ole Owens, du Chelly Canyon, November.

1925 - Idol from Kiva 12, Pecos.

L–R: Ida Sanford, Constance Vaillant, Singleton Moorehead, Mark Howe. Singleton's collection of pottery, later given to the museum at Andover.

1926 - Robert Wauchope (19 years old), Pecos, New Mexico.

1928 - A. V. Kidder and friend, Santiago Atitlán.

Dr. Kidder, Head, archaeological staff of Carnegie Institution of Washington, photo taken in the field, Yucatan.

Earl H. Morris, and A. V. Kidder.

Group E, Uaxactún, G. C. Vaillant, A. L. Smith, S. G. Morley.

1929 - Charles Lindbergh helping Ann [Morrow Lindbergh] into plane, Pecos.

1931 - Wiggins, Bolles, Ruppert, Kidder, Pollock, Stromsvik, Court of the Phalli.

Clark Wissler, J. L. Nusbaum, A. V. Kidder. Laboratory of Anthropology dedication.

Earl Morris' camp, Mummy Cave, Canon del Muerto. L–R: C. A. Amsden, Gustav Stromsvik, ?, ?, J. E. S. Thompson, ?, E. H. Morris, Kidder, Mrs. J. C. Merriam, Ole Owens, Madeleine, Amsden, September.

1937 - A. V. Kidder, Antonio Villacosta, Jane Jennings; Kaminaljuyú.

1938–1939 - Dr. Vannevar Bush; Awatovi.

1939 - Awatovi, A. V. Kidder and Jo Brew.

1943 - Paul Richard, Harriet Cosgrove; cold morning at 9th Avenue Carnegie Institution office, mending pots.

1948 - Pecos Conference, Point of Pines, J. O. Brew.
    Pecos Conference, Point of Pines, Clyde Kluckhohn.
    Pecos Conference, Point of Pines, E. H. Morris.
    Pecos Conference, Point of Pines, Arizona, A. V. Kidder and Harold S. Colton—founder of the Museum of Northern Arizona at Flagstaff, Arizona.
1952 - Ariane Brunel, half Portugese, half Swiss at site 10-50, Point of Pines—burial area. The skeleton she's working on is a female fetus, A. V. Kidder kibitzing.
    Point of Pines, Skeletons at burial site 10-50, A. V. Kidder about to bag cleaned skeletons.
    Richard and Nat Woodbury, Christmas card, 1952-Pecos Mission, Haury presenting A. V. Kidder with little silver trowel, two pictures enclosed in christmas card.
1953 - A. V. Kidder and ?
1954 - Large photograph of A. V. Kidder in front of the Pecos Mission, in case. Inscription on left cover of case reads, "To A. V. Kidder, Together with Sincere Good Wishes, From, Harry Dundahl, Santa Fe, New Mexico, January."
1956 - Point of Pines, Barbara Gandee, I think, A. V. Kidder looking at a skeleton [?].
1960 - A. V. Kidder.

XXIX. Undated Photographs

Will Barker, mountain sheep trap.
Betatakin
Mesa Redonda, L–R: ?, Byers, Kidder, Girard, Ekholm.
Casa Colorado, Chichen Itza, Joe's "Famous Pict"!
Consultation with the natives.
Burton and Hattie Cosgrove, Burton Cosgrove, Jr.
Emil Haury, presenting A. V. Kidder the University of Arizona "Medal of Merit," 41 Holden Street [Cambridge, Massachusetts].
C. E. Guthe at Pecos.
A. V. Kidder [with pipe in hand, sitting in a chair].
Kietsiel
Jack Lavery and Earl Morris near head of Adams Canyon, Gobernador district.
Lindbergh [aerial] views of Pecos, negatives in Santa Fe.
Maya Indian near Coba.
S. G. Morley and A. V. Kidder, Temple of the Initial Series, Chichén [Itzá], photograph by J. C. Merriam.

Earl Morris, entering Danies House, Mesa Verde.

Carrying encrusted plaque in its stone repository from Temple of the Chac Mool to laboratory, Chichén Itzá, Morris ahead, Stromsvik behind Morley on far side, Charlot on near, steadying, Kidder being useless, J. C. Merriam—photographer.

Pictograph, Pajarito.

Temple of the Wall Panels, Chichén Itzá, Yucatan. In the photograph are Francis and Elizabeth Proctor, who supplied funds for the excavation and repair by Karl Ruppert.

Karl Ruppert, [World] War II, American Ambulance.

Gustav Stromsvik, Copan, in Norwegian Free Navy uniform in World War II.

Antonio Tejeda, artist—Carnegie Institution of Washington, the Guatemala office.

Temple E-VII—sub. Uaxactún (Washactoon), Guatemala.

Packing skeletons, Pecos, Chistino Varela, left.

Robert Wauchope (year, location?).

XXX. Unidentified, Undated Photographs

10 photographs

INDEX TO A. V. KIDDER
CORRESPONDENCE,
AMERICAN PHILOSOPHICAL SOCIETY

I. *Letters from Franz Boas to A. V. Kidder*

1921 5 December, 1 page.
1924 14 February, 1 page.
  11 March, 1 page.
  6 November, 1 page.
1926 11 January, 1 page.
  13 January, 1 page.
  6 February, 1 page.
  24 February, 1 page.
  25 February, 1 page.
  7 June, 1 page.
  18 October, 1 page.
  21 October, 1 page.
  3 November, 1 page.
  23 November, 1 page.
1927 8 April, 1 page.
  25 May, 1 page.
  27 June, 1 page.
  18 July, 1 page.
  9 December, 1 page.
1929 3 January, 2 pages.
  4 January, 2 pages.
  7 January, 1 page.

  29 January, 1 page.
  15 April, 1 page.
  19 April, 1 page.
1931 3 February, 1 page.
  16 February, 1 page.
  18 February, 1 page.
  8 April, 1 page.
  22 April, 1 page.
  28 May, 1 page.
  27 June, 1 page.
1932 7 January, 2 pages.
  17 May, 1 page.
  31 October, 1 page.
  1 November, 1 page.
1936 20 May, 1 page.
  17 June, 1 page.
  23 October, 1 page.
1937 23 September, 1 page.
  25 October, 1 page.
  15 November, 1 page.
1941 5 May, 1 page.

II. Letters from A. V. Kidder to Franz Boas

1923 11 May, 1 page.
12 July, 1 page.
1924 16 February, 1 page.
1925 12 February, 1 page.
6 April, 1 page.
1926 12 January, 1 page.
8 February, 1 page.
23 February, 1 page.
9 June, 1 page.
19 October, 1 page.
25 October, 1 page.
26 November, 1 page.
31 December, 1 page.
1927 2 April, 1 page.
25 May, 1 page.
31 May, 1 page.
25 June, 1 page.
5 November, 1 page.
12 December, 1 page.
1928 24 September, 1 page.
1929 3 January, 1 page.
5 January, 1 page.
31 January, 1 page.
2 February, 1 page.
18 April, 1 page.
29 May, 1 page.

6 June, 1 page.
21 October, 1 page.
1 November, 1 page.
[no day] December, 1 page.
1931 8 January, 1 page.
13 February, 1 page.
17 February, 1 page.
19 February, 1 page.
9 April, 1 page.
21 April, 1 page.
20 June, 1 page.
1 July, 1 page.
7 July, 1 page.
1932 11 March, 1 page.
1 June, 1 page.
31 October, 1 page.
9 November, 1 page.
1936 13 May, 1 page.
5 June, 1 page.
19 June, 1 page.
29 October, 1 page.
2 November, 1 page.
1937 18 October, 1 page.
2 November, 1 page.
19 November, 1 page.
1940 4 October, 1 page.

III. A. V. Kidder Report to the National Research Council, Division of Anthropology and Psychology, Commission on the Study of the American Negro

1926 30 October, 3 pages.

IV. Correspondence Between A. V. Kidder and E. R. Riesen

A. V. Kidder from E. R. Riesen
1931 21 April, 1 page.

A. V. Kidder to E. R. Riesen
1931 27 April, 2 pages.

V. Letters from A. V. Kidder to Neil M. Judd

VI. Letters from Neil M. Judd to A. V. Kidder

VII. Letters from A. F. Blakeslee to A. V. Kidder
(in A. F. Blakeslee Papers)

1930 17 June, 1 page.
    24 June, 1 page.
    30 August, 1 page.
    20 October, 1 page.

    28 October, 1 page.
    14 November, 1 page.
1943 21 June, 1 page.

VIII. Letters from A. V. Kidder to A. F. Blakeslee
(in A. F. Blakeslee Papers)

1930 21 June, 1 page.
    28 August, 1 page.
    2 September, 1 page.

    30 October, 1 page.
    20 November, 1 page.
1931 6 January, 1 page.
1943 22 June, 1 page.

IX. Letters from Charles B. Davenport to A. V. Kidder
(in Charles B. Davenport Papers)

1926 21 October, 1 page.
    28 October, 2 pages.
    1 November, 1 page.
    3 November, 3 pages.
    29 November, 1 page.
1927 25 February, 1 page.
    23 March, 1 page.
1929 9 February, 1 page.
    15 February, 1 page.
    26 February, 1 page.
    4 March, 1 page.
    21 May, 1 page.
1930 27 February, 1 page.
    6 March, 1 page.

    17 March, 1 page.
    10 May, 1 page.
    19 May, 2 pages.
    28 August, 1 page.
    3 September, 1 page.
1931 16 May, 1 page.
    19 May, 1 page.
    19 November, 1 page.
1932 11 January, 1 page.
    14 December, 1 page.
    20 December, 1 page.
    22 December, 1 page.
1933 21 March, 1 page.

X. Letters from A. V. Kidder to Charles B. Davenport
(in Charles B. Davenport Papers)

1926 19 October, 2 pages.
    25 October, 1 page.

    29 October, 1 page, with at-
    tached Memorandum to Mem-

bers of the Committee on a Study of the American Negro, post-dated 30 October, from A. V. Kidder, 3 pages.
5 November, 1 page.
27 November, 1 page.
1 December, 1 page.
1927 23 February, 1 page.
28 February, 1 page.
25 June, 1 page.
1929 12 February, 1 page.
16 February, 1 page.
21 February, 1 page.
12 March, 1 page.

23 May, 1 page.
27 May, 1 page.
1930 3 March, 1 page.
7 May, 1 page.
16 May, 1 page.
22 May, 2 pages.
2 September, 1 page.
5 September, 1 page.
1931 18 May, 1 page.
23 May, 1 page.
12 November, 1 page.
1932 8 January, 1 page.
12 January, 1 page.
16 December, 2 pages.
22 December, 1 page.

XI. *Miscellaneous Correspondence in Charles B. Davenport Papers*

Letter from J. I. Goodrich to Kidder
1929 16 February, 1 page.
Letter from Kidder to J. C. Merriam
1932 12 January, 1 page.
Letter from T. R. Johnson to Davenport
1931 23 May, 1 page.

1927 10 March Memorandum to the Members of the Committee on a Study of the American Negro, Division of Anthropology and Psychology (National Research Council) from A. V. Kidder, 1 page.

XII. *Correspondence in Leonard Carmichael Papers*

Letter from Carmichael to Kidder
1962 12 March, 1 page.

Letter from Kidder to Carmichael
1962 7 March, 1 page.

XIII. *Correspondence in Leslie C. Dunn Papers*

Letter from Kidder to Merriam
1936 19 June, 2 pages.
Letter from Dunn to Kidder
1929 25 February, 1 page.
Letters from Kidder to Dunn

1929 21 February, 1 page.
1935 25 May, 1 page.
1 August, 1 page.
1936 17 October, 1 page.
Letter from Dunn to Davenport

1930 28 February, 1 page.
Letter from Davenport to Dunn
1927 27 February, 1 page.
Letter from Laughlin to Kidder
1936 16 June, 1 page, with attach-
ments on budgetary requirements for a special committee on
eugenics and a history of the
Eugenics Record Office, 10
pages.
n.d. "Memorandum for Dr. Merriam re: Meeting of Advisory
Committee on Eugenics Record
Office," A. V. Kidder

XIV. Correspondence in Simon Flexner Papers

Telegrams to Simon Flexner
1931 18 May, 1 page.
19 May, 1 page.

Telegram to A. V. Kidder
1931 19 May, 1 page.

XV. Letters to A. V. Kidder from William E. Lingelbach
(in William E. Lingelbach Papers)

n.d. postcard.

1960 8 February, 1 page.

XVI. Letters to William E. Lingelbach from A. V. Kidder
(to William E. Lingelbach Papers)

1958 12 January, 1 page.
1959 21 March, 1 page.
5 April, 1 page.
9 November, 1 page.
1960 18 January, 1 page.
12 February, 1 page.
22 February, 1 page.
1961 26 April, 1 page.
6 June, 1 page.

INDEX TO THE
A. V. KIDDER–HAROLD S. COLTON
CORRESPONDENCE,
MUSEUM OF NORTHERN ARIZONA

I. Letters from A. V. Kidder to Harold S. Colton

1926 7 October, 1 page, 2 copies.

1928 8 June, 1 page.

4 October, 1 page.

19 October, 1 page.

27 November, 1 page.

10 December, 1 page.

20 December, 1 page.

1929 12 September, 1 page.

1932 7 May, 1 page.

21 May, 1 page.

18 August, 1 page.

1937 [?], 1 page, written from Aztec.

2 December, 1 page.

1939 5 July, 1 page.

31 September, 1 page.

1951 12 May, 1 page.

1953 2 July, 1 page.

1957 5 June, 1 page.

29 August, 1 page.

1960 3 January, 2 pages.

29 August, postcard.

1961 16 May, 1 page.

26 May, 1 page.

6 June, 2 pages.

20 June, 1 page.

12 July, 1 page.

12 December, 1 page.

1962 24 July, 1 page.

II. Letters from Harold S. Colton to A. V. Kidder

1926 11 October, 1 page, 2 copies.

1928 1 June, 1 page.

25 September, 1 page.

17 September, 1 page, carbon copy.

5 December, 2 pages.

16 December, 2 pages.

1932 2 May, 1 page.

14 May, 1 page, with copy of invitation to second Pecos Conference, n.d., from A. V. Kidder, 1 page.

16 May, 1 page.
1939 10 July, 1 page.
9 October, 1 page.
6 December, 1 page.
1953 13 January, 1 page.

23 July, 1 page.
1957 31 May, 2 pages.
13 August, 2 pages.
1958 12 November, 1 page.
1961 5 July, 2 pages.

Bibliography

Archival collections directly cited in the text are identified as follows:

ATM: Alfred M. Tozzer Papers, Peabody Museum Archives, Harvard University

AVK: Alfred Vincent Kidder Papers, Harvard University Archives (Contains A. V. Kidder's unpublished papers and memoirs designated as AVK I, AVK II, AVKIII.)

ELH: Edgar Lee Hewett Papers, Museum of New Mexico

SGM: Sylvanus G. Morley Diaries, Peabody Museum Archives, Harvard University.

TL: Alfred Marsten Tozzer Library, Harvard University

Adams, Richard E. W.
1960 "Manuel Gamio and Stratigraphic Excavation," *American Antiquity* 26(1):99.

Amsden, Charles
1927 "The Pecos Conference," *The Masterkey* 1(4):14–18.
1929 "The Second Pecos Conference," *The Masterkey* 17:317–25.

Ascher, Robert
1961 "Analogy in Archaeological Interpretation," *Southwestern Journal of Anthropology* 17:317–25.

Bandelier, Adolf F.
1881 "Report on the Ruins of the Pueblo of Pecos," *Papers of the Archaeological Institute of America*, American Series 1(2):1–114.
1890a "Contributions to the History of the Southwestern Portion of the United States," *Papers of the Archaeological Institute of America*, American Series 5.
1890b *Investigations Among the Indians of the Southwestern United States Carried on Mainly in the Years from 1880 to 1885, Papers of the Archaeologi-*

191

cal Institute of America, American Series 3, part 1, Peabody Museum of Archaeology and Ethnology, Harvard University, Cambridge.

Batres, Leopoldo

1906 *Teotihuacán o la Ciudad Sagrada de los Tolteca*, Mexico, D. F.

Bastian, Adolph

1876 "Die Monumente in Santa Lucia Cotzumalhuapa," *Zeitschrift fur Ethnologie* 8:322–36, 403–4, Berlin.

Beale, Marie (Oge)

1930 *The Modern Magic Carpet: Air Jaunting over the Ancient East*, J. H. Furot, Baltimore

1932 *Flight into America's Past: Inca Peaks and Maya Jungles*, Putnam and Sons, New York.

Binford, Lewis R.

1968a "Some Comments on Historical Versus Processual Archaeology," *Southwestern Journal of Anthropology* 24:267–75.

1978 *Nunamiut Ethno-Archaeology*, Academic Press, New York.

1968b "Methodological Considerations of the Archaeological Use of Ethnographic Data," in *Man the Hunter*, ed. by R. Lee and I. Devore, pp. 268–73, Aldine Publishing Company, Chicago.

Binford, Sally

1968 "Ethnographic Data and Understanding the Pleistocene," in *Man the Hunter*, ed. by R. Lee and I. Devore, pp. 274–74, Aldine Publishing Company, Chicago.

Boas, Franz

1913 "Archaeological Investigations in the Valley of Mexico by the International School, 1911–1912," *Proceedings, Eighteenth International Congress of Americanists* 1:176–79.

Brew, John Otis

1946 "Archaeology of Alkali Ridge, Southwestern Utah: With a Review of the Prehistory of the Mesa Verde Division of the San Juan and Some Observations on Archaeological Systematics," *Papers of the Peabody Museum of Archaeology and Ethnology, Harvard University* 21:24–30.

Brinton, Daniel G.

1882 *The Maya Chronicles*, Brinton's Library of Aboriginal American Literature, number 6, Philadelphia.

1885 *The Annals of the Cakchiquels*, Brinton's Library of Aboriginal American Literature, number 6, Philadelphia.

Brunhouse, Robert L.

1971 *Sylvanus Morley and the World of the Ancient Mayas*, University of Oklahoma Press, Norman.

Catherwood, Frederick
 1844 *Views of Ancient Monuments in Central America, Chiapas, and Yucatan*, Vizetelly, London.
Charnay, Desiré
 1887 *The Ancient Cities of the New World*, Harper, New York.
Chauvenet, Beatrice
 1983 *Hewett and Friends: A Biography of Santa Fe's Vibrant Era*, Museum of New Mexico Press, Santa Fe.
Colton, Harold
 1928 Letter to A. V. Kidder, 17 October, AVK.
 1932 Letter to Dr. A. V. Kidder, 14 May, AVK.
 1953 Letter to Dr. A. V. Kidder, 23 July, AVK.
Cordell, Linda S.
 1984 *Prehistory of the Southwest*, Academic Press, Orlando, Florida.
Cushing, Frank H.
 1890 "Preliminary Notes on the Origin, Working Hypothesis, and Primary Researches of the Hemenway Southwestern Archaeological Expedition," in *Congrès International des Americanistes, 1889*, Berlin.
Davis, Nuel Pharr
 1968 *Lawrence and Oppenheimer*, Simon and Schuster, New York.
Deuel, Leo
 1969 *Flights Into Yesterday*, St. Martin's Press, New York.
Dixon, Roland B.
 1913 "Some Aspects of North American Archaeology," *American Anthropologist* 15:549–77.
 1930 "Anthropology, 1866–1929," in *The Development of Harvard University*, ed. by Samuel Eliot Morison, pp. 202–15, Harvard University Press, Cambridge.
Eliot, Alexander
 1974 "Eliot of Harvard," *American Heritage* 25(5)(August), American Heritage Publishing Company, New York.
Emory, William H.
 1848 "Notes of a Military Reconnaissance from Fort Leavenworth, in Missouri, to San Diego, in California, Including Parts of the Arkansas, Del Norte, and Gila Rivers," 30th Congress, 1st Session, *Senate Executive Docket 7*, Washington, D. C.
Fewkes, Jesse W.
 1930 *Tepoztlán, A Mexican Village: A Study of Folk Life*, Chicago, University of the Bureau of American Ethnology, part 2, number 11, Washington, pp. 519–742.

Fletcher, John G.

1937 *Life is My Song*, Farrar and Rinehart, New York.

Forstemann, Ernst W.

1906 "Commentary on the Maya Manuscripts in the Royal Public Library of Dresden," *Papers of the Peabody Museum* 4(2):49–266, Cambridge, Mass.

Gamio, Manuel

1913 "Arqueología de Atzcapotzalo, D. F. México," *Proceedings, Eighteenth International Congress of Americanists*, pp. 180–87.

Gann, Thomas W. F.

1900 "Mounds in Northern Honduras," *Bureau of American Ethnology, Nineteenth Annual Report*, part 2:655–92.

Givens, Douglas R.

1982 "The Impact of A. V. Kidder on the Carnegie Institution and American Archaeology," paper read at 81st Annual Meeting of the American Anthropological Association, Washington, D. C.

1989 "Alfred Vincent Kidder and Archaeological Field Work," paper read at "Networks of the Past": The Third Annual Symposium on the History of Archaeology, Annual Meeting of the American Anthropological Association, Washington, D. C.

Gladwin, Winifred, and Harold S. Gladwin.

1928 "A Method for Designation of Ruins in the Southwest," *Medallion Papers*, Number 1, Pasadena.

1929 "The Red-on-Buff Culture of the Gila Basin," *Medallion Papers*, number 3, Globe, Arizona.

1935 "The Eastern Range of the Red-on-Buff Culture," *Medallion Papers*, number 16, Globe, Arizona.

Glock, Albert E.

1985 "Tradition and Change in Two Archaeologies," *American Antiquity* 50(2):468.

Goodman, Joseph T.

1897 "The Archaic Maya Inscriptions," in *Biologia Centrali Americana*, ed. by A. P. Maudslay, part 8, appendix to volume 1, Porter and Dulau, London.

Gould, Richard A., and Patty Jo Watson.

1982 "A Dialogue on the Meaning and Use of Analogy in Ethnological Reasoning," *Journal of Anthropological Archaeology* 1:355–81.

Griffin, James B.

1959 "The Pursuit of Archaeology in the United States," *American Anthropologist* 61:379–89.

Guernsey, Samuel J.
1931 "Explorations in Northeastern Arizona," *Papers of the Peabody Museum of American Archaeology and Ethnology*, vol. 1, number 1, Harvard University, Cambridge, Mass.

Guthe, Carl E.
1917 "The Pueblo Ruin at Rowe, New Mexico," *El Palacio* 4(4): 33–39.

Haag, William G.
1986 "Field Methods in Archaeology," in *American Archaeology Past and Future*, ed. by David J. Meltzer, Don D. Fowler, and Jeremy A. Sabloff, pp. 63–76, Smithsonian Institution Press, Washington, D. C.

Haury, Emil W.
1936a "Some Southwestern Pottery Types, Series IV," *Medallion Paper 19*, Gila Pueblo, Globe, Arizona.
1936b "The Mogollon Culture of Southwestern New Mexico," *Medallion Paper 20*, Gila Pueblo, Globe, Arizona.
1937 "A Pre-Spanish Rubber Ball from Arizona," *American Antiquity*, 2(4):282–88.
1940 "Excavations in the Forestdale Valley, East-Central Arizona," *University of Arizona Social Science Bulletin 12*, Tucson.
1987 Personal Communication, University of Arizona, Tucson.

Hewett, Edgar Lee
1904 "Studies on the Extinct Pueblo of Pecos," *American Anthropologist* 6:426–39.
1909 "Archaeology of Rio Grande Valley," *Out West* 31(2):692–719.
1912 "The Excavation of Quirigua, Guatemala, by the School of American Archaeology," *Proceedings of the XVIII International Congress of Americanists*, London.
1913 "The Rio Grande Valley, New Mexico," in *The Physiography of the Rio Grande Valley, New Mexico, in Relation to Pueblo Culture*, by Edgar Lee Hewett, Junius Henderson, and Wilfred William Robbins, Smithsonian Institution, Bureau of American Ethnology, Bulletin 54, Washington, D. C.
1916 "The School of American Archaeology," *Art and Archaeology* 4(6): 317–29.
1930 *Ancient Life in the American Southwest*, Bobbs-Merrill Company, Indianapolis.
1930[?] Letter to A. V. Kidder, May 14, ELH.
1943 "Making Archaeologists," chapter 20, in *Campfire and Trail*, pp. 149–54, University of New Mexico Press, Albuquerque.

Hinsley, Curtis M., Jr.

1981 *Savages and Scientists*, Smithsonian Institution Press, Washington, D. C.

1986 "Edgar Lee Hewett and the School of American Research in Santa Fe," in *American Archaeology Past and Future*, ed. by David J. Meltzer, Don D. Fowler, and Jeremy A. Sabloff, pp. 217–33, Smithsonian Institution Press, Washington, D. C.

Holmes, William H.

1876 "Report on the Geology of the North-Western Portion of Elk Range," in *Eighth Annual Report, United States Geological and Geographical Survey of the Territories for the Year 1874*, pp. 59–71, Washington, D. C.

1878 "Report on the Ancient Ruins of Southwestern Colorado, Examined During the Summers of 1875 and 1876," in *Tenth Annual Report of the U. S. Geological and Geographical Survey of the Territories, 1876*, pp. 383–408, Washington, D. C.

1886 "Pottery of the Ancient Pueblos," in *Fourth Report of the Bureau of Ethnology*, pp. 257–360, Washington, D. C.

1895–97 *Archaeological Studies Among the Ancient Cities of Mexico*, Field Columbian Museum Anthropological Series, 2(1), Chicago.

1914 Telegram from Holmes to Hewett, 15 January, 1 page, ELH.

Hooton, Earnest A.

1930 "The Indians of Pecos Pueblo, a Study of Their Skeletal Remains," *Papers of the Phillips Academy, Southwestern Expedition*, number 4, Yale University Press, New Haven.

Hough, Walter

1933 "William Henry Holmes (1846–1933), *American Anthropologist* 35:752–64.

Jackson, William H.

1876 "Ancient Ruins in Southwestern Colorado," in *Annual Report of the U. S. Geological and Geographical Survey Report of the Territories, 1874*, pp. 367–81, Washington, D. C.

1878 "Report on the Ancient Ruins Examined in 1875 and 1877," *United States Geological Survey of the Territories for 1876*, pp. 411–50.

Jenks, A. E.

1913 "Report on the Science of Anthropology in the Western Hemisphere and the Pacific Islands," in *Reports Upon the Present Condition and Future Needs of the Science of Anthropology*, presented by W. H. R. Rivers, A. E. Jenks, and S. G. Morley, Carnegie Institution of Washington, Washington, pp. 29–59.

Joyce, Thomas A.

1914 *Mexican Archaeology*, Putnam, London.

Judd, Neil M.

1917a "Archaeological Reconnaissance in Western Utah," in *Smithsonian Miscellaneous Collections*, vol. 66, number 17, pp. 103–8, Washington, D. C.

1917b "Notes on Certain Prehistoric Habitations in Western Utah," in *Proceedings, 19th International Congress of Americanists*, pp. 119–24, Washington, D. C.

1918 "Archaeological Work in Arizona and Utah," *Smithsonian Miscellaneous Collections* 68(12):74–83.

1920 "Archaeological Investigations in Utah and Arizona," *Smithsonian Miscellaneous Collections* 72(1):66–69.

1922 "Archaeological Investigations at Pueblo Bonito, New Mexico," *Smithsonian Miscellaneous Collections* 72(15):106–17.

1954 "The Material Culture of Pueblo Bonito," *Smithsonian Miscellaneous Collections*, vol. 124, Smithsonian Institution, Washington, D. C.

Kidder, Alfred Vincent

n.d. "A Collection of Remembrances of the Maya and Pecos Times," Guatemala City, AVK I.

n.d. Handwritten note on J. C. Meriam, AVK.

n.d. "The Indian-South of Us," typescript, 12 pages, AVK.

1901 "A Bittern at Close Range," *Bird Lore* 3:173.

1904 Diary of A. V. Kidder, pp. 1–120, AVK.

1907a Diary of A. V. Kidder, 14 January-29 July, pp. 1–112, AVK.

1907b Diary of A. V. Kidder, August, pp. 1–51, AVK.

1910 "Explorations in Southeastern Utah in 1908," *American Journal of Archaeology*, 2nd ser., 14:337–59.

1913 "Some Undescribed Ruins of the Historic Period from the Upper San Juan, New Mexico," *American Journal of Archaeology* 17:89–90.

1914 "Southwestern Ceramics: Their Value in Reconstructing the History of Ancient Cliff Dwelling and Pueblo Tribes: An Exposition from the Point of View of Type Distinction," unpublished doctoral dissertation, Harvard University, Cambridge.

1915 "The Pottery of the Pajarito Plateau and of Some Adjacent Regions in New Mexico," *Memoirs, American Anthropological Association* 2(6):407–62.

1916a "The Pueblo of Pecos," *Papers of the School of American Archaeology*, 33:43–50.

1916b "Archaeological Explorations at Pecos, New Mexico," *Proceedings of the National Academy of Sciences* 2:119–23.

1917a "A Design Sequence from New Mexico," *Proceedings of the National Academy of Sciences* 3:369–70.

——— (with M. A. Kidder)

1917b "Notes on the Pottery of Pecos," *American Anthropologist* 19:325–60.

1917c "Prehistoric Cultures of the San Juan Drainage," in *Proceedings of the 19th International Congress of Americanists*, pp. 108–13.

1920a "Ruins of the Historic Period in the Upper San Juan Valley, New Mexico," *American Anthropologist* 22:322–29.

1920b Letter to Edgar Hewett, May, ELH.

1924 *An Introduction to the Study of Southwestern Archaeology With a Preliminary Account of the Excavations at Pecos*, Phillips Academy of Archaeology, Yale University Press, New Haven.

1926 "The Trend of Archaeological Research," *Art and Archaeology* 22:223.

1927a "Southwestern Archaeological Conference," *Science*, 66:489–91.

1927b "Early Man in America," *Masterkey* 1(5):5–13.

1928a "The Present State of Knowledge of American History and Civilization Prior to 1942," *Bulletin Des Sciences Historiques* 1:749–53.

1928b Letter to Harold S. Colton, 17 October, AVK.

1929a "Air Exploration of the Maya Country," *Bulletin of the Pan American Union* 63:1200–1205.

1929b "The Discovery of Ruined Maya Cities," *Science* 70:xii–xiii.

1929c Telegram to Madeleine Kidder, 10 October, AVK.

1929d Letter to Colonel Lindbergh, no month or day, AVK.

1930a "Annual Report of the Chairman, Division of Historical Research," in *Carnegie Institution of Washington, Year Book 29*, pp. 91–121, Carnegie Institution of Washington, Washington, D. C.

1930b "An Archaeological Research and Its Ramifications," *Scientific Monthly* 21:145–50.

1930c "Conference at Chichén Itzá," *Science* 71:391–92.

1930d Letter to Colonel Lindbergh, 25 June, AVK.

1930e Letter to Colonel Lindbergh, 15 July, AVK.

1930f Kidder, Diary, 1930:25–32.

1931a "The Pottery of Pecos," *Papers of the Southwest Expedition, Phillips Academy*, Robert S. Peabody Foundation for Archaeology, Yale University Press, New Haven.

1931b *Year Book 30*, Carnegie Institution of Washington, Washington, D. C.

1931c "The Future of Man in the Light of the Past: The Viewpoint of an Archaeologist," *Scientific Monthly* 22:289–93.

1932a *The Artifacts of Pecos*, Phillips Academy of Archaeology, Yale University Press, New Haven.

1932b Letter to Harold S. Colton, 7 May, AVK.

1932c Letter to Harold S. Colton, 18 August, AVK.

1933 Diary, 1–351, AVK.

1935a "Annual Report of the Chair of the Division of Historical Research," *Year Book 34*, Carnegie Institution of Washington, Washington, D. C.

1935b "Notes on the Ruins of San Agustín Acasaguastlán, Guatemala," *Contributions to American Archaeology*, number 15, Carnegie Institution of Washington, Washington, D. C.

1935c "The Development of Maya Research," in *Proceedings of the 2nd General Assembly, Pan American Institute of Geography and History*, pp. 218–25.

1936 "The Pottery of Pecos," vol. 2, *Papers of the Phillips Academy of Archaeology*, Yale University Press, New Haven.

1937 "The Development of Maya Research," in *Proceedings of the Second General Assembly, Pan American Institute of Geography and History, 1935*, pp. 218–25, U. S. Department of State Conference Series, number 28, Government Printing Office, Washington, D. C.

1939a "The Pottery of Pecos," vol. 2, in *Papers of the Southwest Expedition*, number 7, Department of Archaeology, Phillips Academy, pp. 596–611, Yale University Press, New Haven.

1939b Diary, 1 January–31 December, pp. 1–250, AVK.

1940 "Looking Backward," *Proceedings* 83:527–37, American Philosophical Society.

1946a "Memorandum Regarding Future Archaeological Activities," Division of Historical Research, Carnegie Institution of Washington, typewritten, dated 16 December, pp. 1–59, AVK.

1946b "Memorandum for the Advisory Committee on the Division of Historical Research," Carnegie Institution of Washington, typewritten, dated 16 December, pp. 1–105, AVK.

1949 "With H. S. and C. B. Cosgrove, the Pendleton Ruin, Hidalgo County, New Mexico," *Contributions to American Anthropology and History*, Carnegie Institution of Washington, Publication 585, Washington, D. C.

1953 "Comments," in *An Appraisal of Anthropology Today*, ed. by Sol Tax, pp. 257–58, University of Chicago Press, Chicago.

1954 "Rambling Reminiscences," preliminary draft by Alfred Vincent Kidder concerning his family, background, childhood, education, and professional colleagues, pp. 1–163, AVK II.

1957 [1956 or 1957] "Personal Remembrances," tape-recorded interviews with Alfred Kidder, Gordon R. Willey, J. O. Brew, and Fay-Cooper Cole, transcribed by Katherine [Willey?], pp. 1–83, AVK III.

1958 "Pecos, New Mexico: Archaeological Notes," *Papers of the Robert S. Peabody Foundation for Archaeology*, vol. 5, Phillips Academy, Andover, Mass.

1959a "Middle American Archaeology since 1906, " in *Pan American Union*, pamphlet, pp. 1–10, Organization of American States, Washington, D. C.

1959b "The Diary of Sylvanus G. Morley," *Proceedings of the American Philosophical Society* 103:778–82.

1960 Letter to Harold Colton, 3 January, AVK.

1961 "Archaeological Investigations at Kaminaljuyú, Guatemala," *Proceedings of the American Philosophical Society* 105:559–70.

———— and Samuel J. Guernsey

1919 "Archaeological Explorations in Northeastern Arizona," *Bureau of American Ethnology*, Bulletin 65, U. S. Government Printing Office, Washington, D. C.

———— and Anna O. Shepard

1936 "Pottery of Pecos" (The Glase-Paint Culinary and Other Wares), *Papers of the Southwest Expedition, No. 7, Vol. II*, Department of Archaeology, Phillips Academy, Andover, Mass.

———— , Jesse D. Jennings, and E. M. Shook

1946a "Excavations at Kaminaljuyú, Guatemala," *Carnegie Institution of Washington*, Publication 561, Washington, D. C.

———— and E. M. Shook

1952 "Mound E-III-3, Kaminaljuyú, Guatemala," *Carnegie Institution of Washington*, Publication 596, Contribution 53, Washington, D. C.

———— and J. E. S. Thompson

1938 "The Correlation of Maya and Christian Chronologies," in *Carnegie Institution of Washington*, Publication 501, pp. 493–510, Washington, D. C.

1958 "The Correlation of Maya and Christian Chronologies," in *Cooperation in Research*, Carnegie Institution of Washington, Washington, D. C.

Kidder, Homer H.

1899 "Ojibwa Myths & Halfbreed Tales Related by Charles and Charlotte Konawgam and Jacques la Pique, 1893–1895," unpublished, archives of the American Philosophical Society, Philadelphia, 323 lvs., Recorded with notes, 398.2/k534.

Kirchoff, Paul

    1953 "Mesoamerica," *Acta Americana* (Mexico, D. F., 1943) 1:92–107.

Kluckhohn, Clyde

    1940 "The Conceptual Nature of Middle American Studies," in *The Maya and Their Neighbors (Essays on Middle American Anthropology and Archaeology)*, ed. by Clarence L. Hay, et al., Dover Publishing Company, New York, pp. 41–51.

Kroeber, Alfred L.

    1915 "Frederic Ward Putnam (1839–1915)," *American Anthropologist* 17:712–18.

    1916 "Zuni Culture Sequences," *Proceedings of the National Academy of Sciences* 2:42–45.

Lindbergh, Charles

    n.d. Letter to Dr. Kidder, handwritten on Hotel Pancoast stationary, Miami, Florida, AVK.

    1929 Letter to Dr. Kidder, 18 December, AVK.

    1930a Letter to Dr. Kidder, ca. 1930, no day or month, AVK.

    1930b Letter to Dr. Kidder, 15 July, AVK.

    1930c Letter to Dr. Kidder, 2 December, AVK.

    1939 Letter to Dr. Kidder, 8 February, AVK.

Linton, Ralph

    1969 *The Tree of Culture*, Alfred A. Knopf, New York.

Lister, Florence C. and Robert H. Lister

    1968 *Earl Morris and Southwestern Archaeology*, University of New Mexico Press, Albuquerque.

Lothrop, Samuel K.

    1926 "Stone Sculptures from Finca Areuelo," *Indian Notes, Museum of the American Indian* 3:147–71, New York.

Maler, Teobart.

    1901 *Researches in the Central Portion of the Usumatsintla Valley*, Memoirs of the Peabody Museum 2(1), Cambridge, Mass.

    1903 *Researches in the Central Portion of the Usumatsintla Valley*, Memoirs of the Peabody Museum 2(2), Cambridge, Mass.

    1908 *Explorations of the Upper Usumatsintla and Adjacent Region: Altar de Sacrificios, Seibal, Itsilmte-Sacluk, Cankuen*, Memoirs of the Peabody Museum 4(4), Cambridge, Mass.

Mark, Joan
    1980 *Four Anthropologists: An American Science in its Early Years*, pp. 23–150.
Martin, Paul S., Laurence Roys, and Gerhardt Von Bonin
    1936 "Lowry Ruin in Southwestern Colorado," *Field Museum of Natural History Anthropological Series* 23(1), Chicago.
————, John Rinaldo, and Marjorie Kelly
    1940 "The SU Site Excavations at a Mogollon Village, Western New Mexico, 1939," *Field Museum of Natural History Anthropological Series* 32(1), Chicago.
Mason, J.
    1963 "Alfred Vincent Kidder (1885–1963), *Year Book of the American Philosophical Society*, Philadelphia, pp. 176–172.
Maudslay, Alfred P.
    1889–1902 *Biologia Centrali Americana*, 4 vols., Porter and Dulau, London.
McGee, W. J., William H. Holmes, et al.
    1900 "Frank Hamilton Cushing (1857–1900)," *American Anthropologist* 2:354–80.
McGregor, John C.
    1965 *Southwestern Archaeology*, 2d ed., University of Illinois Press, Urbana.
McNitt, Frank
    1957 *Richard Weatherill: Anazasi*, University of New Mexico Press, Albuquerque.
Merriam, J. C.
    1928 "Report to the President," in *Carnegie Institution of Washington, Year Book 27*, pp. 1–38, Washington, D. C.
Merwin, Raymond E. and George C. Vaillant
    1932 *The Ruins of Holmul, Guatemala*, Memoirs of the Peabody Museum 3(2), Cambridge, Mass.
Mindeleff, Cosmo
    1896 "Aboriginal Remains in Verde Valley, Arizona," in *Thirteenth Report of the Bureau of Ethnology*, pp. 179–261, Washington, D. C.
Mindeliff, Victor
    1891 "The Study of Pueblo Architecture: Tusayan and Cibola," in *Eighth Report of the Bureau of Ethnology*, pp. 3–228, Washington, D. C.
Morley, Sylvanus G.
    n.d. Letter from Morley to Hewett, 15 February, 4 pages, ELH.
    n.d. Letter from Morley to Hewett, 1 November, 2 pages, ELH.

1907a Diary, 1–31 July, pp. 1–32, SGM.

1907b Diary, 1–31 August, pp. 1–32, SGM.

1913a "Excavations at Quirigua, Guatemala," *National Geographic Magazine* 24:339–61.

1913b "Archaeological Research at the Ruins of Chichen Itza, Yucatan," in *Reports Upon the Present Conditions and Future Needs of the Science of Anthropology*, presented by W. H. R. Rivers, A. E. Jenks, and S. G. Morley, Carnegie Institution of Washington, pp. 61–83.

1914a Diary, 1 January-27 January, pp. 1–27. SGM.

1914b Letter from Morley to Hewett, 28 July, 1 page, ELH.

1919 Diary, 1 May, SGM.

1920 Diary, 2 July, pp. 94–106, SGM.

1923a Diary, 27 February, pp. 58–73, SGM.

1923b Diary, 29–30 August, pp. 420–55, SGM.

1946 *The Ancient Maya*, Stanford University Press, Stanford.

1947a Diary, 16 March, pp. 1–6, SGM.

1947b Diary, 1 April, pp. 8–9, SGM.

———— and Alfred V. Kidder

1917 "The Archaeology of the McElmo Canyon," *El Palacio* 4:41–70.

Nelson, Nels C.

1909 "Shellmounds of the San Francisco Bay Region," *University of California Publications in American Archaeology and Ethnology* 7(4):319–48.

1910 "The Ellis Landing Shellmound," *University of California Publications in American Archaeology and Ethnology* (5):357–429.

1914 "Pueblo Ruins of the Galisteo Basin, New Mexico," *Anthropological Papers of the American Museum of Natural History*, vol. 15, part 1, New York.

1916 "Chronology of the Tano Ruins, New Mexico," *American Anthropologist*, 18:159–80.

1917 "Excavation of the Aztec Ruin," *American Museum Journal* 17(2): 85–99.

1919a "The Archaeology of the Southwest: A Preliminary Report," *Proceedings of the National Academy of Sciences* 5:114–20.

1919b "The Southwest Problem," *El Palacio* 6(9):132–35.

Nordenskiöld, Gustav

1893 *The Cliff Dwellers of the Mesa Verde*, trans. by D. Lloyd Morgan, P. A. Norstedt and Soner, Stockholm.

Nutall, Zella

1910 "The Island of Sacrificious," *American Anthropologist* 12:257–95.

Parsons, Elsie Clews
    1940 "Relations Between Ethnology and Archaeology in the South-
    west," *American Antiquity*, 5:214–20.
Peckham, Stuart
    1982 Letter to D. R. Givens, 15 June, in author's possession.
Pepper, George
    1920 "Pueblo Bonito," *Anthropological Papers of the American Museum of
    Natural History* 27, Washington, D. C.
Phillips, Philip
    1955 "Alfred Marsten Tozzer," *American Antiquity* 21:72–80.
Pollock, H. E. D.
    1949 Memorandum to Division Staff, 20 April, AVK.
Prescott, William H.
    1843 *History of the Conquest of Mexico*, Harper, New York.
Prudden, T. Mitchel
    1903 "The Prehistoric Ruins of the San Juan Watershed in Utah, Ari-
    zona, Colorado, and New Mexico," *American Anthropologist* n.s. 16(1):
    33–58.
Putnam, Frederick W.
    1979 "Reports Upon Archaeological and Ethnological Collections from
    the Vicinity of Santa Barbara, California and from Ruined Pueblos in
    Arizona and New Mexico, and Certain Interior Tribes," *Report of the
    U.S. Geographical Surveys West of 100th Meridian*, vol. 7, Archaeology,
    Washington, D. C.
Redfield, Robert.
    1930 *Tepoztlán, A Mexican Village: A Study of Folk Life*, Chicago, Univer-
    sity of Chicago Press.
——— and Alfonso Villa Rojas.
    1934 *Chan Kom: A Maya Village*, Carnegie Institution of Washington,
    Washington, D. C.
Rivers, W. H. R.
    1913 "Report on Anthropological Research Outside America," in *Re-
    ports upon the Present Conditions and Future Needs of the Science of Anthropol-
    ogy*, presented by W. H. R. Rivers, A. E. Jenks, and S. G. Morley, pp.
    5–28, Carnegie Institution of Washington, Washington, D. C.
Roberts, Frank H. H., Jr.
    1929 *Shabi'eshchee Village, a Late Basketmaker Site in the Chaco Canyon, New
    Mexico*, Bureau of American Ethnology, Bulletin 92, Washington, D. C.
    1931 *The Ruins of Kiatuthlanna, Eastern Arizona*, Bureau of American
    Ethnology, Bulletin 100, Washington, D. C.

1932 *The Village of the Great Kivas on the Zuni Reservation New Mexico*, Bureau of American Ethnology, Bulletin 111, Washington, D. C.

1935 "Survey of Southwestern Archaeology," *American Anthropologist* 37:1–33.

Rohn, Arthur H.

1973 "The Southwest and Intermontane West," in *The Development of North American Archaeology*, ed. by James E. Fitting, pp. 185–211, Anchor Books, New York.

Sapir, Edward

1916 *Time Perspective in Aboriginal American Culture; a Study in Method*, Geological Survey of Canada, Anthropological Series, number 13, Ottawa.

Sapper, Karl

1895 "Altindianische Ansiedlungen in Guatemala und Chiapas," *Publications of the Königlichen Museum fur Volkerkunde* 4:13–20, Berlin.

Saville, Marshall H.

1892 "Explorations on the Main Structure of Copan, Honduras," *Proceedings of the American Association for the Advancement of Science* 41:271–75.

Schmidt, Erich F.

1928 *Time Relations of Prehistoric Pottery Types in Southern Arizona*, Anthropological Papers of the American Museum of Natural History 30(5).

Schwartz, Douglas

1981 "Four Exceptional Men: The Foundation of Northern Rio Grande Archaeology," *Archaeological Society of New Mexico Papers* 6:251–73.

Shepard, Anna O.

1942 "Rio Grande Glaze-Paint Ware: A Study Illustrating the Place of Ceramic Technological Analysis in Archaeological Research," in *Contributions to American Anthropology and History-Carnegie Institution of Washington*, ed. by Anna O. Shepard, Carnegie Institution of Washington, Washington, D. C.

1956 *Ceramics for the Archaeologist*, Carnegie Institution of Washington, Publication 609, Washington, D. C.

Simpson, J. H.

1850 "Journal of a Military Reconnaissance from Santa Fe, New Mexico, to the Navajo Country," in Reports of the Secretary of War, 31st Congress, First Session, Senate, Ex. Doc. 64, pp. 56–139, Washington, D. C.

Spier, Leslie

1918 "Notes on Some Little Colorado Ruins," *Anthropological Papers of the American Museum of Natural History* 28(4):333–62.

1919 "Ruins in the White Mountains, Arizona," *Anthropological Papers of the American Museum of Natural History* 18(5):364–87.

1931 "N. C. Nelson's Stratigraphic Technique in the Reconstruction of Prehistoric Sequences in Southwestern America," in *Methods in Social Science*, ed. by S. A. Rice, pp. 275–83, University of Chicago Press.

Spinden, Herbert J.

1913 *A Study of Maya Art*, Memoirs of the Peabody Museum 6, Cambridge, Mass.

1928 *Ancient Civilizations of Mexico and Central America*, American Museum of Natural History Handbook Series, no. 3. New York.

Stephens, John

1837 *Incidents of Travel in Egypt, Arabia Petraea and the Holy Land*, 2 vols., Harper and Brothers, New York.

1838 *Incidents of Travel in Greece, Turkey, Russia and Poland*, 2 vols., New York.

1839 *Incidents of Travel in Egypt, Arabia Petraea, and the Holy Land*, 10th Edition, Harper, New York.

1841 *Incidents of Travel in Central America, Chiapas and Yucatan*, 2 vols., New York.

1843 *Incidents of Travel in Yucatan*, 2 vols., New York.

Steward, Julian H.

1942 "The Direct Historical Approach to Archaeology," *American Antiquity* 7:337–44.

1973 *Alfred Kroeber*, Columbia University Press, New York.

Stocking, George W.

1982 "The Santa Fe Style in American Anthropology: Regional Interest, Academic Initiative and Philanthropic Policy in the First Two Decades of the Laboratory of Anthropology, Inc.," *Journal of the History of the Behavioral Sciences* 18:3–19.

Tax, Sol

1953 *Penny Capitalism: A Guatemalan Indian Economy*, University of Chicago Press, Chicago.

Taylor, Walter W., Jr.

1948 *A Study of Archaeology*, Memoir 69, American Anthropological Association, Menasha.

1954 "Southwest Archaeology, Its History and Theory," *American Anthropologist* 56:561–75.

1967 *A Study in Archaeology*, Southern Illinois University Press, Carbondale.

Thompson, Edward H.

1897 *The Chultunes of Labna, Yucatan*, Memoirs of the Peabody Museum 1(3), Cambridge, Mass.

1898 "Ruins of Xkichmook, Yucatan," *Field Columbian Museum Anthropological Series* 2(3):209–29, Chicago.

1904 *Archaeological Researches in Yucatan*, Memoirs of the Peabody Museum 3(1), Cambridge, Mass.

Thompson, J. Eric S.

1960 *Maya Hieroglyphic Writing: An Introduction*, 2d ed., University of Oklahoma Press, Norman.

1961 Letter to A. V. Kidder, 29 April, TL.

Tozzer, Alfred M.

1910 Letter of Gardner M. Lane, 28 October, ATM.

1911 "A Preliminary Study of the Prehistoric Ruins of Tikal, Guatemala," *Memoirs of the Peabody Museum* 5(2):93–135, Cambridge, Mass.

1913 "A Preliminary Study of the Prehistoric Ruins of Tikal, Guatemala," *Memoirs of the Peabody Museum* 5(3):137–201, Cambridge, Mass.

1926 "Chronological Aspects of American Archaeology," *Proceedings of the Massachusetts Historical Society* 59:283–91.

Tylor, Edward Burnett

1874 (orig. 1871) *Primitive Culture. Researches into the Development of Mythology, Religion, Language, Art, and Custom*, 2 vols., Estes and Lauriat, Boston.

Vaillant, George C.

1927 "The Chronological Significance of Maya Ceramics," unpublished Ph.D. Dissertation, Harvard University.

Watson, Patty Jo, Steven A. LeBlanc, and Charles L. Redman

1984 *Archaeological Explanation: The Scientific Method in Archaeology*, Columbia University Press, New York.

Wauchope, Robert

1965 "Alfred Vincent Kidder, 1885–1963," *American Antiquity*, 31(2) (pt. 1):149–71.

Webb, George E.

1983 *Tree Rings and Telescopes: The Scientific Career of A. E. Douglass*, University of Arizona Press, Tucson.

Willey, Gordon R.

1967 "Alfred Vincent Kidder," in *National Academy of Sciences Biographical Memoirs* 39:292–322, Columbia University Press.

1968 "One Hundred Years of American Archaeology," in *One Hundred*

Years of Anthropology, ed. by J. O. Brew, pp. 29–53, Harvard University Press, Cambridge.

———— and Phillip Phillips

1959 *Method and Theory in American Archaeology*, University of Chicago Press, Chicago.

———— and Jeremy A. Sabloff

1980 *A History of American Archaeology*, W. H. Freeman and Company, San Francisco.

Woodbury, Richard B.

1960 "Nels C. Nelson and Chronological Archaeology," *American Antiquity* 25(3):400–401.

1973 *Alfred V. Kidder*, Columbia University Press, New York.

1981 "From Chaos to Order: A. V. Kidder at Pecos," in *Exploration* (Annual Bulletin of the School for American Research), pp. 15–22.

1982 "The Small Conference as Personal Network," paper presented at "Roots of Modern Anthropology Symposium," 81st Annual Meeting of the American Anthropological Association, Washington, D. C.

1983a "Looking Back at the Pecos Conference," *The Kiva* 48(4):251–66.

1983b Letter to D. R. Givens, 23 September, in author's possession.

Wylie, Alison

1982 "An Analogy by Any Other Name Is Just As Analogical," *Journal of Anthropological Archaeology* 1:382–401.

Year Book 28

1929 Carnegie Institution of Washington, Washington, D. C.

Year Book 29

1930 Carnegie Institution of Washington, Washington, D. C.

Yellen, John E.

1977 *Archaeological Approaches to the Present*, Academic Press, New York.

INDEX

Adams, J. P., 43
Agassiz, Alexander, 1
Aldana, Barbara Kidder (daughter of Kidder), 27–28, 111
Alfred Vincent Kidder Award, ix
American Anthropological Association, ix, 77
American Bureau of Ethnology reports, 2
American Museum of Natural History (New York), 33, 41, 50
American Philosophical Society, x, xi
American Society of Naturalists, 109
Americanist archaeology, xi, 78, 99, 118; as envisioned by Kidder, 68–69, 73–76; Kidder impact on, 121–29; pre-Kidder climate of, 37–38
Amsden, Charles, 73
Amsden, Monroe, 147
analogies, ethnographic, debate over, 127
Anasazi, 17, 20, 150
The Ancient Maya (Morley), 113
Anderson, Charlie, 146
Andrade, Manuel J., 108, 160
Antiquities Act of 1906, 23
Antiquity law of Mexico, 87
Archaeological Institute of America, 10, 23, 26, 31, 34, 36

Archaeological Studies of Ancient Cities of Mexico (Holmes), 80
archaeology: administration of, Kidder contribution to, 69–70, 100, 104, 128–29; aerial, in Middle America, 100–104; Americanist. *See* Americanist archaeology; core attack in, 125–26; Cushing/Fewkes era of, 31–33, 40; direct historical approach, 38, 63–64, 126–27; dirt archaeology, 121–22; expedition attitude, 42; and history, Kidder contribution to, 127–28; intensive investigation in, 127; location analysis in, 127; multidisciplinary approach, 41, 70, 93–100, 124–26; pre-Kidder in Middle America, 78–89; salvage, 111; teamwork in, 104–5, 109, 154
ash-boy, 144
A. V. Kidder (Woodbury), 76

bag tests, 66–67
Bandelier, Adolph F., 31, 47, 69, 146
Bandelier National Monument, 20
Bastian, Adolph, 80
Batres, Leopold, 80, 91
Beale, Mrs. Truxton, 116
Bennett, Wendell, 117